The Mindful Teacher's Toolkit

This book is dedicated to all teachers, everywhere.
You make the world a better place.

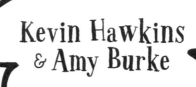

Kevin Hawkins & Amy Burke

The Mindful Teacher's Toolkit

Awareness-based Wellbeing in Schools

Activities for 4-18 year olds

CORWIN

SAGE Publications Ltd
1 Oliver's Yard
55 City Road
London EC1Y 1SP

CORWIN
A SAGE company
2455 Teller Road
Thousand Oaks, California 91320
(0800)233-9936
www.corwin.com

SAGE Publications India Pvt Ltd
B 1/I 1 Mohan Cooperative Industrial Area
Mathura Road
New Delhi 110 044

SAGE Publications Asia-Pacific Pte Ltd
3 Church Street
#10-04 Samsung Hub
Singapore 049483

Editor: Jude Bowen
Senior assistant editor: Catriona McMullen
Production editor: Katherine Haw
Copyeditor: Tom Bedford
Proofreader: Leigh C. Smithson
Indexer: Martin Hargreaves
Marketing manager: Dilhara Attygalle
Cover design: Wendy Scott
Typeset by: C&M Digitals (P) Ltd, Chennai, India
Printed in the UK

Library of Congress Control Number: 2021935489

British Library Cataloguing in Publication data

A catalogue record for this book is available from
the British Library

ISBN 978-1-5297-3177-4
ISBN 978-1-5297-3176-7 (pbk)

At SAGE we take sustainability seriously. Most of our products are printed in the UK using responsibly sourced
papers and boards. When we print overseas we ensure sustainable papers are used as measured by the PREPS
grading system. We undertake an annual audit to monitor our sustainability.

Contents

List of Figures

About the Authors

 Kevin Hawkins has worked with children and adolescents in various contexts for over 40 years as a teacher, school head and social worker, in the UK, Europe and Africa. In London he worked as a counsellor for drug users and as a resettlement worker for homeless young people. He has taught across the age ranges in state schools and in international schools, with a focus on developing the whole child through balancing academic, social and emotional aspects of learning. He was Head of the Arusha Campus of the International School Moshi in Arusha, Tanzania, and for 10 years was Middle School Principal at the International School of Prague in the Czech Republic.

Kevin started teaching mindful awareness to students, teachers and parents in 2008, and in 2012 he co-founded MindWell Education (www.mindwell-education.com) which supports educational communities in developing awareness-based wellbeing through mindfulness and social-emotional learning. His first book, *Mindful Teacher, Mindful School: Improving Wellbeing in Teaching and Learning*, was published by SAGE/Corwin in 2017. Kevin works independently as a speaker, consultant and teacher trainer. He has three grown-up children and is based in Valencia, Spain, where he lives with his wife and co-author, Amy Burke.

 Amy Burke is an educational consultant who spent 15 years as a high school teacher and guidance counsellor in Canada and The Netherlands. She holds a Master's Degree in Contemplative Education from Naropa University and in 2012 co-founded MindWell Education. Amy is a facilitator for the CARE program (Cultivating Awareness and Resilience in Education), a teacher trainer for the Mindfulness in Schools Project, and a Mentor for Inward Bound Mindfulness Education (iBme UK). Amy works internationally providing workshops and retreats for educators, students and parents, with a focus on self-care and stress management.

 Krysten Fort-Catanese is a contributor to this book and the author of Chapter 1. She has taught and led in progressive and innovative schools for over 20 years. In 2012, Krysten became the founding Director of Social and Emotional Learning and Mindfulness at Phuket International Academy, now the United World College, Thailand. She is a teacher trainer with the Mindfulness in Schools Project and joined the MindWell Education team in 2013. Currently, Krysten is the Head of Friends Elementary School in Boulder, Colorado, USA.

≋ Acknowledgements ≋

Heartfelt thanks to all educators who have already taken steps to bring greater awareness and wellbeing to themselves, their colleagues, students and school communities – this book would not exist without your efforts. Our hope is that in some way our book will reflect and support these efforts and might also encourage others who feel drawn to this work to take their own first steps on this unfolding global journey to greater awareness, wellbeing and peace for our planet.

For helpful feedback on our early drafts we sincerely thank:

Michael Anderson, Susan Burbidge, Paul Fisher, Lucy Hawkins and Rachel Read

For their generous contributions and kind permission to use their words, experiences, ideas and images we are greatly indebted to:

Judson Brewer, Christa Turksma, Leandro Johner, Terry Taylor, Maike Wagner, Adam Avin, Jake Holgate, Kat Holgate, Kara Smith, Charlotte Record, Michael Anderson, Adrian Bethune, Linda Lantieri, Vicki Zakrzewski, Chris Willard, Otto Scharmer, Arawana Hayashi, David Treleaven, Ellie Kimber, Kareem Ghandour, Doug Worthen, Simoon Franzen, Bree Greene, Sarah Silverton, Claire Kelly, Clare Winter, Terry Taylor, CASEL, Jessica Morey, Pauline McKenna, Chrystal Kelly, Andy Ashton, Karim Vergnes, Simone Morelos Zaragoza Wotherspoon, Isabela Canavati, Yixin Zou, Amberly Adema, Helen Maffini, Bart Dankaerts, Josipa Mihić, Tovi Scruggs-Hussein, Tracy Heilers and Arnie Bieber.

Special thanks to Julia Coto for kind permission to use the valuable work of Juan Coto.

A warm shout-out to our heartfriend, Kevin Fong, whose vision and wisdom continue to influence our work.

Huge thanks to Mark Greenberg, not just for writing the Foreword but also for the wonderful work you and Christa do for educators and for your support and friendship (and for use of the Mouse House!)

Mega thanks to the team at SAGE/Corwin, especially Cat McMullen, Jude Bowen, Katherine Haw and Dilly Attygalle for your professionalism, encouragement and support. We love working with you!

We are especially grateful to our dear friend and MindWell colleague Krysten Fort-Catanese, who wrote Chapter 1. We have so much appreciated your contributions, support and transatlantic encouragement! Warm, heartfelt thanks also to our other MindWell colleagues Kara Smith and Lina Paumgarten for your friendship and fellowship over the years as well as for your direct contributions to this book. What a Team!

From Kevin:
Special thanks for their continual encouragement, love and support to my wonderful children, Lucy, Billy and Rosa (sorry we couldn't quite squeeze in that 'All About Rosa' subtitle!); my Superb Sisters, Anne and Julie, and their lovely families; Mum and Dad; and above all, to Awesome Amy, my wife, co-author and travelling companion on this incredible journey! Where to next? ...

From Amy:
Thank you to my family for loving me always and not just because you have to.

To my mama, growing with you is super cool.

To John for always being with me. Still.

To my Ladeez for embodying generosity of spirit and true friendship.

To Morry for Seeing me.

And to the Love of my Life, Kevin, for your truly unconditional love and support. Thanks for letting me hitch my wagon to your star. I'll go anywhere with you.

MindWell Education Weblinks

Visit
www.mindwell-education.com

The MindWell Education website includes a dedicated page for

The Mindful Teacher's Toolkit with resources to further support readers:

www.mindwell-education.com/mtt-resources

Kevin Hawkins and Amy Burke are co-founders of MindWell Education, which supports the integration of mindful awareness training and social-emotional learning in whole school communities in order to foster wellbeing for all.

Amy and Kevin offer a range of training courses in Being Mindful, Teaching Mindfully, and Teaching Mindfulness, as well as dedicated courses for school leaders in Mindful Leadership and Implementing Awareness-based Wellbeing in Schools. For further information on courses, see www.mindwell-education.com/courses.

Foreword

'I am very interested, but where do I begin?', 'How do I begin?' These are questions I hear from many educators regarding nurturing the mindful awareness and social and emotional competence of their students. Kevin Hawkins and Amy Burke, both education visionaries, have created a developmentally focused toolkit for educators from PreK-12 that provides practical support and practices that teachers can begin to use tomorrow. Many educators are puzzled about the similarities and differences between mindful awareness practices and social and emotional learning. Should I focus on awareness? Should I focus on Social-Emotional Learning (SEL)? With many years of experience in both teaching and teacher professional development, Kevin and Amy have seamlessly integrated mindful awareness practices and social and emotional learning. This integration is key because developing mindful awareness provides essential support for deepening our ability to care for ourselves and for others, as well as to engage joyfully in learning.

A great strength of this book is its carefully designed developmental approach which begins with simple calming and attentional practices for young children and extends to the developmental needs of teens, including supporting practices to reduce anxiety and helping youth to find their sense of purpose and meaning. Although the core abilities of mindful awareness and attention are important at every developmental phase (including adulthood), how to skilfully support these practices at each age is essential.

Of course, using the various practices in the book effectively depends on the development and embodiment of these values, attitudes and behaviours on the part of the teacher. Here, and in Kevin's previous book (*Mindful Teacher, Mindful School*), there are clear directions for educators to develop their own personal mindful awareness practice and ideas for how to embody and integrate these practices in their teaching. Wisely, the authors conclude the book with a valuable chapter on how to support whole school transformation in which mindful awareness is central to providing a 'true education' for all learners, both adults and children. Reading this book I have feelings of delight and anticipation as teachers find new avenues to cultivate awareness in their students and themselves in support of a more caring and compassionate world for all. Welcome and enjoy!

Mark Greenberg PhD
Emeritus Professor, Human Development and
Family Studies, Penn State University
Chairperson of the Board, CREATE for Education

How to Use This Book

Our book is a structured selection of activities and practices that can be used to introduce mindful awareness training to students in age-appropriate ways across the full range of education. Built into the exercises are notes on how to deliver them as well as advice on issues that might arise based on varied experiences from training students and teachers around the world. Intertwined within the activities and notes are various ways of encouraging and advising teachers on keeping their own practice of mindful awareness alive and connected to their work with their students.

   We have set the book up in a way that makes it easy for you to dip into sections that interest you most. We would encourage you to read the **Introduction** first in order to set the scene and establish some common understandings used through-out the book. Then, if you want to get straight into the activities most appropriate for the age group you teach, you will find those in Section I.

Pick `n Mix: Section I

We have divided this section into four different age bands:

   Early Years (EYs): 3-6 years

   Primary Years (PYs): 7-10 years

   Midde Years (MYs): 11-13 years

   Secondary Years (SYs): 14-18 years

These divisions are both real and somewhat arbitrary. It makes sense of course to vary the approach and content according to children's stages of development. But these age categories also overlap with each other. Individual students of the same chronological age differ widely in maturity and engagement levels and we have all had the experience of feeling that some classes seem much 'younger' than others of the same age. Some 13 year olds may be very interested in hearing about research, while some 17 year olds may appreciate a theoretical approach similar to what we would use with adults. Almost all of the activities are adaptable by language, tone and content, so we recommend you start by exploring the most relevant age range and adapt it to suit your students. **Be sure to take a look at the activities in the bands above or below your age group too – there are exercises and approaches there that can also be adapted for your students.**

Experience and research show that students learn these kinds of activities best when presented with a combination of routine and variety, so don't feel you have to keep making everything 'new'. There is a lot to be said for familiarity and deepening through consistency.

 # Pick 'n Mix: Section II

Section II is mainly structured by role and specialism rather than age group. We encourage you to explore and dip in and out as you like. There are so many areas that overlap in these chapters that they will likely be of interest to all mindful educators. For example:

- An upper elementary class teacher or a secondary PSHE/Life Skills teacher may well be interested to learn about how their students could apply mindful awareness in sports and performance activities.

- Likewise, a PE teacher with an interest in using mindfulness in sports will benefit by finding out about how awareness training is introduced to students and what opportunities there are to apply these skills in other subject areas.

- All teachers have students with neuro-divergent learning needs in their classes so it is well worth any teacher looking over the section on 'Students with Special Educational Needs'.

- Mindful Leadership is not restricted to those with titles and responsibilities – we all take up leadership roles in certain contexts – and so learning about how to sustain our energies whilst embodying self-care and contributing to whole school wellbeing can benefit us all.

What we are saying here goes somewhat beyond the idea of 'How to make best use of this book'. We are advocating for approaches to fostering wellbeing in our students that connect across age ranges and subject divisions and that build bridges between teachers of different subjects and ages in the pursuit of developmentally appropriate and coherent approaches to greater wellbeing in our school communities.

In the latter part of Section II and the Conclusion we broaden our perspective to consider important issues and challenges around implementation, school culture, systems change and alignment with global trends in education and beyond.

Features

This book contains a number of recurring features to help guide you on this journey:

- **Skills Icons** indicate which social-emotional competencies are supported by a particular activity or practice (see **Introduction** for details).

Self- Awareness	Self- Management	Social Awareness	Relationship Skills	Responsible Decision- Making
(Self-A)	(Self-M)	(Soc-A)	(Rel. Skills)	(Resp. D-M)

- **Teacher Scripts** will give you a feel for how we deliver activities and practices but they aren't necessarily designed to be read word for word. They can be seen more as guideposts to support you at the start, and as you continue to develop your personal mindfulness practice and your experience in leading these exercises, you will soon find your own authentic voice.

- **Teaching Tips** are based on practical experiences of delivering specific activities to an age group.

- **Top Teaching Tips** apply to all or most age groups and can be found at the end of Section I (see Chapter 5).

- **Teacher Reflections** invite you to pause, journal and reconnect with your personal practice and experience.

- **Further Reading and Resources** at the end of each chapter highlight additional sources of guidance and ideas. In Section I you can draw from these to further develop activities and approaches that best suit you and your students.

- **Featured Boxes** include Expert Advice, Author Voice, Educator Voice, Student Voice, Case Studies, and Research. These are spread throughout the book and offer experiences and advice from a range of teachers and leaders in wellbeing, SEL and mindfulness in education from around the world.

Taken together, these features offer more than a simple 'toolkit'. The combination of tools, guidance manual and real-life examples provide mindful teachers with everything they need in order to be able to develop their own mindful classroom and contribute to improving wellbeing in their school community.

Key Terminology

This book is primarily designed for educators who have already taken those first steps towards cultivating their own mindful awareness and social-emotional competencies. We focus on showing you how to start and then how to develop **Mindful Awareness Training (MAT)** for your students and we show you how this training connects with **Social-Emotional Learning (SEL)**.

Seasoning Activities are short calming or energizing moments that can be sprinkled through the school day, allowing teachers and students to pause and reboot.

As you work to help raise your students' awareness and relationship skills, you will most likely feel motivated at some point to collaborate with others in your school community to embed deeper changes into your school systems and culture. **Awareness-based Wellbeing (ABW)** encompasses these broader efforts and is our way of defining the combination of programmes, initiatives, approaches and processes that serve to consciously foster wellbeing in a school community through nurturing understanding of self, each other and the overall school ecosystem and culture.

Be Mindful, Teach Mindfully, Teach Mindfulness ...

Meaningful systemic and cultural change in education *is* possible. In fact, it's essential. In the concluding chapter of this book, we show how people and organizations around the world are already working to achieve this change. As educators we can all play a part in this process, and we can start right here, right now by focusing on *being the change we want to see* in ourselves.

Being Mindful

This core component of mindfulness in education refers to fostering self-care through the development of personal mindfulness meditation practice. Such practices can be approached in various ways, but in general include elements of **formal practices** such as sitting, walking or doing a body scan while lying down; along with **informal practices** applying mindful awareness to everyday activities, learning to live and work more mindfully.

Learning mindfulness meditation is best done with an experienced and certified trainer, either in person or online, but there are also some great self-taught resources available. Through this personal mindfulness training we can begin to develop greater self-awareness and improved emotional regulation, actively sustaining and supporting our positive mental health and resilience. This is what we mean when we talk about **self-care** and its impact on our wellbeing.

We highly recommend that teachers take this first step to establish their own mindful awareness before teaching mindfulness to students.

At the end of the next chapter we offer some recommended resources to help you get started on this amazing journey.

 # Teaching Mindfully

Once you have begun your training in mindfulness you will likely begin to notice ways in which it starts to impact your work, family and relationships in general. Without even mentioning the word 'mindfulness' in your classroom, you may begin to take with you a heightened sense of awareness and a more embodied presence that subtly begins to change the learning environment for your students. The increased ability to sense into the body can help teachers step out of overthinking, improve emotional regulation and bring greater warmth and even joy to our connections with students and colleagues. We can also use this increased sensitivity to respond more skilfully to challenging moments and to making subtle changes in our teaching to respond more sensitively to the needs of individuals and the group.

Mindfulness is not a magic pill and it does not make your irritability, frustration or over-reactions suddenly disappear. However, we have noticed a profound impact in our own lives and as well as the research that supports this, we have heard from so many other educators about the positive effects of taking a little time for self-care and nourishment through developing a personal practice.

Teaching Mindfulness

...is the subject of this book. Read on!

Introduction

Awareness-based Wellbeing in Schools

Our first book, **Mindful Teacher, Mindful School: Improving Wellbeing in Teaching and Learning** (Hawkins, 2017), was designed as an introduction for teachers and school leaders who may be curious and wanting to find out more about this kind of work, and in that book, we set out three key aspects of mindfulness in education:

Being Mindful

Teaching Mindfully

Teaching Mindfulness

We especially wanted to highlight the foundational aspect of **Being Mindful**, that essential first step we all need to take before learning to deliver Mindful Awareness Training (MAT) to students. It is this foundation that allows us to **Teach Mindfully**, impacting the way we are and how we connect with our students.

This book focuses primarily on the third aspect, **Teaching Mindfulness**, and is aimed at educators who have already established a personal mindfulness practice. If you don't yet have a practice and are a curious beginner, don't worry, we will show you how to get started on that crucial first step.

In the final pages of our first book we raised a challenge for school leaders and educational policy makers around the crucial need to transform education to help create a wiser, more compassionate and sustainable society. We want to pick up on that challenge here by proposing that:

- Given the complex environmental, societal and spiritual challenges of our time;
- Given the sense of isolation and disconnectedness experienced by many people and, in particular, young people around the world;
- Given the loss of any compelling narrative that guides our educational systems in meeting the real needs of students and of society in the 21st century;

- Given all of this, it is time now to consider *a new narrative for the purpose of schooling in the 21st century*, a narrative that clearly articulates 'What Really Matters' in life and learning.

We need a narrative that unites teachers, parents and students around the world with a sense of purpose that can be drawn on every day in everything that is done in school. Something that has the potential to make school relevant for all learners.

If we were to agree on a succinct, universal, underlying purpose for education for the forseeable future, perhaps it might be something like this:

To help our students, in the context of this community, learn how best to share the planet.

In a world where humans as a species are undeniably clever and technologically powerful but, in general, appear to lack wisdom, we need to harness our educational systems to support the healthy growth of young people, providing them with the opportunities to develop a more balanced sense of mind, heart and body. Young people who are wise as well as clever. Because despite our 'cleverness' we are not so smart, are we, when it comes to sharing this planet with each other. And we are not so clever when it comes to sharing the planet with other species, or indeed, with all life on Earth. But we can be. We know enough now about how humans grow and develop, about how we learn best and about our own needs and the needs of the planet.

It is time to consciously shape our educational systems to effectively foster wellbeing, alongside academic achievement, in learning environments that provide children with experiences that give them purpose and that connect them to those deeper universal values that we all want for our children:

- To be safe, healthy and happy.
- To be able to relate and collaborate effectively with each other.
- To be able to care for themselves, each other and our amazing, but threatened, planet.

Redefining 21st Century Skills

At the start of the century, *21st Century Skills* was a significant movement designed to help prepare students for a post-industrial information age. In particular, it has been up to now mainly about helping students gain the necessary skills and competencies to be able to manoeuvre in a career landscape that is always changing. While this still remains relevant, there is another, deeper layer to 21st Century Skills. Much of what we thought only a few years ago about an uncertain future being off in the distance is, in fact, already here. In the face of climate crisis, biodiversity extinction, systemic racism, global pandemics and other forms of major disruption, there is an immediate need to equip our children more effectively for this fast-changing world. In re-defining 21st Century Skills we need to include approaches to learning that help cultivate wisdom, compassion and wellbeing in our young people.

The key to producing a generation of young people who are well-equipped to embody these qualities is to not just provide them with academic qualifications based on the ability to regurgitate memorized information in examination rooms, but to design systems of learning that actually address what it is to be a human being at this point in our history and that consciously cultivate *all* our capacities in programmes that are truly designed to foster human development.

The World *is* the Curriculum

Inversion means turning the inside out and the outside in.

- 'Inside out' in this case means that learners leave the classroom and engage with the major hotspots of societal innovation in their own cities, regions, and ecosystems. In short: the city, the region, and the global ecosystem is the classroom.

- 'Outside in' means that the problems, the challenges of the world, are brought back onto the campus where they can be at the center of study and scientific inquiry.

In short: the challenges of the world, and of societal transformation, are the curriculum.

(Scharmer, 2019)

It's not actually so hard to see how all school learning could be reimagined to make every day at school another step towards more effective sharing of the planet. The artificial compartmentalization of knowledge into separate silos of specialist learning (our traditional school subject areas) needs to be broken down. Many schools have begun to explore approaches such as Project-Based Learning and Systems Thinking that see education and the acquisition of knowledge, skills and understanding in more holistic ways. Even within traditional subjects we can see how, for example:

- Geography and History can become learning vehicles that help develop global understanding, cooperation and the fostering of equality.

- Technology, Maths and the Sciences can be focused on understanding how complex ecosystems function and designing approaches that help students learn how to think in more naturalistic, holistic and integrative (as opposed to reductionist) ways.

- The Arts and Literature can be highly significant areas to explore self and collective expression and can provide meaningful opportunities to foster a deeper understanding of the human condition.

But all this still leaves a large gap in learning if we really want schools to foster and tap into the full range of human capacities. We have to begin to investigate these areas of study in ways that truly foster growth and understanding of the learner's mind, heart and body as well as understanding of the external world. By including the subjective, internal experiences of the learner as valued areas of discovery, alongside the objective study of the external, we can help our children grow up with a more balanced understanding of themselves and of the world. Only when we begin to also study and work on ourselves as educators, learners and human beings, will we fully develop the perspectives and collaborative qualities necessary to achieve lasting change.

Expert Voice: 'Silence Is a Part of the Conversation'

Australian aboriginal leader Professor Colleen Hayward made a memorable comment about silence during an online discussion on dealing with global disruption (GAIA, 2020). She said she had noticed that people living in modern cultures seem to find silence uncomfortable. 'But', she said, 'silence is a part of the conversation. Part of listening to the land and to each other' (GAIA, 2020).

Professor Hayward reminds us of the importance of quiet reflection and inner knowledge and also that traditional peoples offer rich sources of wisdom and understanding of how to live sustainably and in harmony with the planet. Such wisdom offers a valuable resource for helping our young people learn how to best share the planet.

In addition to cultivating this awareness of self and other, there is a third element of awareness that is equally integral to deep change. That is building **awareness of the systems and the environments in which we work and live**. Experience has shown that it is highly possible to put a group of well-intentioned individuals into a flawed system and produce results that harm those the system is intended to serve. We will develop this theme further in the final chapter, but for now we want to point out that some of the most powerful contemporary business and systemic change approaches now incorporate some form of emotional intelligence, self-awareness or mindfulness as critical elements of instigating systemic change.

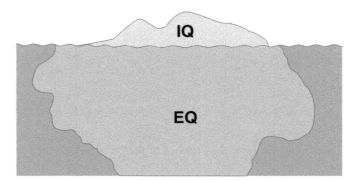

Figure 0.1   EQ/IQ Iceberg: There is increasing recognition of the importance of Emotional Intelligence.

We all know from personal experience how personality issues can get in the way of effective collaboration. The worlds of science, business, and more recently even education, are waking up to the importance of those social and emotional competencies (EQ) that underly everything we do. Since the 1990s neuroscience has helped us understand that, thanks to the neuroplasticity of the brain, these socio-emotional skills are trainable and thus eminently suited to being incorporated in skills-based learning systems in schools.

- So what do we already know and have available to schools that can support teachers, leaders and policy makers who want to redesign our school systems for greater balance and wellbeing by incorporating a more holistic emphasis on social and emotional aspects of learning?

- And, what evidence-based programmes and frameworks are out there that might provide us with a secure scaffolding to support this rebuilding of our curricula and approaches?

Thankfully, there are already many examples of alternative approaches that have been tried and tested in educational settings. We have the whole history of progressive education to draw from and we can also look to numerous contemporary organizations and approaches that help show us how to educate the whole child and how to nurture these essential social-emotional qualities. One model that we will draw on throughout this book comes from the Collaborative for Academic and Social and Emotional Learning (CASEL) in the USA. They have developed the most succinct and coherent categorization of social and emotional competencies that we have come across.

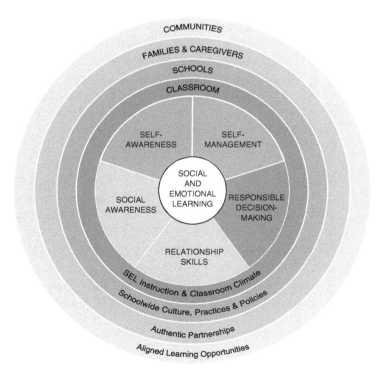

Figure 0.2   The CASEL SEL Framework

Core Social–Emotional Competencies: The CASEL 5

Self-awareness: The abilities to understand one's own emotions, thoughts, and values and how they influence behaviour across contexts. This includes capacities to recognize one's strengths and limitations with a well-grounded sense of confidence and purpose.

Self-management: The abilities to manage one's emotions, thoughts, and behaviours effectively in different situations and to achieve goals and aspirations. This includes the capacities to delay gratification, manage stress, and feel motivation and agency to accomplish personal/collective goals.

Social awareness: The abilities to understand the perspectives of, and empathize with, others, including those from diverse backgrounds, cultures, and contexts. This includes the capacities to feel compassion for others, understand broader historical and social norms for behaviour in different settings, and recognize family, school, and community resources and supports.

Relationship skills: The abilities to establish and maintain healthy and supportive relationships and to effectively navigate settings with diverse individuals and groups. This includes the capacities to communicate clearly, listen actively, cooperate, work collaboratively to problem solve and negotiate conflict constructively, navigate settings with differing social and cultural demands and opportunities, provide leadership, and seek or offer help when needed.

Responsible decision-making: The abilities to make caring and constructive choices about personal behaviour and social interactions across diverse situations. This includes the capacities to consider ethical standards and safety concerns, and to evaluate the benefits and consequences of various actions for personal, social, and collective wellbeing.

Many school systems and educational organizations around the world are now using these CASEL competencies as a valuable framework to help organize learning in these areas. These competencies can help provide schools with a tangible reference point, a Social-Emotional North Star, which can guide their journey towards greater balance and wellbeing. The fostering of this area of learning, commonly known as **SEL** (Social-Emotional Learning), is increasingly being seen by educators and policy makers to be one of the central functions of education in the 21st century. The importance of positive social-emotional interventions cannot be overstated. This was brought home to Prevention Research specialist Mark Greenberg when he and his co-researchers analysed data that tracked students in the USA over 19 years from kindergarten into early adulthood. They found a strong correlation between the development of early social-emotional competencies and related wellbeing outcomes across a range of domains in adulthood, including education and employment, levels of mental health, criminal behaviour and substance abuse (Jones et al., 2015).

Mindful Awareness or Social–Emotional Learning?

In our own teaching experience and in working with schools around the world, we have learned that it actually doesn't matter if your starting point is SEL or Mindfulness. You might start with SEL skills and later augment that with **Mindful Awareness Training (MAT)**, or you may start with Mindfulness and later develop your scope to include social-emotional competencies. Many schools are also now

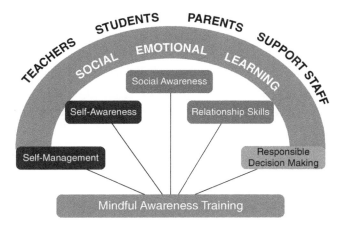

Figure 0.3   Awareness-based Wellbeing Framework

Source: © MindWell

using Positive Psychology as an effective starting point in their approach to this work and they sometimes then include MAT in their programmes. Regardless of where you start, what matters is that you explore and practice whatever it is you are teaching first for yourself in a meaningful way.

Periodic reflection on your intentions, 'What do I want, deep down, for my students?', and on your own practice, 'What are my strengths and challenges in this area?', will keep you connected to the realities of teaching and learning in this area. In this book we focus on a holistic approach to MAT that encompasses social and emotional aspects of learning.

The combination of **MAT + SEL** is the foundation of what we term **'Awareness-based Wellbeing' (ABW)** in schools.

Integrating SEL and Mindfulness

In their article exploring 'How SEL and mindfulness can work together', Linda Lantieri and Vicki Zakrzewski (2015) show how, when you integrate SEL and mindful awareness training, the practical training of mindfulness supports, enhances and enlivens SEL, while the SEL focus on life skills can help provide learners with real-world opportunities to apply and try out their growing skillset:

- **Self-awareness:** *Students' self-awareness deepens when enhanced by the mindfulness practices of focusing attention and self-compassion.*

- **Self-management:** *Mindfulness increases students' emotion regulation skills, which enhances their ability to resolve conflict more creatively or to say how they're feeling in an emotionally balanced way.*

- **Social awareness:** *Mindfulness increases students' empathy by helping them to regulate their emotions rather than get emotionally overwhelmed when faced with a difficult situation. As a result, their capacity to notice another person's suffering and respond to it increases.*

- **Relationship skills:** *Mindfulness increases compassion. Thus, when students practice SEL skills such as creating a win-win solution with someone who challenges them, they are doing so with more compassionate understanding.*

- **Decision-making:** *Mindfulness increases cognitive flexibility and creativity, which gives students a wider range of responses to challenging situations.*

By helping students become aware of and then embody the connection between their emotions, thoughts, and bodily sensations, students are better able to regulate their emotions, which then impacts things such as their behavior, stress levels, relationships, and ability to focus. In short, mindfulness practices connect students' inner and outer experiences and help them see the congruence between the two.

Italicized excerpts reproduced with permission from an article that originally appeared in *Greater Good*, the online magazine of the Greater Good Science Center at UC Berkeley. Read more at https://greatergood.berkeley.edu/

Mindful awareness training can be used to improve our attention but it is also much more than just bare attention training. When taught by embodied teachers who are developing their own capacity to be more aware and more present, we begin to see the broader and deeper potential of a training that helps us understand how our minds, bodies and emotions function and especially how we can tap into our natural curiosity and enliven our natural qualities of kindness and caring. In the context of social and emotional skills development we begin to find ways to apply these profound learnings in multiple areas in school and beyond. And of course, if we want to help create healthy learning ecosystems that really make our school communities places where children and adults thrive and flourish, we have to start with ourselves.

Expert Voice: Educator Self-Care

Many of us choose to become educators because we believe in the power of a good education. We love instilling in our students a love and enthusiasm for lifelong learning. As educators we are skilled at supporting our students and their families, but we often forget to take care of ourselves.

- As a teacher you may often feel sequestered with your students in a classroom that gives you little time or space for some breathing time. Your day is full, filled with all the demands of a classroom full of young people who demand not only your time and attention, but also for you to be flexible and patient and to be able to deal with whatever 'storm' is blowing in your classroom. In addition, the curriculum keeps growing and you may feel there is no time to really develop relationships with your students and create the kind of caring, supportive classroom that you yearn for. This can be exhausting and if we don't learn to take care

(Continued)

of our own needs it can lead to a feeling of lack of accomplishment and burn-out. As the teacher, you are the most important person in that classroom. If you are not doing well, nothing will run well.

- As a principal there are many demands on your plate and you often feel pressure from many sides. You feel responsible for the wellbeing of your students, teachers, and other school staff. Your most important job is to create a school environment where all thrive, and this includes your teachers, staff, the students and their parents. In most contexts, principals are also feeling the pressure of curricula and academic performance scores.

All these demands can take a toll on our health and wellbeing. As a result, self-care for educators is not a luxury but a necessity. If we want to create school environments where everyone feels valued and at home, an environment where our students feel a sense of belonging in which they can succeed, we need to pay attention to the health and wellbeing of all of our educators.

Christa Turksma - Co-Developer of the CARE program, Director of Training, createforeducation.org

Christa's message here brings us back to the core, foundational aspect of **being mindful**.

Self-care means more than taking regular bubble baths, even though this may be a great way of relaxing! In the context of this book, self-care for teachers and school leaders is about nurturing our mental, emotional and physical health, fostering resilience and sustainability in a challenging career. Although this book focuses on ways of effectively bringing mindful awareness training to students, we will keep coming back to the importance of self-care for ourselves as educators.

We said at the outset that this book is for teachers who have already started a personal mindfulness practice. But we also want to reassure you that, if you haven't already done so, you can begin to take small steps now to get started. Below we list various options that you can explore to get started. Find a route that feels right for you, and enjoy the journey! You won't regret it.

Further Reading and Resources

Training Courses for 'Being Mindful'

CARE - Cultivating Awareness and Resilience in Education, https://createforeducation.org/
MBSR Home Study Course - www.soundstrue.com/
Mindful Schools - 101: Mindfulness Foundations, www.mindfulschools.org/

Mindfulness in Schools Project – '.begin' course, https://mindfulnessinschools.org/

Mindfulness-Based Stress Reduction Courses – check local mindfulness centres or live online options.

MindWell Education – 'Be Mindful, Teach Mindfully, Teach Mindfulness', www.mindwell-education.com/

Books

Hawkins, K. (2017) *Mindful Teacher, Mindful School: Improving Wellbeing in Teaching and Learning*. London: SAGE.

Jennings, P. (2020) *Teacher Burnout Turnaround: Strategies for Empowered Educators*. New York: W.W. Norton & Company.

Williams, M. and Penman, D. (2011) *Mindfulness: A Practical Guide to Finding Peace in a Frantic World*. London: Piatkus.

Video

Amy Burke, TEDx Talk, *Mindfulness in Education: Learning from the Inside Out*, www.youtube.com/watch?v=2i2B44sLVCM&t=5s

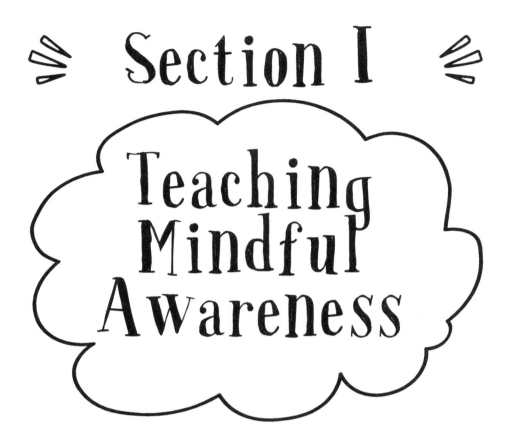

Section I

Teaching Mindful Awareness

Mindful awareness training is a **unique subject that is also uniquely subjective**. Many students are not used to this kind of experiential learning and exploration in school. Because of this, and because we are asking them to investigate and observe how their minds, bodies and emotions work, mindful awareness training can sometimes be challenging, and even at times uncomfortable for some.

Guiding children and young people in an exploration of the human condition takes great sensitivity and understanding. There is no 'one size fits all' approach and it is important to provide activities and practices that are both developmentally appropriate *and* engaging.

1.

Mindful Awareness in the Early Years Classroom (3-6 year olds)

In this chapter we provide you with:

Awareness Building Activities	Activities
Establishing Breath Awareness	Seeing Breathing
	Watch the Wind!
Energizing Activities	Tickling the Sky
	Clap and Connect!
Calming Activities	Pebble Practice
	Breath Buddy
Reflecting Activity	Glitter Mind Jar
Seasoning Activities	Jump or Run!
	Slow It Down
	Seashell Breathing
	Mmm, Nice!
Classroom Resource	Calm Corners
Conflict Resolution	Peace Begins with Me
Teacher Practices	Clarifying Intentions
	Relax, Release, Return
	Pause, Reflect, Plan

Working With This Age Group

'Early Years' is defined in different ways around the world and here we are using it to signify the 3-6 year age span.

The Early Years (EYs) are a precious and precocious time, full of wonder and curiosity. Oftentimes, children at this age are already present in the moment and full of questions about the world around them. They are natural seekers, love to explore, and are especially sensitive to the emotional weather of the classroom. It is critical that teachers are walking their talk when teaching mindfulness to 3-6 year olds. The most effective way to bring mindfulness to this age group is for the adults around them to be embodying it. Teachers practising mindfulness themselves is the essential foundation that will help young children develop mind-body awareness whilst learning the language of how to express their oftentimes strong and varying emotions in a safe and supportive atmosphere. Whether children are feeling frustration, anger or excitement, educators can be at the ready to help them deal with these powerful emotional experiences through mindful awareness.

Developmentally, this age group learns best through play, music and connecting with nature. 'Learning by doing' is key. They enjoy repeating activities and hearing things over and over again. Bringing mindfulness into an EYs classroom is ultimately about planting seeds of awareness in children as they begin to build up a toolkit that will help them explore their experiences with curiosity and kindness.

Awareness–Building Activities

In this chapter we unpack some activities that you can use to help begin to isolate and integrate the senses, and in Chapter 2 we explore using the full range of senses as the main gateway to building awareness. The overall intention here is to share experiential exercises that are responsive, useful and practical. **Teaching mindfully** is about 'reading the field' – sensing the mood of the classroom and applying what is needed in any given moment. You might feel that an energizing, fun activity will be most helpful or you may turn towards more calming and soothing practices, depending on the mood and feel of the class. These practices can help build up that mental and emotional toolkit, allowing your students to see that mindfulness can be useful in times of excitement as well as in times of sadness or anger.

As mentioned in the Introduction, we always start with ourselves, with **Being Mindful**, so let's now take a few moments to check in with our personal motivations and intentions:

Teacher Reflection: Clarifying Intentions

- First take some moments to ground yourself.
- Perhaps taking a few conscious breaths; connecting with the body; noticing the sensations of sitting; the movement of breath in the body; or the sounds around you ...

- What is motivating you to try this with your students?
- What is your intention?
- Stay curious for a moment longer and see if anything else, perhaps a deeper, underlying motivation arises ...
- Make a note of what came up for you.

The question 'Why am I doing this?' is an important one to keep in mind throughout this journey. Try to revisit this brief reflection from time to time and before guiding an exercise or practice.

Getting Started

The following activities are designed to be foundational in building up a mindful classroom culture. You can also **'season the day'** with these practices, sprinkling moments of calm and connection in the classroom whenever helpful. After the introductory Breath Awareness Practice, the activities are labelled as Energizing, Calming or Reflecting, and you can mix and match them as you wish to suit the needs of your classroom and the moment.

The scripts provided in this chapter are written as we would deliver them for 3-6 year olds so feel free to adapt the language and tone to suit your class. As usual, make sure to try these activities out before you introduce them to children. Most importantly, continue to practise yourself, nurture a growth mindset, and have FUN!

Establishing Breath Awareness

To a young child, 'Just breathe' or 'Pay attention to your breath' are quite nebulous instructions! The younger the child, the more tactile they need to be and the more modelling they need from the caring adults around them. With that said, there are a number of activities that can help children start to explore their breath.

 Self-A   Self-M   ### Seeing Breathing

There are various ways we can help children actually 'see' and feel their breath. Depending on where you live, for example, you might be able to refer to seeing the exhaling breath outdoors on a really cold day or breathing onto a cold window and noticing the condensation. You can also set up fun acvtivities to explore this, for example:

- Blowing soap bubbles.

- Making a feather move with your breath.

- Pushing a cardboard toilet roll cylinder across the desk using only the breath.

(Continued)

You could structure any of these activities by adapting the script provided here:

     ## Watch the Wind!

This activity requires handheld toy windmills which can be bought or made in class as a craft activity — see here for an example of how to make them: www. makeandtakes.com/garden-pinwheel-craft

*   Invite the children to sit in a circle.

 *Today, we are going to have fun with our breath. Your breath is always there for you, like a good friend, to support you through your ups and downs. We are going to use these windmills to help us to 'see' our breathing in action.*

Now let's sit with our backs straight and our bodies relaxed.

*   Model this so they can mirror you.

Now, let's gently blow on our windmills together using long, deep breaths, and see what happens.

*   Model this yourself with a nice, even in-breath and a slower, more deliberate out-breath. Allow them to experiment with this.

Is it easy or hard to make your windmill move? How does that feel on the inside?

*   Allow some sharing with children taking turns and giving their attention to each other.

Now, let's see what it's like to not change our breathing at all. Let's just see if we can breathe in our usual way. Not trying to make it faster and not trying to make it slower.

*   This will be challenging for this age group as they will automatically want to change and experiment with their breath. Allow some space for that to happen and just gently bring them back to the instruction.

So, what did you notice about your breath this time? How did that feel? What happened to your windmill?

Wow, we can really use our windmills to experiment with our breath and then see how it feels on the inside of our body. Let's keep them in our Calm Corner so that when we need to take a moment to cool down or just explore our breath, we can use our windmills to check in.

Well done, everyone. This activity showed us how different types of breathing can tell us a lot about how we are feeling on the inside.

Sample Practices: Energizing, Calming, Reflecting

Energizing

       Tickling the Sky Practice

Today we are going to tune into our hearing as we learn to reach up to tickle the sky.

What does it mean to hear? What does it mean to listen?

- Take some moments for them to take turns sharing.

  And now I am sure some of you are wondering, tickle the sky! How will we do that?

- Bring out the chime (preferrably one with a long ringtone).

  I am going to show you what it means to 'tickle the sky'. First I need to create my own personal bubble.

  Move into a space where you can hold out your arms and spin slowly around making sure to not touch any furniture.

  Watch me as I get my body close to the floor.

- Model getting into a ball on the floor for them.

  Then, I will ring the chime and as I hear the sound, I am going to move my body to stand up and then reach – reach – reach on my tippy-toes and wiggle my fingertips to tickle the sky! Then take a deep breath.

  As I start to notice the fading of the chime, I will slowly melt down, down, down to the floor and move back into the same spot where I began. And then I will take another deep breath.

  Now, let's try it together!

  Find a space and create your personal bubble by stretching out your arms and moving in a slow circle.

- Continue going through the entire practice again with the class.
- Doing this practice three times in a row can be very energizing as the children tune their attention to the chime and respond with their body to the sound.

(Continued)

TEACHING TIP

Lean in! Students will most likely giggle during this activity since they are 'tickling the sky'. Try to lean into the silliness, have fun, and just keep giving instructions as you move them through the practice.

  Clap and Connect!

- Invite students to sit or stand in a circle (depending on where your class is with their spatial awareness development, you may find this works better sitting down).

Ok, friends, today we are going to do an activity that requires us to really pay attention and give our full focus to our neighbours. Can you look to each side of you and say hello?

- Give them a moment to do this – it's really about knowing who is actually next to them.

Now, we are going to play 'Clap and Connect!' Watch me as I look into Michelle's eyes for a moment before we clap our hands together at the same time. It's okay if you do not clap your hands at the exact same time, the point is to connect with your eyes and then clap together as best you can.

- Model this moment of making connection through eye contact before clapping hands together.

After we clap together, Michelle will pass the clap to the person on the other side of her. And then we will pass the clap in this way all around the circle until it makes its way back to me. Let's try it and remember to wait until you connect with your neighbour's eyes before clapping!

- Try doing this around the circle once. There will be moments of laughter, connection, and some will rush but that is okay – try to hold it all with a sense of fun and encouragement.

Wow, that was tricky to look into my neighbour's eyes and clap with them. I really had to pay attention and focus! How was that for you?

- Listen to some experiences and then try it again.

Wonderful focus, friends! You really tuned into each other and connected on those claps! Let's try this again but now we will challenge ourselves with going in the opposite direction. Let's give it a go!

- Listen to what they notice. Find out what helped them to clap at the same time. Be responsive to their sharing and encourage kindness and compliments.

Way to work together as a community! You really paid attention to your neighbours right here, right now, which is what made this activity so successful. Well done!

(This activity is based on a Drama exercise and there are various versions available online.)

Calming

Pebble Practice

Supply, or have students gather, four small stones each, ones that can be painted and fit in a small pouch. Have students paint their four stones different colours of their choosing: one representing water, one representing a flower, one representing a mountain, and one to represent sunshine. Once their pebbles are dry, have students keep them in a special pouch with a drawstring.

Today we are going to learn about Pebble Practice. This is a calming practice that we can do on our own or together to help us feel peaceful.

- Hand out their pouches.

We are now going to pick up our pouch and carefully take out our four stones, one at a time.

- Model doing this ever so gently, showing them how to reach in and intentionally take out one at a time, examining each stone as they place it down in front of them.

Let's take a few moments to look at our stones. What do we notice? ...

- Now model picking up the flower pebble carefully with one hand and placing it gently in the palm of the other hand.

Look at your pebble, take a deep breath and slowly say, 'Breathing in, I am a flower ... Breathing out I feel fresh'.

Pause for a moment. Set the stone down gently, starting a new pile.

Continue to pick up and look at each pebble in turn:

Look at your pebble, take a deep breath and slowly say, 'Breathing in, I am a mountain ... Breathing out I feel strong'.

(Continued)

Look at your pebble, take a deep breath and slowly say, 'Breathing in, I am water … Breathing out I feel calm'.

Look at your pebble, take a deep breath and slowly say, 'Breathing in, I am sunshine … Breathing out I feel warm and happy'.

- Now they can give themselves a hug and take one more deep breath.

What did you notice when you were holding your stones?

- Allow for answers and sharing. Their sharing can be full of deep understanding and wondering so make time for this whenever possible. Not all children need to share; just a few responses can be helpful for the group to connect with their personal, as well as the wider group's, experiences.

Let's now carefully put our stones back in your pouch and gently bring them to the basket in the centre of the rug.

- Give verbal feedback as you notice them taking extra care.

We will try this practice again soon. We will keep our pebble bags handy in the Calm Corner.

Any time you feel angry or frustrated you can pick up the flower pebble, take a breath, close your eyes and feel that freshness inside yourself.

Or when you feel frightened or worried you can pick up the mountain stone and feel stronger.

When you feel upset or muddled up, you can pick up the water pebble and feel calmer and clearer.

When you feel sad or lonely you can pick up the sunshine stone and try to feel that warmth and happiness inside yourself.

This is how the Pebble Practice can help us take care of our feelings.

(Adapted from the orginal practice by Thich Nhat Hanh, *Happy Teachers Change the World*, reprinted by permission of Parallax Press.)

TEACHING TIP

You might get a feel for the pace of this practice by watching a version led by Thay Phap Luu, www.youtube.com/watch?v=Pc1pdjPG9BM

Extension Activity

There is a lovely, calming song by Betsy Rose, 'Breathing In, Breathing Out', that you could use to accompany this practice:

- Lyrics: www.betsyrosemusic.org/lyrics/
- Audio: www.youtube.com/watch?v=jFgLvpHUjYk

  Breath Buddy Practice

When we help younger children connect with their breathing in simple, fun ways, they often find it quite calming. There are various ways to help them feel into their natural belly breathing. In this activity, adapted from Susan Kaiser-Greenland (2010), we show how we have used stuffed animals to help the students tune into their breathing. We have also found this works quite well using bean bags or flat river stones which can be personalized as Breath Buddies by painting them.

Invite students to bring in a small stuffed animal, or you can provide them in order to make sure the size is just right. The stuffed animal should be able to fit on their tummy while lying down without any problems of it being too big. If you do have your students bring in their own, take time to let them share about their toys with one another. Before beginning this practice, you may also want to have some mats of some kind where the children can lie down around the room. Before you begin the practice, gather students together in a circle and show them what they are about to do. You can also have eye pillows for each child. These can help immensely with encouraging children to tune into their own experience. However, you know your students best so make sure to take their personal histories into consideration. If trauma is in their sphere of experience, then do not use the eye pillows or 'make' them close their eyes. These should both be optional anyway.

Note: Children who have experienced trauma may sometimes find some awareness activities uncomfortable. See Chapter 5 for information on trauma-sensitive teaching.

Good morning, friends. Today we are going to learn a practice called 'Breath Buddy'. This is a gentle breathing practice where we will be lying down. What do you think we will be doing with our toys during this practice? (Gather a few responses.) Great ideas – now, let me show you.

- Show them your 'buddy' – and then lie down in the centre of the circle. Place your buddy on your belly.

I am going to place my buddy on my belly as I lie down. I want to make sure my buddy is safe and secure so I am going to find a spot where it won't fall off. Now that my buddy is feeling ready, watch as I breath in (buddy goes up) and watch as I breathe out (buddy goes down). Notice how my buddy goes up and then it goes down, ever so carefully.

- Model this for a few more breaths. Then sit up and have children find a spot to lie down. It is best if you have prearranged spots with mats already placed around the room.

(Continued)

Now, let's all go to our spots and lie down on our back. Take a deep breath once you settle into your spot and then see what it is like to find that spot on your belly where your buddy will be safe and secure.

- Once most students are settled with their buddy, you can guide them through this gentle, calming practice.

Let's all now take a deep breath, seeing if we can really tune in to our buddy on our belly going up. Now letting our breath go, we notice our buddy going down as we slowly breathe out. See if you can pay attention to the up and down rhythm of your breathing and notice how it calms your buddy.

- Continue to model all of these steps for them. Go through at least five to ten cycles of breathing. The first few you can guide, and then in the last few you can just allow them to fully be in their own experience.

Let's now just notice what we notice when each one of us really gives our full attention to our buddy …

- Allow for some silence. Exaggerated breathing is bound to happen − you can walk around the room and guide individual students if they need encouragement or reminders to give their buddy all their care and focus. After this tuning in, you can have them go through one last breath for the practice.

Let's take one last breath together and then slowly come up to sit. From sitting, let's look at our buddy, give it a hug, and then come back to our circle. Your buddy can sit in your lap.

- Take some time to share experiences and what they noticed with the buddy on their belly.

Extension Activity

In all of these activities we are trying to bring a kind and loving quality of attention. Some teachers like to help their students consciously develop kindness for self and others, and one way to do this could be to extend the Breath Buddy activity. After students have had some time to settle themselves and their buddy, you can add a compassion practice, encouraging them to focus on sending kind thoughts and wishes to their 'buddy', then perhaps to a friend, a family member and then to themselves. You can find a good example of this in the activity *Sending Friendly Wishes* (Kaiser-Greenland, 2010: 68−9), from which this is adapted.

Extension Activity

The Belly Breathe song from Sesame Street is a fun, energetic way to follow-up with some singing and dancing: www.youtube.com/watch?v=_mZbzDOpyIA&t=4s

Reflecting

 Glitter Mind Jar Practice

This practice can really bring us into the moment by offering a strong anchor point. It can help us to rest, reflect, and even turn our attention to gratitude. You can make glitter jars ahead of time, or if you decide to make them *with* your class, just remember that you will need lots of assistance or parent volunteers! As messy as it might get, it is definitely worth it as the children feel a true sense of ownership with this powerful mindfulness tool. (See for example, 'How to Make Your Own Glitter Jar': www.mindful.org/how-to-create-a-glitter-jar-for-kids/)

This practice gives children the space and time to calm down and learn how to pay attention to what is going on inside their body and in their surroundings. Regularly practising this with the glitter jar can increase their sense of self-efficacy with strong emotions. Glitter jars are a very useful mindfulness tool both at school and at home. Watching the glitter swirl around and then settle on the bottom of the jar gives an individual, or the class, the time to calm down and reframe their attention. This is done in silence as much as possible. Your tone during the guidance should match the calm space.

Today we are going to learn the Glitter Jar practice. We now get to add it to our toolkit of practices.

Let's take the jar and give it a good shake.

- Model doing this and then guide the students to safely do the same.

Do you see how the glitter swirls around in the water, it's hard to see through isn't it? That can be how we feel inside sometimes. Our mind might be all mixed up and our body might feel wild like this glitter – going this way and that way.

Now, let's stop shaking up our jar and put it down. (Model this for them.) Let's watch the glitter settle to the bottom. As the glitter starts to sink to the bottom, let's place one hand on our belly and one hand on our heart. Feel your breathing.

- Model each step – one hand on belly, one hand on heart – the children will look to you for this guidance and will mirror what you do.

Keep watching closely until all the glitter has settled. Ok, now that most of the glitter is at the bottom, let's take one, long deep breath. (Do this with them.) Did you notice that the glitter didn't go away? It's still at the bottom of the jar but we can see clearly now. How are you feeling right now? What do you notice? Do you feel a bit more calm?

(Continued)

- Allow for some varied responses.

How might the Glitter Jar be like our busy bee bodies and minds? How might this practice help us when we are feeling mad or sad or even excited?

- Allow for some responses and examples of their own experiences with feelings.

It's hard for us to see clearly in the jar when the glitter is moving around. When we take the time to calm ourselves, our bodies and minds slow down and settle just like the glitter.

- Have them shake their glitter jars once more, put them down, place hands on belly and heart to breathe and then watch the glitter settle.

The Glitter Jar can help us calm down and see more clearly how we are feeling and how we can help ourselves. We will put some in the Calm Corner to be part of our mindfulness toolkit.

Extension Activity

After you have established this practice, you can show this beautiful video – 'Just Breathe': www.youtube.com/watch?v=RVA2N6tX2cg&t=7s – so students can continue to connect the Glitter Mind Jar with supporting their emotional wellbeing.

Educator Voice: Glitter Mind Jar in Action

After introducing the glitter mind jar to my students, they made their own jars as well as a community one for the class. Students took their personal one home so they could use it whenever they needed it, which also provided a strong link between school and home. It reinforced that these practices are for our everyday lives and not just in the classroom.

One morning we were having a 'Rose and Thorn' check in circle and one little 5 year old boy, Jeremy, talked about a problem (thorn) he had in a public playground over the weekend. Another little boy had come over and pushed Jeremy off the slide. Jeremy told our class, 'I got so angry and wanted to go push him down but my mom said to remember my mindfulness. I stopped and thought about my glitter jar, I just imagined it swirling around in my mind. I put my hand here (on his belly) and took deep breaths. I could see the glitter going down, down, down to the bottom and I felt good in my heart'. He took another deep breath and then Jeremy got his mom's help to go over to the boy so he could tell him how he felt about the push. Jeremy finished by asking the boy if he could be more careful next time and the boy agreed.

Everyone in the class was listening so intensely to every word that Jeremy was saying and when he was finished, one little girl even started to spontaneously clap for him. The whole class followed, applauding with big smiles, they were so proud of him. This story became a very important one for our class.

Many children would often refer to it when we would talk about the power of mindfulness. Every student eventually had a glitter jar story to share ... so many you could fill a book! This showed me how meaningful this tool was in connecting the dots for them and for me, providing a way for these children to calm themselves and illustrating that peace really does begin with each one of us.

Krysten Fort-Catanese – Head of Elementary, Friends School, Boulder, CO

  ## Other Seasoning Activities

Choose any simple, short activity to help your class Calm, Energize or Reflect, whichever is most needed at the time. For example:

- **Jump or Run!** Do star jumps or run on the spot for one minute, then place your hand on your heart and pay attention to your how your heartbeat and your breathing feels. Check in again a few moments later and see if anything has changed. How do you feel?

- **Slow It Down:** Choose any familiar action and just do it really slowly, for example: Dreamy Dancing, Swimming in Syrup (or 'Moving in Molasses!'), Walking in Water. Then come to a stop and notice how you feel.

- **Seashell Breathing:** Place your hands flat against each ear and breath in and out slowly. Listen to the sounds. Does it sound like sea?

- **Mmm, Nice!** Think of something that smells nice – maybe a flower or a freshly baked cake. Breathe in through the nose to really smell it, and as you breathe out, make a gentle 'Mmmm' sound.

There are also lots of great movement and breathing activities (for example Rainbow Breathing) available at the www.gonoodle.com/ website.

TEACHING TIPS

- Try to develop a combination of repeated core practices to support awareness along with the occasional introduction of new activities to maintain interest and engagement.

- Don't forget to look at the other chapters in Section I for more ideas to draw from and adapt for your students.

- You will find lots more general teaching advice and pedagogical tips in Chapter 5.

(Continued)

Expert Voice: We Are Not Trying to Create Little Meditators!

Many heart-warming images show small children meditating in a still, crossed-legged posture, eyes closed. Whilwst not discounting the value of this experience, mindfulness can be introduced to children and young people with more relevance to their everyday experience and lives. Mindfulness has much broader potential than simply as a form of relaxation, or a way to 'fix' things. Practising mindfulness to develop attitudes of curiosity, friendliness and allowing is more valuable than only practising while sitting still with the focus inside us, with eyes closed. We need to teach ways to create connections, resilience and effective responsiveness within ourselves, with other people and with the world we inhabit. Learning theory tells us that we learn best when the learning is clearly connected to where we can apply it. Could we expand our understanding of mindfulness to fully, and equally, value practising awareness in everyday life? Practising as we walk, talk, play, work, move and be still? Because mindfulness is about practising living mindfully rather than developing little meditators: it's about 'being mindful' rather than 'doing mindfulness'.

Sarah Silverton – Mindfulness teacher and trainer, UK,
www.thepresentcourses.org/

Setting the Weather

If you become frustrated or agitated with children during any of these activities, try to anchor yourself with a few deep breaths. Doing so can transform the entire feeling and mood of the room and prevent a potential 'power play' between yourself and a child. By doing this, teachers can *co-regulate* the room, which can have a profound impact on classroom management in general. Don't be afraid to let go of the activity if it's not feeling right. Maybe they are too distracted, finding it hard to settle and focus, or maybe there are external factors that are affecting the classroom environment. Whatever the reason, it's okay to acknowledge that now is not the best time to do the activity and save it for another time. Trying to force these types of activities when the time isn't right could end up putting them off completely.

> I've come to a frightening conclusion that I am the decisive element in the classroom. It's my personal approach that creates the climate. It's my daily mood that makes the weather. As a teacher, I possess a tremendous power to make a child's life miserable or joyous. I can be a tool of torture or an instrument of inspiration. I can humiliate or heal. In all situations, it is my response that decides whether a crisis will be escalated or de-escalated and a child humanized or dehumanized. (Ginott, 1994 [1972])

'Relax, Release, Return' Practice

Try this practice if you find yourself really struggling, especially if this age group is not 'doing as they are told' and you are frazzled. This is a highly versatile practice that can last anywhere from 20 seconds with eyes open to 20 minutes with eyes closed or lowered, and it can be done standing or seated.

1. **Relax:** Notice the body and any areas of tension. See if you can relax those muscles a little, especially in the shoulders, back, and jaw.

2. **Release:** Shift attention to the breath – this breath coming in, this breath going out. See if you can make the out-breath just slightly longer. Notice the busy mind and just keep releasing through the out-breath.

3. **Return:** Open up your attention to the whole body, from the top of your head to the tips of your toes, grounding yourself. Stay curious right here, right now. Take in your surroundings and return to the task at hand, asking yourself, *What kind of weather do I want to set?*

(From Cultivating Emotional Balance program, adapted with permission from
Dr Alan Wallace)

Calm Corners — Creating a Safe Space

We highly recommend creating a Calm Corner (or 'Peace Corner') in your class-room or school where children can go to take care of their needs, settle their bodies, calm their minds, and feel peaceful and safe. This doesn't need to take up much space – it can even be a low, small table with cushions around it. The table can hold different resources that children can access at any time, such as glitter jars, windmills, mini-Hoberman spheres ('Breath Balls'), sand timers, markers and paper to express their feelings/experiences, conflict resolution tools, and books with social-emotional and mindfulness themes rich with illustrations. A poster of some of the foundational practices that they have learned with you can also be put on the wall.

When setting up this space in your class, it is important to teach your students that this is not a place for 'Time Out', which often has negative connotations, but rather it is a place to help them better understand themselves – body, mind, heart – and how they are feeling in a given moment. It is essential to establish the Calm Corner as a positive, designated space for their own flourishing.

 'Peace Begins with Me ...'

The Calm Corner can also be used for taking a first step before entering into any conflict resolution. When issues arise with friends, they can begin to use their mindfulness resources and this space to help them come to a place of more peace and calm in themselves.

- Students can learn to let you know when they are having difficulty with something or someone.

- They can be supported to learn how to choose one of their mindfulness skills to self-calm before going any further.

- If needed, the next steps of mediation can take place in the Calm Corner.

- Help them take turns listening, sharing, and then coming up with a plan to move ahead together.

Mindful awareness practices can thus dovetail beautifully with the use of Calm Corners and in this way exemplify the cultivation of kindness and compassion through self-awareness and awareness of others that we are seeking to promote in our school communities.

Educator Voice: Calm Corner Connection

I recently visited a preschool classroom where one little 4 year old girl was clearly struggling with her emotions during my visit. Her grandmother had just passed away and her teacher had only found out during an activity on expressing emotions. The teacher was able to reach out to the parent to share some tips to help her daughter deal with her loss and to offer a story book about loss to share with her.

Later in the day, the teacher had been using the Hoberman Sphere* with the class to practice noticing the breath during a circle time activity. The sphere is a useful way to help young children connect with the physical movement of their breathing. The teacher later left the sphere in the mindfulness corner of the classroom where students go to spend quiet or reflective time. There they can choose to perhaps listen to audios, read mindful books, look at the goldfish, smell lavender pots or watch snow globes settle.

The young girl visited the corner at one point in the day and she independently took the sphere and started breathing in and out while playing with it. When one of her classmates joined her and asked what she was doing, she said, 'This can help you feel better – you breathe in and out – do you want to try it?' Together the two girls practiced their breathing using the sphere. Smiles appeared and they decided to watch the glitter jars settle before moving on to other activities. These brief moments of self-care, using resources to manage feelings and to notice and respond to emotions is becoming a key part of learning for these children.

Dr Helen Maffini – Mindfulness in the Early Years, Consultant and Trainer, www.mindbe-education.com

*See this article for detailed tips on using the Hoberman Sphere with students: www.mindful.org/a-mindful-kids-practice-the-breath-ball/

Pause. Reflect. Plan.

Now that you have got started, where you go next depends on how much time and space you have available and also on your deeper intentions about **what you really want for your students**. This is a good time to pause and reflect again on where you are heading with this work and on how you can continue to sustain yourself on this journey.

To help you reflect on this, please turn now to the **'Teacher Reflection' on p. 45**.

Ultimately, Early Years education is a time of exploration and play. Introducing mindful awareness in ways that can be joyful is essential. Helping children to ground themselves in their body is a powerful way to begin. The above practices are just a few ideas to help students build up their ability to aim and sustain their attention as well as cultivate kindness and compassion. Keep returning to your intentions and motivations. Be aware of your own need to make things go your way or to be 'right' versus following the needs of the class and responding to the children right in front of you. The most important piece is that you are coming from a place of *Being Mindful*. See for yourself what it is like to 'Relax, Release, and Return' in these moments so that you can truly practise being present. Above all, keep it joyful, stay curious, and cultivate a sense of wonder. This will lead to new and exciting discoveries for both yourself and the children in your care. You are setting them up with the foundations of an emotional toolkit that they can return to again and again throughout their lifetime.

Chapter Summary

In this chapter we have:

- Shown you examples of how to introduce mindful awareness activities to 3–6 year old students.

- Provided some practices you can try out to begin to extend students' practice in developing these skills and to 'season' their school day.

- Highlighted the importance of a Calm Corner space in your classroom and/or school.

Further Reading and Resources

Curriculum Training

Dots Curriculum (Mindfulness in Schools Project) – for 3-6 year olds, https://mindfulnessin schools.org/teach-dots-3-6/dots-curriculum-ages-3-6/

Kindness Curriculum – Center for Healthy Minds at the University of Wisconsin-Madison, 12-week program for pre-kindergarten, https://centerhealthyminds.org/join-the-movement/sign-up-to-receive-the-kindness-curriculum

MindBE Preschool Curriculum – for 2–6 year olds, https://mindbe-education.com/

The Present Curriculum – for children ages 3–12+, www.thepresentcourses.org/the-present-courses/for-primary-schools/

Books

Kaiser-Greenland, S. (2010) *The Mindful Child: How to Help Your Kids Manage Stress, Become Happier, Kinder and More Compassionate*. New York: Free Press.

Nhat Hanh, T. (2011) *Planting Seeds: Practicing Mindfulness with Children*. Berkeley, CA: Parallax Press.

Books to Read Aloud

We show just a few examples here and you can see a longer list at www.mindwell-education.com/mtt-resources

MacLean, K. (2009) *Moody Cow Meditates*. Boston, MA: Wisdom Publications.

O'Leary, W. and Willard, C. (2019) *Breathing Makes it Better: A Book for Sad Days, Mad Days, Glad Days and All the Feelings in Between*. Berkeley, CA: Shambhala Publications.

Rechtschaffen, D. and Willard, C. (2019) *Alphabreaths: The ABCs of Mindful Breathing*. Boulder, CO: Sounds True.

Verde, S., Illustrated by Peter Reynolds (2017) *I Am Peace: A Book of Mindfulness*. New York: Abrams Books for Young Readers.

Songs

Mindful Songs for Children – www.mindfulteachers.org/2016/05/songs-for-children.html

2.
Mindful Awareness in the Primary Years Classroom (7-10 year olds)

In this chapter we provide you with:

Mindful Awareness Training	Activities
Awareness of the Senses	Sense 1: Listening
	Sense 2: Touch
	Sense 3: Sight
	Senses 4 and 5: Taste and Smell
Senses Extension	Combining Senses
	Savouring Sounds
Mindful Movement	Water Walking
	Feather Walking
	Crunchy Walk
Seasoning Activities	Standing Seaweed Sensation
	30-Second Listening
	Freezing and Melting
	Feather Breath
	Back-to-Back Breathing
	Shoulder Rolls
	Foot Stamp
	Hand Hug and Brush
Teacher Practices	Intentions and Senses Reflection
	Pause, Reflect, Plan

Working With This Age Group

In this chapter we have focused on the practical use of Mindful Awareness Training (MAT) with 7-10 year olds. In general, young children are already quite good at living in the moment, so with these sessions we tap into this ability, consciously enlivening their natural awareness through the senses and helping them understand how they can use these skills to self-calm and focus. Children at this age benefit from repeating activities, movement and practices that help strengthen the synaptic connections between the hippocampus and the developing prefrontal cortex, helping them to find ways to exert executive control and learn how to regulate and express their emotions.

We love introducing mindfulness to children of this age, opening a door for them into understanding how they access present-moment awareness through their senses.

- Right from the start we are laying the foundations, both intellectually and experientially, for a whole range of 'slowing down and pausing' activities that our students will be able to draw on in the course of our time together in class. This **'seasoning the day'** will enable us to punctuate busy schooldays with moments of calm.

- By leading students to encounter these moments consciously we are helping them develop the capacity to ground themselves and self-soothe through engaging their parasympathetic nervous systems. Over time, we can help provide them with a toolkit of practices and skills that they can draw on to support positive mental health habits and contribute to overall wellbeing.

- In addition, this learning to consciously cool down is the first step towards any effective approach to conflict resolution.

Developmentally, this group covers quite a wide span. The activities and scripts are written as guides to how we deliver them to children approximately in the middle of this range, so you will need to adapt the language and tone to suit your class. Keep it light and fun, encouraging your children to stay curious. Being aware of what is developmentally appropriate is key. Make sure to try the activities out before you introduce them to students - and enjoy exploring!

Before you actually start teaching this, let's check in with personal intentions:

Teacher Reflection: Intentions and Senses

- Why do you want to try this out with your students?
- What is your intention?

Take a moment to reflect and journal on this.

- Be open to asking yourself the same question once more: *Why am I doing this?*
- See if anything else, perhaps a deeper, underlying motivation arises.

Now, finally, let's check in with your own connection to the purpose of these activities – that is, consciously connecting with sensory experiences:

- When was the last time you just took a moment to listen, taste, look, touch, smell?

If you haven't done so recently (and are honest enough to admit it!) try taking a moment to do so now …

Whilst reading this paragraph, can you allow yourself to slow down a little, continue to read a little more slowly, whilst also becoming aware of sensations in your body, your feet, your hands, your seat; sounds and silences around you; temperature; the breath coming and going …

Just continue to notice sensations and at the end of this sentence, look up, may be stretch, look around, take a moment to breathe, and notice …

'Noticing what you notice' is such an important foundation for this work, and the more we can bring our attention back to our own present moment experience, the better prepared we will be to lead others in these important awareness activities.

So, if you are ready, let's now explore bringing this to your students!

Awareness of the Senses Activity

Intention: To provide a series of brief but active experiential exercises that show students how to consciously engage with sensory experiences.

This activity runs through a series of different sense exercises and could take around 30-40 minutes depending on the age group. Alternatively, you could adapt this and shorten it to just focus on one sense at a time, using each activity as a 5-10 minute starter for any class. You could then revisit this same sense in various ways of your choosing over the week.

Today we are going to learn about our senses and how they help us to be more alive and awake to what is happening around us and inside us. Who can name one of our senses?

- Continue to elicit all the senses.

 ## Sense 1: Listening

Let's see, where will we begin? Let's start with our ears and our sense of hearing. I'm going to keep quiet for about 30 seconds and I'd like you to also stay quiet and just notice any sounds that you hear. When the time is up, I will ask you to remember any sounds you noticed. Okay? Let's see how good we all are at listening …

(Continued)

So just sit quietly and notice what you hear without speaking for 30 seconds starting from, now ...

- In this last sentence you may find that you are naturally slowing down the cadence of your speech and perhaps lowering the volume a little as you ease yourself and your class into quiet listening mode. This embodiment helps set the tone for your students. As the group listening continues, do your best to stay embodied. Don't worry too much or react too strongly if some students are fidgety or making noises, just do the best you can to manage these individuals through eye contact, gestures, etc.

Okay, what did you hear?

- Take offerings one at a time from students using horizontal inquiry **(see Chapter 5 Top Tip 11)**, perhaps commenting:

Oh I see others nodding. Did you also hear that?

- Try to get as many different sounds as you can, congratulating the group:

Wow, you guys are such good listeners. What a lot of sounds you heard! I didn't even notice the clock ticking or the bird outside.

- This is an activity you can repeat from time to time. Often children enjoy these listening activities and they like to be praised on how their listening skills are developing. You can also help them link this to the importance of listening in learning, languages, music, relationships, etc.

- Moreover, without forcing it, you have created a shared moment of quiet in the classroom - highly unusual in normal school life! You may decide to address this overtly:

How does it feel to be silent like this together in class? We ask you to listen all the time but we don't often teach you how to listen carefully. That's what we are beginning to do here.

Sense 2: Touch

Let's explore our sense of touch next! What do we mostly think of when we think of touch? Yes, our fingers. In these sense exercises try to be very curious, just like scientists, exploring whatever you experience.

Let's do the next activity standing up. Rub your hands together like this.

- Hold hands up palm to palm and rub them back and forth.

Of course our different sense experiences are not separate, they overlap. So while we are rubbing our hands let's also listen to the sounds they are making right now ...

Tune into your hands and fingers, notice the movement, perhaps they are getting warmer ...

Now let's stop and gently place one hand on your chest or heart area and one on your belly. See if you can be very curious now about what your hands are experiencing. Almost like you are listening with your hands.

Can you feel the clothes touching your hands? ...

Any movement in the heart/chest area? ...

And the belly? ...

Now let your hands just hang gently by your sides. And tune in again to any sensations you can notice in your fingers ...

hands ...

arms ...

shoulders ...

or anywhere else in your body right now ...

How are the insides of your body feeling?

Now that we are all quiet, can you maybe notice the movement of breathing in your body?

in your belly ...

in your chest ...

or in your nose ...

- At this point you can close the exercise by asking them again to:

Notice how you feel, notice how the room feels.

- Then, time permitting, you could do another short debrief inviting them to ask a partner, as a curious scientist, what they noticed, emphasizing practising careful listening. Then ask for one or two students to share with the whole class.

- You might also add here a moment to reflect on the purpose of this type of activity, for example:

How might using this sense of touch help us?

(Continued)

- Elicit their ideas, then consider adding a personal example. Here is one of ours:

Sometimes, if I notice I am worrying too much about something, I can use a short focus on my sense of touch to help me worry less. And you can try this with me right now if you want to.

I'm going to try putting my attention into my feet and notice how they feel.

See if you can feel your feet now - from the inside - your toes, maybe the socks and shoes around your feet ...

And now, just notice how you are feeling ...

You may not notice anything different first time. Different practices work for different people at different times. For me, I noticed that when I felt my feet for a moment then I was not worrying about anything and now I feel a little bit calmer.

This activity, or your own variation of it, can be also used as a **Seasoning Activity** at any point during the day. Explore using it at different times and you may find that a short activity, even one minute, can change the atmosphere of the classroom and help students move, settle and re-focus.

TEACHING TIP

Throughout this type of activity, monitor your own experience whilst guiding the children. This is another fundamental principle of MAT. It is our own noticing of sensations in the present moment that can make these short guided practices come alive. This very literal 'embodiment' can also help us maintain flexibility of response when, for example, a sudden noise distracts everyone and we incorporate it into our guidance.

Of course, with a class full of energetic and distractible 8 year olds, there are limits to how much internal monitoring we can maintain! We have to learn how to balance a degree of self-awareness with the need to maintain effective classroom management. This may create a degree of inner tension, but an outer alertness to the realities of the classroom can help us stay focused whilst we can sometimes use our inner ability to 'soften' in order to respond more sensitively to challenging student behaviour.

Keeping a sense of humour can also be very helpful!

 ## Sense 3: Sight

One sense we may sometimes take for granted is our sight. We use our eyes so much that we often forget what an amazing thing it is to be able to see. The world is full of so many beautiful colours, shades and shapes.

Let's just try now for a minute to see if we can explore using our eyes with curiosity. Let's all stand up and move into your own space so you are not too near anyone else.

Take a deep breath in and as you breathe out slowly close your eyes or look down at one spot on the floor ...

Now gently open your eyes and, standing in the same place but turning around very slowly, let's see if we can focus on noticing all of the things in the room that are red (or whatever colour is most obvious in your room).

Without talking, see if you can notice, just with your eyes, different shades of red. Some might be more pinky-red, some might be more orangey-red. Keep looking and noticing.

Now what about blue? Shades of blue. Darker blue. Lighter blue. (If you have a window, you can also include anything you see outside the room.)

And now green.

Now just for a moment look at all the colours around you and see what you notice ...

How do they all look together? What lovely colours we have in our room!

Well done everyone. As I said at the beginning, it's not always easy to appreciate how wonderful it is to be able to see. How beautifully coloured our world is. Some people aren't able to see some colours because their eyes and their brains don't detect them. Do you know anyone like that? And of course some people are born unable to see or they may have lost their sight later on in life. How lucky we are to be able to see.

Remember, our senses are like doors that open to the world and help us understand and connect with everything around us and with all the people in our lives.

TEACHING TIP

Most primary classrooms are quite colourful, but if you happen to be in a bland room, try picking one main colour, even if it is grey or white or brown, and encourage students to notice subtle shades of this colour. Or notice where the light is coming into the room and how it is lighting up different areas. Shapes can work too. It's sometimes shocking to see how many right angles you can find in one room!

Children will naturally want to call out what they are seeing, but we are trying in these practices to help them move towards being able to listen inwardly, so guiding them to 'answer on the inside' may be helpful. We often start these kinds of exercises by saying:

Different people like different activities, and this one may or may not work well for you, but please do your best to not look at others because that might distract them when they might be learning something really important.

Senses 4 and 5: Taste and Smell

- This may work best as a separate activity as it does take some preparation and management. If instead you are wanting to finish off the senses introduction now with a short taste activity, you can do so in a simple way, not drawing it out too much, with just a brief settling and then handing out a piece of chocolate or alternative to each student. Ask them to *really* focus on the sense of taste as they quietly enjoy it.

- Here we show how mindful eating can be used as a separate concluding activity, taking some time to pull together everything we have covered so far:

Today we are going to explore two senses we haven't yet focused on. What do you think they are? ... That's right, smell and taste. First though, can you tell me why you think we have been doing all these sense activities? ...

Yes, as we were saying last week, we are so fortunate if we have all of our senses working well and it is really good for us to appreciate them and to be thankful. But there is also another reason. We know from scientists that when we choose to notice what is happening in our bodies through our senses, we can help the brain to focus in a more relaxed way. This can be very good for our minds and feelings and even our bodies. For example, it can help us when we might be worrying too much about something. Let's look at this short animation of someone you may already know worrying about something ...

- In their **'.b'** (Stop and Breathe) course for 11–18 year olds the Mindfulness in Schools Project makes inspired use of a lovely clip from *Kung Fu Panda*. You can use it here as a nice focus for introducing the tasting activity: www.you tube.com/watch?v=BwqSraJpqfs (YouTube: Search 'Kung Fu Panda, Today is a Gift').

- We have also used this clip to good effect when introducing the Awareness of the Senses activity. (It also works well with older teens, and even university students and adults seem to really enjoy it!)

- The clip ends with Po (the Kung Fu Panda) about to mindfully eat a peach.

Is Po looking as worried now as he was at the start? What was Master Oogway, the wise old turtle, telling Po about the 'gift of the present'? When Po heard that, he looked at the one peach that had fallen into his hand and he now understands that he has the choice to eat that one peach slowly, carefully, really enjoying it, noticing everything about it. Not just stuffing his face as he was doing when he was upset.

In a moment we will try to see if we too can eat something very carefully, with all our sense doors open. Remember I said that we have learned from scientists who have explored how our minds, bodies and emotions work and you know that you are all scientists too. You can use your attention and curiosity to explore things mindfully, with your senses.

As we do this final exploration we will be using all the senses we have investigated up until now. We will look, listen, touch, and yes, smell and taste.

- This eating exercise can be done with almost any food but we have enjoyed using tangerines. They are very good for eliciting all of the senses. If you feel the students have been sitting for too long and need to move, invite them to come up and take a tangerine from a basket (and a napkin), returning to their desk and placing the tangerine on the napkin. It's helpful, but not necessary, to have them in the fridge so they are cold.

TEACHING TIP

You will also have a tangerine and will be doing the same things you ask your students to do. Your present experience of doing this will model the practice to students, and also help inform how you direct the questions, as well as your pacing of the instructions.

Sometimes teachers lead tasting practices without doing it themselves and may either miss opportunities to make it more real and engaging or, as in one case we saw, continue to describe sensations long after the students' (quickly dissolving) treats had gone!

Now that you all have your tangerine in front of you, let's first use our sense of sight to investigate this tangerine.

- You can encourage students to keep the answers to the following questions to themselves, or invite some answers to be shared out loud. The key to this exercise, like so many of them, is to pique their interest - and also of course to make it enjoyable!

What do you notice about the colour? Is it the same colour on the whole tangerine? What about the texture? Is it smooth or rough? And how about the light shining on the tangerine? Are there any reflections? Get to know your tangerine. In fact, get to know your tangerine so well that if I collected all of these and put them back into the basket, you would be able to find yours again!

Don't worry! I'm not going to do that! Just try to notice as much as you can about this tangerine, by using your sense of sight. Everyone has a tangerine in front of them. But only you have this one. It's unique. Just like you.

Now pick up the tangerine and place it in one of your hands. What do you notice from your sense of touch? Is there any temperature to the tangerine? What about weight. Maybe move it gently from one hand to the other and notice how heavy or light it is. Is it smooth or rough to the touch?

(Continued)

Do tangerines make any sounds? Let's hold it up to an ear. Nothing there yet but what if we gently begin to peel the tangerine? Take a moment to get ready to peel it ... now bring it back to your ear and let's just listen as we all begin to peel our tangerines together.

- Allow some peeling and listening time ...

Wow! Do you notice another sense coming alive as we peel this? That's right - smell! What do you notice about the smell? Can you sense it in your nostrils? And what about your mouth now - is it getting ready to eat this tangerine? How do you know? So keep peeling now and keep noticing smell as you gently tear away one section of your tangerine, like this. (Demonstrate by holding one section up.)

Don't eat it yet - but let's do a quick investigation of this section. Hold it up to the light. Feel its weight and texture. And now, put it in your mouth between your teeth on one side - but don't bite it yet!

- Do this yourself at this point. It is difficult to speak with a section of tangerine in your mouth, but it is also humorous and the students can get a kick out of your playfulness.

Notice again what is happening in the mouth. Maybe there's more saliva there? Now, in your own time, start to chew this section of tangerine very slowly, noticing any of the senses as you eat it ...

Keep noticing, tasting ... You may even notice other senses again. There is touch involved in tasting - the tongue touching the tangerine, the insides of the mouth ... Sometimes you might hear chewing ...

- Allow them some time to finish eating and sensing.

And now turn to your learning partner and find out from them what that experience was like for them. You may both eat the rest of your tangerines normally while you take turns sharing about what eating with our sense doors open feels like ...

Do we normally eat like this? Of course we couldn't eat like this all the time, but perhaps you can try to eat really using your senses carefully every now and then, even just a few mouthfuls. You may even want to teach your parents how to eat a tangerine like Po!

TEACHING TIPS

- Introducing food into a class activity brings with it a heightened excitement level which requires careful classroom management. Be clear with instructions and frontload steps on what's to come and what to expect. Try your best to prepare things in advance and go with the flow!

- Don't forget to check about allergies and have some alternatives if necessary.

- Having the tangerines and napkins ready but hidden is helpful so the students don't see them until you are ready to begin the exercise.

(For more tips and pedagogical advice on teaching mindfulness, see **Top Teaching Tips, Chapter 5**.)

Of course, part of what we are doing here with our students is instilling a sense of appreciation and gratitude for the wonderful things that we have and the ways we can connect through our senses. We know from the research (Emmons, 2010) that bringing conscious attention to feelings of appreciation and gratitude can have a positive effect on our wellbeing.

Teacher Voice: What Went Well?

In my classroom, every Friday we do a 'What Went Well?' activity where we reflect on our week in school and remember three small things that went well for us and why. We write these down on a sticky-note, stick these onto the 'What Went Well?' board and celebrate the positive week we have had.

From my experience of embedding wellbeing practices into the schools I have worked in, what I find most effective is explaining succinctly why the practices are important for wellbeing and then helping make it as easy as possible for teachers to adopt the practices too. So, I invited colleagues to my classroom and showed them the board. I briefly explained the research behind the activity and gave them a handout with some links to further reading if they wanted to explore the evidence. Finally, I gave them a stack of sticky-notes and a 'What Went Well?' banner for them to create a display easily in their own classrooms. Busy teachers need to know why something is worth doing and it needs to be easy to implement. That's why this wellbeing practice can work so well in schools.

Adrian Bethune - part-time primary school teacher, Aylesbury, UK and author of *Wellbeing in the Primary Classroom: A Practical Guide to Teaching Happiness*, www.teachappy.co.uk

Senses Extension Activities

Combining Senses

In follow-up activities you may sometimes want to explicitly focus students on combining different senses. For example:

- Can they listen to the ticking of the clock and other sounds and be aware of the physical movement of the breath at the same time? You can guide them

(Continued)

gently into these brief practices, for example starting with sounds and then including the awareness of breath movement.

- Can they look at the tree outside the window and notice their breath moving in their body at the same time?

- Can they feel their feet 'from the inside' while listening to the clock?

     ## Savouring Sounds

If you want to take the introductory listening activity further, then on another day you could try this:

> Let's go back to practising our listening skills. Remember how useful learning to be a good listener is? And how helpful it is to our bodies, minds, and feelings to sometimes just take a moment to be quiet? In a minute I'm going to ring the chime bar so let's sit (or stand) in a way that helps remind us to pay attention. If you feel comfortable you might want to close your eyes. Some people find their listening sense works better when they don't use their sight sense. If you prefer to keep your eyes open, that's fine, just look gently towards a spot in front of you on the floor or the desk.

> Now listen to the sound of the chime as it fades away, and when you can't hear it any longer, just see if you can stay quiet, relaxed and awake and simply notice any other sounds or silences that come to your attention …

> No need to try too hard, just allow the sounds to come to you. This time you don't have to remember what you hear, just see if you can enjoy listening to the sounds themselves. Be curious …

> Notice loudness… softness … high sounds … low sounds … sounds outside the room … sounds inside the room …

> To close, I will ring the chime bar once more, and when you no longer hear the sound, just gently open your eyes.

> Notice how you feel. Notice how the room feels. Maybe stretch a little.

> How was that? Turn to your learning partner (or someone close to you) and ask them what they noticed. Not just which sounds they heard, but also how did they feel doing that activity?

- If the activity went well, reinforce this with the group:

> You know, that was a really lovely silence you guys created while doing that activity. Well done!

- If it was a bit bumpy, then:

> Okay, thank you for having a go at this. Mindful listening is not always easy to do. It's actually a skill that needs practice. Some times are easier than others. This is something that we can practice again together.

TEACHING TIP

- Don't prolong this activity too much when you do it for the first time. Feel free to use your own words and allow short pauses throughout the activity. Use your own awareness to sense into when to close it.

Having completed our introduction to the senses, where we go next depends on how much time and space we have available each week and also on our deeper intentions.

What do we really want for our students?

Take the time now to pause and reflect again on where you are heading and how you can continue to sustain yourself on this journey.

Teacher Reflection: Pause, Reflect, Plan

If you are working through this book with colleagues, this could be a good focus activity for pair or group work. If reflecting alone, collect your responses in your journal.

1. What do I really want for my students?

Explore this question for a moment, checking in with any previous intentions and see-ing whether anything new arises or whether you want to reconfirm your original ideas.

2. Realistically, how much class time can I make available for:
    a. Regular mindfulness lessons?
    b. Short Seasoning Activities?
3. What other opportunities might there be to connect what my students are learning here with other school classes and activities?
4. What support might I be able to get from colleagues, school leaders, and parents?
5. How can I develop and sustain my own wellbeing and self-care at school?
6. How can I find support for sustaining my wellbeing outside of school (e.g. local meditation groups, retreats, yoga classes, tai chi, Qi Gong, online courses, etc? See The Contemplative Tree diagram, Figure 4.2 in Chapter 4.)

As you continue to develop and explore your work in this area you are becoming what we call a 'Champion Teacher', in the sense that, through your personal under-standing of the value of self-care and awareness-based wellbeing, you are modelling this in yourself, as best you can. In Chapter 8 we explore further questions and challenges related to your development of this work in schools and how this can contribute to a larger shift of focus in your school community.

Mindful Movement

Having introduced your students to a range of conscious sensory experiences you may want to try out other activities to build and apply present-moment awareness in other fun ways. This next activity is one example of how to do just that.

 ## Water Walking

Intention:

- After investigating the senses and how to focus our minds we can also bring that same focus to movement, practising waking up the senses whilst also paying attention to each other.

  This activity requires the use of water and cups. If your school cafeteria has reusable plastic beakers, you may want to use these. (See below for alternative ways to approach this activity without using water.)

Preparation:

- This can be done in the classroom, but it can also be useful to do this activity in a bigger space or even outside.

- Fill the cups with drinking water, almost to the brim. Make sure to have one per student plus one for you and any assistants.

- Have a pitcher ready filled with more drinking water.

- If indoors, bring a towel to clean up any spills!

Activity:

- Invite students to take one cup of water each and walk around the room slowly - the intention is to try not to spill any water.

- Children will naturally look at the water as they walk - it helps them focus on not spilling it.

- Continue to guide them with verbal instructions using a light, playful tone:

  Walk as slowly as possible to ensure the water stays in the cup.

  Notice your classmates as you walk near to each other.

  Are you holding your breath? If so, let it out slowly as you continue to walk.

  Are you gripping the cup very tightly? See if you can loosen your grip a little.

- As you continue to guide them allow for moments of silence here and there.

- Walk around and use the pitcher of drinking water to fill up random cups a little bit more. This will create a buzz and some students will want more water and some may avoid you! No need to fill up all cups. The random nature of it is part of the fun.

- At a certain point, you may want to ask students to carefully exchange cups with the child nearest to them.

- Continue with slow walking around and then bring them to a final stop.

- One way to end is by bringing their attention to their bodies and breath and then briefly focus on appreciating having clean drinking water. For example:

Now that we have stopped walking, notice if your muscles feel tight. Maybe your shoulders and arms are tight. Try relaxing your shoulders down while still holding the cup. Now, using your sense of sight, bring your attention to the water in the cup. You are standing still but is the water still? Do you notice any movement in the water? And how are you feeling right now?

- Then you can direct students to pour water back in the pitcher or sink or, better still, if there are plants in the room they can water them. If you are doing this activity outside, students can choose to give some water back to the earth or plants nearby.

Optional extension:

Do you notice any temptation to drink the water? Maybe, or maybe not. Our bodies need water every day to help us stay healthy. We are very lucky that we can drink water whenever we want to. If you want to, feel free to slowly take a sip or two of water and use your sense of touch - inside your mouth, like we did with our tangerines - to taste the water. If you do not want to drink, no problem.

  ## Water-Walking Variations

- Instead of walking you may have students pass one cup of water around a circle, standing or sitting.

- You can have the whole class do it together, or in small groups. Introduce one cup at the beginning then add more cups to be passed around. Consider changing directions!

Alternative (Dry!) Activity: Feather or Marble Walking

This has a similar intention to Water Walking. Try it out for yourself first and see if you think marbles or feathers would work best for your class.

- Give each student a small feather or marble.

- Model yourself holding the feather/marble in an open palm and encourage them to try to not close the hand around it to secure it. Help them focus before moving; perhaps putting their attention in their feet; tuning in to the sense of touch of the object in their palm without looking at it, etc.

(Continued)

- Then start to move slowly enough that the feather/marble stays in the open palm while they are moving, without needing to close their hands.

- You could even give half the class marbles while the other half has feathers and exchange part way through.

Crunchy Walk

- Make a trail on the floor using crumpled-up newspaper or tissue paper.

- Invite students to walk carefully along the trail, focusing on the 'crunchy' sensations with their feet and ears.

- You can consider making a few different trails with different materials, colours and sensations using scarves, cotton balls, etc., and breaking the class into smaller groups of 'explorers'.

- If possible, try this one outside in the autumn on crunchy leaves!

Educator Voice: Our Wellbeing Journey

I was very fortunate to be Principal of a new public (state) school in Canada and we decided, after lots of research and planning, that mindfulness and wellbeing would be the foundation of our school culture from the beginning.

Through research, we discovered that the MindUP curriculum was a good fit for our school. In order to implement the program all staff participated in three days of training on mindfulness in which they also gained valuable insight into their own wellbeing. Teachers started to notice differences with themselves – they felt calmer in the classroom, they were better able to recognize their emotions and how best to care for themselves. We asked our students if they found the breathing strategies helpful:

They are helpful, if you're mad, you can use it to calm yourself down. Also it gives you a chance to have some time when nobody is annoying you.

Grade 4 Student

I feel more relaxed and ready to learn or else I would totally go off-topic and not do my work. Every day, whenever I get mad, I always take a moment to breathe and forget about it so that it won't be stuck in my head for the rest of the day.

Grade 5 Student

It makes me realize how hyper I actually am. When I do realize, I know that I need to calm down. When I don't realize, I keep on going crazy.

Grade 6 Student

They make it easier for you to focus and they calm you down but you have to actually do the exercises for it to work.

Grade 5 Student

Every classroom has a Calming Corner with mindfulness tools available for students and despite limited space in the school we have a dedicated room for staff mindfulness practices. I will do my very best not to give up this space as it is a refuge for teachers during a busy school day!

Maintaining a focus on wellbeing in the school is a journey and it doesn't happen overnight. Clear communication, professional development and teacher support are key. I am committed to providing time for staff to be trained – it is a continual challenge but this is critical! We can't expect students to practice if WE don't practice mindfulness and our own self-regulation. It is not always easy to find the time for this in a busy school but we always begin our staff meetings with mindfulness and make it a priority in our learning.

Pauline McKenna – Principal, Kanata Highlands Public School, Ottawa, Canada

Seasoning Activities

Once you have laid a foundation for whole-class sensory activities you can build on this by introducing short Seasoning Activities to help students self-calm and/or energize. These brief exercises can be used at the beginning or end of a class; for a transition exercise between activities; or whenever you want the class to pause for a moment. With any age group it is important to provide opportunities for movement and physical grounding, and with 7-10 year olds we need to find ways to allow them to move around frequently. By doing movement with an awareness component we can help students find ways to consciously self-soothe and self-calm. These simple activities can help equip them with a self-care toolkit that they can draw from when needed.

Below are a few sample activities. Once you have a sense of the combination of physical, emotional and mental awareness these activities provide, you will be able to create your own, perhaps even inviting students to suggest exercises that might work for them. At the end of this chapter we point you towards other resources that you can draw from to extend your range of Seasoning Activities.

  ## Standing Seaweed Sensation

- Invite students to spread themselves around the room, spaced away from each other and facing you.

- Tell them about seaweed and in particular kelp – how it is like an underwater forest, each long strand anchored to the bed of the ocean.

(Continued)

- Model standing tall and loose like kelp and invite them to sense into their feet, the root of the kelp, anchored to the sea bed.

- Close eyes or lower gaze to sense more clearly this feeling through the feet.

- Imagine the sea gently moving around them, back and forth, gently beneath the waves, being pushed and pulled slightly from side to side as well.

- As the waves build, the bodies are rocked more powerfully by the water, but the roots keep their feet in place.

- As the waves begin to gradually calm, the movement slows down until there is just a very slight, gentle rocking movement.

- Finally the waves stop moving altogether and they can stand still – a quiet forest of kelp.

- Invite them to notice whether there are any tiny movements in the body even standing still.

- If their eyes were closed, invite them to open them and notice how they feel. Maybe stretch the arms up high, taking a deep breath in, and bringing the arms down as they breathe out. Then invite them to return to their seats, keeping this sense of being 'calm kelp'.

- If appropriate, congratulate them on how well they participated, how much like a kelp forest they really were and remind them that the seaweed activity is one of the ways we can tune into our senses through the body and that these short moments are really good for helping us stay calm and healthy.

TEACHING TIP

For this activity we sometimes have a background video of kelp swaying in the sea because the visual movement and sounds can help students calm more easily and connect them with the sense of nature and natural movement. For example: www.youtube.com/watch?v=DCWJPrGTLtU (YouTube Search: 'Spring Seaweeds').

       ## 30-Second Listening

- This was first introduced in the 'Awareness of Senses' introduction above and can be used as a stand-alone activity at any time.

- Consider extending it by a few seconds each time.

- You can also vary it in the way you draw attention to the sounds, for example: *Let's focus just on sounds from outside the room*, or *notice today if some sounds are continuous, and some just come and go*, etc.

Freezing and Melting

- This can be done sitting or standing.

- Gradually squeeze-freeze the whole body tight, tight, tight, solid like a block of ice.

- Then slowly 'melt', loosening and releasing the tightness bit by bit, perhaps guiding them through one body area at a time.

TEACHING TIP

Some students might automatically hold their breath as they are 'freezing'. Mention this possibility in the moment, as an object of curiosity rather than a 'mistake'. You can also then guide them to notice how we often naturally exhale more deeply when we begin to 'melt'.

 Feather Breath

- This can be done with a real or imaginary feather.

  Hold it between thumb and index finger.

  Blow on the feather – as gently as possible – with the intention to maintain a flow of breath, having the feather move, but as little as possible.

  Do this a few times, taking a long breath in (careful not to inhale the feather!), then exhaling slowly with gentle blowing.

  Notice how you feel.

- Remind them that when we want to slow down a little or calm ourselves, a longer, gentle out-breath helps the body to relax and rest. Slowing down the body can also help slow down the mind when we get over-busy or worried.

TEACHING TIPS

- Watch out for hyperventilating! If children seem to over-breathe or try too hard, just help them to breathe and blow more easily and gently. Even their natural breath will move the feather slightly.

- Prolonged silences and a focus on the breath can be uncomfortable if a student has any trauma in their past. Please refer to the end of Chapter 5 for more information on trauma-sensitive teaching.

(Rel. Skills) ## Back-to-Back Breathing

Sit with your back resting against your partner's back. Sit up straight and be still and silent.

One person starts breathing in and out slowly and deeply. The other person tries to sync their breathing to their partner's.

Notice how you feel. Ask your partner what they noticed.

For more Breath Awareness practices, see Chapters 1 and 3.

Shoulder Rolls

Choose a comfortable sitting position.

As you take a slow deep breath in through your nose raise your shoulders up towards your ears ...

Breath slowly out through your mouth, rolling your shoulders back and down as you exhale.

Repeat slowly, rolling your shoulders up and down in time with your breath.

Foot Stamp

- This can be done sitting or standing.

  Stamp the feet, starting slowly and building to stamping as quickly and as fast as possible.

- Guide them a little, like an orchestral conductor.

  Then begin to slow down, coming to stillness and quiet.

- Draw students' attention to any sensations they might notice in their feet and toes (e.g. warmth, tingling, fizzing, prickling).

  Just notice!

Hand Hug and Brush

Rub hands together to create warmth.

Squeeze different parts of your body noticing how they feel before and after.

Pretend your hands are brushes, firmly 'brushing' arms, neck, belly, lower back and legs.

Stand still, lower or close your eyes, notice any sensations left over from the brushing.

Once you have a feel for what works for your students, you can try out some of your own activities or draw from the rich range of resources available in this area. You will find some examples in the Further Reading and Resources at the end of this chapter. And don't forget to consider 'Pick 'n Mixing' some adapted activities from the other chapters in this section.

In Section II you will find many ideas to help you create opportunities for your students to begin to apply the new skills they are learning across the curriculum and throughout the school day. As you begin to contribute to a shifting of your school culture and processes to focus more on awareness, wellbeing and balance, don't forget to keep your own balance and wellbeing at the heart of everything you do.

Chapter Summary

In this chapter we have:

- Shown you how to introduce sensory awareness activities to 7–10 year olds.

- Laid the foundation for building attention, listening and emotional regulation skills.

- Provided a range of exercises you can try out to 'season' the school day and extend your students' practice in further developing these skills.

Further Reading and Resources

Curriculum Training

Holistic Life Foundation - various programmes, https://hlfinc.org/
Mindful Schools - for ages 5-10, www.mindfulschools.org/
MindUP - for ages 3-13, https://mindup.org/
PATHS Program – for ages 3–10, evidence-based SEL Program, (CASEL certified) https://pathsprogram.com/
Paws b (Mindfulness in Schools Project) - for ages 7-11, https://mindfulnessinschools.org/teach-paws-b/
Still Quiet Place - for ages 5-18, www.stillquietplace.com/sqp-10-week-online-training/

Books

Bethune, A. (2019) *Wellbeing in the Primary Classroom: A Practical Guide to Teaching Happiness.* London: Bloomsbury Publishing.
Nhat Hanh, T. and Weare, K. (2017) *Happy Teachers Change the World: A Guide for Cultivating Mindfulness in Education.* Berkeley, CA: Parallax.
Rechtschaffen, D. (2014) *The Mindful Way of Education: Cultivating Well-Being in Teachers and Students.* New York: W.W. Norton & Company.

Books to Read Aloud

DiOrio, R., illustrated by Eliza Wheeler (2010) *What Does It Mean to Be Present?* San Francisco, CA: Little Pickle Press.

Edwards, N., illustrated by Katie Hickey (2019) *Happy: A Children's Book of Mindfulness.* London: Little Tiger Press.

Muth, J. (2002) *The Three Questions*. New York: Scholastic Press.

Willard, C. and Weisser, O. (2020) *The Breathing Book*. Boulder, CO: Sounds True.

App

Inner Explorer - https://innerexplorer.org/
90 days of short accessible guided audio practices for 5-10 year olds (CASEL certified).

Websites

Go Noodle - Movement activities and mindfulness practices, www.gonoodle.com/
Mind Yeti - Mindfulness practices, www.mindyeti.com/

3.

Mindful Awareness in the Middle Years Classroom (11-13 year olds)

In this chapter we provide you with:

Mindful Awareness Training	Activities
Session 1: Mind and Body • Using attention to connect mind and body.	Framing Your Introduction Tapping Into the Body Feet Seat Hands
Session 2: Anchoring • Using the body and sounds as ways of grounding. • Applying attention skills to listening to others.	Relaxed and Alert Short Opening Practice Shake it Off 'Listen In' Losing Attention – The Balloon Pairs Whispering Tuning In to Tunes
Session 3: Breath Awareness • Using the breath as another way of anchoring. • Applying breath awareness to regulating emotions.	Using Alternative Anchors Loosen Up The Breath Hot Chocolate Breath
Session 4: Using The Tools • What we have learnt and how to apply skills. • Exploring positive emotions. • Closing the course.	Dropping Anchor Toolkit Activity Feedback Survey Paper Clouds Circle Up Savour and Share

(Continued)

(Continued)

Mindful Awareness Training	Activities
Extension Activities	Mindful Walking
	Body Scan
	Letting the Body Lead
	Guess Who?
	Sensory Safari
Teacher Practices	Clarifying Your Intention
	Pause, Reflect, Plan

Working With This Age Group

A fellow middle school principal once opened her address to new parents by stating: 'The Middle School years are characterized by a time of rapid transition. When your children come to us, they are still babies; when they leave us, they can *have* babies.' Guaranteed to set parent alarm bells ringing, there is nevertheless truth in her description of the huge range of biological and developmental experiences within such a relatively narrow chronological age band. While there is no 'average' Middle Years (MYs) student, there are some general characteristics that are common to these years. For example:

- Self-consciousness grows (not always in a positive or comfortable way).
- Peer relationships often become a high priority.
- Physiological changes can lead to a roller coaster of moods and emotions.

Students at this stage are often caring, idealistic and energetic. Some experience excitement, or a sense of horror, about their rapidly changing body (or lack thereof!) and for many this can create a sense of physical and social awkwardness. A growing interest in *Who I am* and *How my mind, body and emotions work* can be harnessed and explored in line with these changes.

Younger children often take quite naturally to mindful awareness activities, but it can sometimes be more challenging in the MYs. In structuring their learning, pace and variety become increasingly important for many students as their 'wandering minds' find more and more to wander about! Authenticity is critical for engaging MYs students on a deeper level and it takes a teacher with both mindfulness and age-appropriate teaching skills to be able to find ways to open this door effectively for students. Many students at this age are developing close relationships with their peers (and with their technology), but connection with adults is still the key to their learning. Middle Years teachers often become adept at establishing the special kind of rapport that works best with this sometimes frustrating but ultimately highly rewarding age group.

Throughout your exploration of teaching mindfulness to students we strongly recommend that you keep checking in with your own experience, with your personal mindfulness practice and with your intentions:

Teacher Reflection: Clarifying Your Intention

First, settle yourself by sitting with a grounded, alert posture and take three conscious breaths.

- Why do you want to explore this area with your students?
- What is your intention?

Take a moment to reflect on this ...

Now, ask yourself the same question once more: *Why am I doing this?* and see if anything else, perhaps a deeper, underlying motivation arises.
    Write down anything that has arisen.
    Pause and repeat and see if any new feelings or images arise.
    Revisiting your intentions from time to time can be very helpful in guiding you through this work.

Mindful Awareness Training Sessions

As you begin to introduce these new skills to your students you will be guiding practices and leading reflections, so you will need to be able to bring to this, as best you can, an 'embodied presence', along with all your teaching and classroom management skills (see **Chapter 5 Top Teaching Tip 1**). If you have not yet developed a personal mindfulness practice we strongly recommend you wait until you have this established before embarking on introducing the following sessions. You can find support and resources for developing your personal practice at the end of the **Introduction** (pp. 10-11).

Getting Started

There are so many ways of introducing mindful awareness to MYs students, so we set out in this chapter examples of how to get started and then look at how you can best develop your own way forward.

- We offer here a suggested format for four sessions, but this could also be effectively delivered as eight to ten shorter sessions.

- With the younger end of this age group, you could consider starting with some of the **Awareness of the Senses** activities in Chapter 2, modifying the language to fit.

Framing Your Introduction

We offer below one way of introducing the training, but it is worth giving some consideration to how you can best frame your own introduction to make it as accessible as possible for your students. For example, some schools prefer labels such as 'Mental Fitness' to 'Mindfulness' as ways of describing their approach to supporting wellbeing and mental health. A comparison with physical fitness can be easily understood by MYs students, and because we are talking here initially about skills development, analogies like 'brain gym' and 'performance training' are also appropriate. It is also important though to emphasize the community values of training in this area for growth, connection and ethical behaviour. This is not just about bare attention training. Try to help your students get a feel for the broader benefits of nurturing curiosity and kindness in themselves and their relationships.

Session 1: Mind and Body

Intention:

- To frame and introduce the training sessions, giving students various access points and a rationale for this work.

- To provide students with an invitational experience using mindful awareness as a way to start to train the attention through connecting the mind and body.

The sample scripts are written as we would deliver them to 12 year olds, so feel free to adapt the language and tone to suit your class. The introduction could be done with or without slides depending on your class. Sometimes it's easier to build a focused environment without using a screen, but visual aids can also be really helpful for maintaining students' attention. We like to use slides with interesting images and not too much text.

This short course that we are starting today is designed to help us understand more about the connection between our mind and our body. This is a subject that has fascinated scientists and philosophers throughout history. Understanding ourselves – how our minds work, how our bodies work, how our feelings work – and understanding how these three aspects of being human work together, and can sometimes trip us up and cause us problems, is a central part of our journey to becoming mature adults.

As we find out more about how this understanding is used in the world we will learn how important developing our own self-understanding and selfawareness is for our growth and our health and wellbeing. One of the primary functions of family and school is to help us develop solid foundations in life. And for this we need a balance of physical, emotional and mental health. As we develop our awareness we can use it to make better connections with other people, friends and family and this can also help us understand better how to cope with difficult situations and difficult feelings like anxiety and anger. These social-emotional skills can then become a kind of 'toolkit' available in both our personal and working lives.

- Here you might share some examples of applying Mindful Awareness Training (MAT) in professional work. We outline examples from sports and policing that you can use or adapt and you may find others that you think will be relevant for your students.

Sports:

These days many top athletes use the research and understanding from sports psychology to help develop their abilities. In individual sports like tennis or golf, your inner thoughts and criticisms can really get in the way of your game. You may have all the physical skills you need but that is at most only half the battle. Even champion tennis player Novak Djokovic has to struggle sometimes with his inner thoughts and feelings while in the middle of a competitive match, and if he hadn't learnt how to work with his mind then he would never have been able to achieve such success. Also, in team sports, MAT has been very helpful to many professionals. For example, basketball coach Phil Jackson, who took his teams, including the LA Lakers and the Chicago Bulls, to win a total of 11 NBA Championships, incorporated mindfulness into his training routines to help his players really be present and tune into each other. Some coaches and sports psychologists call this type of training 'mental fitness' because it is just as important as physical fitness and equally necessary to achieve your best as a sportsperson. (See Chapter 6 for more information on applying MAT in Sports and Performance.)

Policing:

Many employers these days are looking for people who have emotional intelligence skills because these enable us to be effective team members and leaders. Even in areas like policing there is a growing interest in using MAT to support policemen and -women with their highly challenging work, helping them learn how to manage stress and to not overreact or use unnecessary force in moments of conflict.

- There are a number of studies that have been done on using MAT in policing – here are a couple of places where you can find further information:

(Continued)

Research Case Study: Mindfulness and Policing

Many countries have now carried out research into the potential of MAT for police officers with positive results, and some have developed their own training courses.

- Mindful Policing: The Future of Force.

  With police violence in the news, and public scrutiny on the rise, cities turn to mindfulness to help officers deal with the stress of the job. (Yeoman, 2017)

This article explores some of the research and benefits arising from initiatives using mindfulness training with police forces in the USA, Canada and Finland.

- The Royal Canadian Mounted Police.

  Research conducted by Pacific University demonstrated improvements in a number of dimensions: perceptions of administrative stress, operational stress, sleep, pain management, anger (emotion regulation), reactivity, burnout, resilience and acting with awareness. (Goerling, 2014)

As we learn more about how our minds work we can also improve our ability to learn, not just in school, but wherever we want to acquire new skills. What we know from scientific research and from people who have spent a lot of time observing their own minds through meditation is that the mind does not easily pay attention unless there is something really important happening to us. If something is dangerous we might immediately wake up and pay attention because our survival may depend on our reaction. Sometimes we don't have to work so hard to pay attention, for example because we might be learning something that we are naturally interested in. But we aren't naturally interested in everything and even the things that might really appeal to us - for example, playing guitar in a band - involve lots of work and practice that isn't so exciting. And of course these days our attention is pulled all over the place because of social media, the internet and our phones.

So, given all of this, how can we learn to use our brains more effectively and be able to put our attention where we choose to put it? In this training we are going to draw from what has been learnt since ancient times by people practising how best to use the human brain, mind and body, combined with scientific research in neuroscience, meditation and psychology from the last 30-40 years. We will start with learning how to train our attention and we can do this by exploring the connection between the mind and the body.

- Use the following diagram to help introduce this:

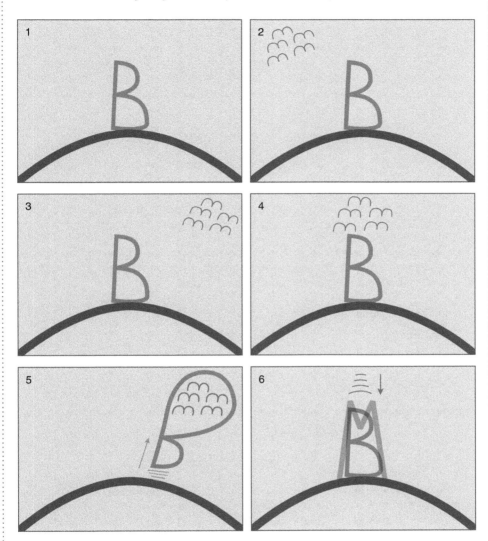

Figures 3.1-3.6 Mind-Body Diagrams

1. This is our Body, sitting on the earth.
2. We also have a Mind. One of the things our Mind does is think. It thinks about the past, remembering things.
3. It thinks about the future – imagining, planning...
4. The Mind also likes to chatter about the present – commenting, judging, liking, disliking...
5. When the Mind gets filled with thoughts, for example worrying about the future, the Body gets disconnected from the Earth.
6. To get re-connected, we can use our awareness of what is happening in the Mind and Body to notice what's going on. We can let go of all the chattering and bring the Mind to rest on the feeling of the Body. We can feel our shoulders, feel our face, feel the soles of our feet. Wherever there is sensation, we can feel that.

(Continued)

Now let's try actually using this understanding in a practical way to help us connect our mind and body. I want to encourage you to approach this for yourself as an explorer or a scientist, bringing curiosity to your own experience. First let's wake up our bodies whilst tuning in with our minds.

 ## Movement: Tapping Into the Body

You may develop your own way of helping students warm up the body in a mindful way. We offer readers a short video (www.mindwell-education.com/mtt-resources) that models how to introduce the short movement activity below. Each student will need a small space to stand in and a chair ready to sit on directly after the movement activity. Try to maximize the space between students as much as you can.

A great way of doing this is by using some simple movements from Traditional Chinese Movement. The Chinese have centuries of experience of using these exercises to bring Mind and Body together:

1. Hip twist – arm swing.

2. Body tapping.

3. Standing still, noticing sensations.

4. Move silently to sit, still noticing.

(These movement activities will make more sense after you have seen the video!)

 ## Feet Seat Hands (FSH) Practice

This introductory seated practice should be kept simple and fairly short as it is the first formal practice you are offering. You will be able to offer slightly longer versions of this practice in later sessions. It is really just about aiming the 'spotlight of attention', as Mark Williams (Williams and Penman, 2011) calls it, at the Feet, Seat and Hands, and noticing physical sensations. We have recorded this for you so you can experience it for yourself before guiding your students (www.mindwell-education.com/mtt-resources).

Coming to sit now in a way that feels both relaxed and alert. Connected with the chair and the floor and also with a sense of sitting well; an uplift through the spine; the hands relaxed on the desk or lap... Allowing your eyes to look gently onto the desk or floor, or, if you feel comfortable to, allowing the eyes to close and just tuning in again to any physical sensations left over from the movement.

And now I invite you to bring your attention, like a spotlight, down to your feet. Can you just feel the feet from the inside... the socks and shoes around the feet; the connection with the floor underneath... If it helps just wiggle the toes a little and then seeing if, when they are still, you can continue to notice any sensations.

And now lightly scanning that spotlight of attention up the lower legs, and the upper legs until you can focus now on the connection with the chair beneath you. The pressure through your seat on the chair, being pulled down by gravity. What does that feel like right now?

And finally, from feet, to seat to hands. Wherever your hands are now, can you shine that spotlight of attention on them as you did with the feet? How do your hands feel? Can you sense the palms of the hands? ... the backs of the hands? ...

Bringing a kind curiosity to your experience; not worrying if you can't really feel anything right now; just doing the best you can to point the spotlight of attention on the hands. Perhaps noticing the spaces between the fingers. Any sensation of heaviness or lightness. Of warmth or coolness. Any tingling or pulsing...

And now letting go of that focus on the Feet, Seat and Hands, and becoming aware of anything else that comes to your attention... Perhaps the breath coming and going... the sense of quiet or sounds around you...

If your eyes were closed just gently opening them, noticing how you feel, notice how the room feels. Perhaps stretching a little...

Pair Share: *What Did You Notice?*
Encourage them to be honest – if they couldn't focus on anything or thought it was boring, then that was their experience! If you prefer, they could do a personal reflection in a journal instead. Some might like to draw rather than write. Consider building short journaling reflections into your sessions after practices.

Whole Group: Ask some simple questions that are invitational and normalizing but not too penetrating. The aim is to establish a safe space and for students to feel that whatever they notice is what they notice and that is OK. It's more important to feel they can be honest about their experience (e.g. 'I felt really tired/bored') than to worry about 'doing it right'. Be open to anyone commenting about a wandering mind and normalize this (*That's what minds do...*), and let them know we will explore this more next time.

Some groups may not be very responsive in front of their peers. For suggestions on leading these types of 'inquiry' after practices, see **Chapter 5 Top Teaching Tip 11**.

Depending on the group, you may have students who would be interested in hearing about some of the research on using MAT in schools, for example:

(Continued)

Research Case Study: Middle School

In the USA in 2018 a group of scientists from Harvard University and the Massachusetts Institute of Technology tested a group of middle school students to see if this kind of training actually produced measurable results. They taught students exactly the same type of exercises we just did and got them to practice a few times a week for eight weeks. The results, which included brain scans of some students, showed that, compared to the control group, these students had:

- Increased ability to focus in the moment.

- Expanded capacity to learn and regulate emotions.

- Amygdala less sensitive to negative stimuli.

(Gutierrez et al., 2019)

It may also be helpful for your students to hear comments from peers who have taken this type of training. Here are some from a group of 13 year olds:

'I have trouble dealing with stress and emotions. I found it helpful because it helped me calm down.'

'I found it helpful because when I was in a conflict I would take a minute to lower my stress levels by breathing, and I would count my breath.'

'I joined just for the experience but it helped me out with a lot of academic work and relationships with others.'

'It literally opened my eyes to the most simple, yet the most important things in my life.'

TEACHING TIP

If you don't have enough time in your first session to do all the activities, you could consider just using one or two simple practices to give students a feel for mindful awareness. For example, the 'Hand Clap Activity' as demonstrated by Richard Burnett in this TEDx: www.youtube.com/watch?v=6mlk6xD_xAQ

Home Practice

We try to avoid prescribing 'Home Work' from these sessions, but many teachers have found, especially with MYs students, that some structure is helpful in providing regular opportunities for students to have a go at practising what they are learning outside of lessons. Not all students will engage with this but some really do get a lot out of trying out practices in the quiet of their own room, where they don't need to worry about what their peers are doing and thinking!

TRY THIS OUT!

Try two to three times this week to bring attention to the hands, holding that spotlight there for a few minutes and just 'notice what you notice'.

Notice during this week any times when you can feel your attention in your body while walking, sitting or moving.

Session 2: Anchoring

Intention:

- To use the body and sounds as anchors for mindful awareness practice, noticing when mind and body feel more connected and when attention has wandered off.

- To apply these attention skills to listening with awareness to each other.

Many teachers like to start each lesson by checking in on home practice or other experiences during the week. This may be done as an informal class chat or in a structured format such as journaling or Pair Share. The focus should be on encouragement rather than 'policing'. As we know, establishing a personal practice is not easy!

Figure 3.7   Mind–Body Anchoring

Source: Adapted from original creation by Arawana Hayashi, and licensed by the Presencing Institute – Otto Scharmer, under a CC-SA 3.0 license https://creative commons.org/licenses/by-sa/3.0/

(Continued)

Last week we discovered that bringing the mind's attention to the body helps us develop an **anchor**, grounding us and allowing us to be more present. Our senses are like windows to the external world around us but we can also notice sensations inside the body. Let's see now if we can explore this sense of aliveness through the body.

Relaxed and Alert (R&A)

- Invite students to slouch in their seats as much as they can. Exaggerate this as you model it yourself.

What message is this giving to your mind?

Yes, time to switch off and sleep!

- Order them, military style, to sit very upright, like a soldier on guard duty.

How does that feel? ... Are you still breathing?

- Finally, ask them to find a sitting position that is in-between those two, 'sitting well', feeling both relaxed and alert.

Grounded through the seat and feet, and a sense of gentle uplift through the spine and the neck. Tucking the chin in slightly, allowing the eyes to look down slightly or close them gently if you feel comfortable to do so.

- Then slide straight into the practice below:

 ## Short Opening Practice

- Guide them gently and briefly to explore Feet Seat Hands.

Scan attention lightly through the body, noticing if there are any other places where it is quite easy to feel sensations.

Which places are harder to sense directly?

- Bring practice to a close.

It's important to note that there's nothing wrong with you if you find this hard to do. Some people might find it easy to put their attention into their feet and feel them, while others find it very difficult. We are each different and the good news is that the neuroscience shows we can train our attention to increasingly make these connections. This is actually what we are doing, making connections in the brain and the body through the nervous system.

Pair Discussion: *Why are we bothering to do this?*

- Then elicit some responses.

We are developing our ability to sustain our attention and this can be useful in many areas of our lives (e.g. studying, managing stress, avoiding excessive worrying) and we will look at this again after the next practice.

There are other sense anchors that we can use to help us to be more present, such as listening to sounds.

Movement: Shake it Off

Today we are going to start with anchoring in the body and then move to listening.

First let's wake up the body so we can connect with it more easily.

1. Stand up in a space.
2. Body Shake Activity (do your own or see video, www.mindwell-education. com/mtt-resources).
3. Sit down, with awareness in the body.

 ## 'Listen In' Practice

- Start again with the R&A posture and Anchoring - e.g. do a brief FSH or invite them to tune in again to anywhere in the body where they can notice a sense of aliveness...
- Transition to sounds:

Now moving the spotlight of attention to notice any sounds you can hear...

If you feel comfortable to do so, allowing your eyes to close so you can just listen.

Allowing the sounds to come to you, no need to try too hard, just sitting here and letting the sounds come... and go.

Sounds from in front of you... from the left side... from the right side... from behind... from above...

Sounds that are coming from nearby... and from further away...

Constant sounds... sounds that come and go...

Enjoy just hearing the physical sounds.

Maybe even notice subtle sounds like your own heart beating, or your breathing...

(Continued)

When you notice the mind has wandered off, you can choose to go directly back to noticing sounds, or you can explore first anchoring again through the Feet, Seat or Hands and then moving back to sounds...

Now bringing your attention to the whole of the body breathing.

And if your eyes were closed, gently opening them, stretching...

Pair Share: *What Did You Notice?*
Whole Group: Pick up on, or suggest if necessary, the possibility of noticing that the mind might have wandered off into thinking or daydreaming and away from noticing the sounds. Make sure they understand that this is perfectly normal, that all of our minds wander, but we don't always notice it.

A big part of this training is to notice this and then to bring our attention back to the anchor we have chosen for the practice. We are beginning to become more familiar with this fascinating aspect of the human mind – the way it is forever going off into thinking mode, even when we hadn't intended to think about something.

Now this isn't to say that there's anything wrong with thinking – it's a key aspect of being a human. Nor is there anything wrong with daydreaming, this can actually be helpful sometimes and even creative. Musicians and poets often get ideas for a new song or poem when they let their minds wander. But there are also many times when our repeated patterns of thinking are quite negative, and this type of thinking can be very critical of ourselves and of others and really not helpful. So training our attention can help us notice when our thoughts are dwelling on negative things and making us feel bad or making a bad situation seem worse.

It's important to become aware of when we are paying attention and when we are not. And also of how we can bring a kind and curious quality of attention to our practice:

Losing Attention – The Balloon

This video (www.mindwell-education.com/mtt-resources) shows one way of demonstrating for students that the repeated bringing back of a wandering mind to our anchor, with curiosity and kindness, is actually the way we build that mindfulness muscle of attention.

Encouraging the qualities of curiosity and kindness are key elements of our practices.

It is important at this stage that they all get the message that we are not trying to stop our thoughts and that it is totally normal for the attention to wander off. It is this noticing and the intentional 'bringing back' of the attention that *is* mindful awareness training. This takes practice!

Pairs Whispering Activity

- Get them into pairs and each take a chair, spreading out as much as possible in the room.

- Pairs sit shoulder to shoulder, facing in opposite directions, not looking at each other.

- They decide who will speak (whisper) first when you ask them to.

- Ring the chime bar and do a short sounds practice to get them tuned in to listening.

- Tell them that you will ring the chime again, and when they can no longer hear it, the first person will whisper very quietly, so only their partner can hear.

- They will speak only for a short time, about a minute, and the topic will be, for example, 'My favourite food' or 'Why is listening important?'.

- The listener will not look at their partner or speak or make movements, just focus on careful listening.

- After a minute or so ring the bell and ask them to return to silence for a moment.

- Then ring again and ask the other person to speak while the partner just listens.

- Ring again and then ask them to have a 'normal' conversation (they can move their chairs to face each other) about what was said and how it felt to do that activity.

- Group debrief: *How was that?*

- If possible, explore together the importance of listening, hearing and being heard.

- *How might the ability to listen well be useful?* e.g. learning in general; foreign and additional language learning; music; relationships; listening to yourself.

  ## Using Pairs Listening Across the Curriculum

Once you have established the rationale for developing listening skills and given the class opportunities to try out pair work and practise applying their skills, this becomes a useful teaching tool that you can employ in any of your classes. You can play with how you arrange the seating, e.g. as above or side by side ('driver and passenger' position) or face to face.

You can choose the best prompt to suit the situation, for example:

- What has been your biggest challenge in working on this project?

- What have you enjoyed most about it?

- In the story we just read, which character do you most identify with? Why?

(For more ideas on using mindful listening and speaking in structured group settings see Chapter 7.)

Additionally, if you use a chime bar to signal collective silence then you are continuing to build up mindful awareness skills outside of these discrete training sessions as well as 'seasoning the school day' with moments of calm and quiet. This is actually an important outcome of these sessions, helping students feel more comfortable with moments of communal quiet. (But see 'No Bell Banging Please!' in **Chapter 5 Top Teaching Tip 6**).

Students can self- and peer-assess these non-academic skills and, as these types of approaches are incorporated into our reporting systems, we gradually begin to change the culture of our schools in ways that underline the importance of skills such as attentive speaking and listening and that explicitly value the experiences and perspectives of the learners.

Teacher Voice: Quiet Times

The most crucial breakthrough moments in my mindfulness groups have been when a class has fully engaged in communal quiet practices. They often emerge from the experience fully sold on the benefits and the program. Furthermore, COVID-19 brought to light for me the experience of introverted students who suffer and struggle quietly through the extroverted world of school and then thrived in the distance learning model. I feel there will be a call for schools to build more quiet times and spaces into the school day to meet these students' needs.

Michael Anderson - Middle School Art Teacher, Austria

 ### Listening Extension Activity: Tuning In to Tunes

- Choose a popular song to play.

- Play a few bars, stop and invite students to choose ONE aspect of the song to focus on like the drums or the intonation of the voice. This becomes their anchor while listening. If their attention wanders, notice where it has gone and then bring it back.

- Pair Share: What Did You Notice? + Whole Group Discussion.

TRY THIS OUT!

Pay attention to sounds. This week, try sitting by a window or in nature if you can and just notice sounds. Keep coming back to the physical sensations of sounds.

Try 'Tuning In to Tunes' at home this week. Explore and enjoy the particular quality of the sounds you have chosen to pay attention to.

Session 3: Breath Awareness

Intention:

- To explore following the breath as another potential anchor of attention.

- To experience and understand how to use the breath to self-calm and manage stress.

Expert Advice: Sensitivity to Trauma

Silence and breathing exercises can sometimes bring up strong emotions, especially in children (and adults) who have experienced some form of trauma. Please read the advice from educator and trauma expert David Treleaven on pp. 128–9 before leading these practices and keep an eye out for any students who may appear to struggle with this.

Brief Opening Practice

Now that you have some experience guiding these practices, try leading a brief arrival practice without a script. Just a few minutes, incorporating a short settling and grounding.

Using Alternative Anchors

Next, before starting the following movement and breath awareness practice, make sure that those who might feel uncomfortable focusing on the breath can resource themselves with alternative anchors:

We can use our growing ability to pay attention to our experience with any of our senses. We can eat or drink something and really notice it. We can observe something with our eyes and really take it in. And what many people find helpful for developing these attention skills is to focus on the

(Continued)

breath as an anchor. Breathing is a physical activity that we can sense into just like we did with FSH.

For some people it's an interesting anchor to use because the breath is always changing - from in, to out, to in - and we can watch this flow with our awareness by bringing our attention to it. We will try doing this now, but if at any time you don't feel comfortable focusing on the breath you can choose something else from your toolkit - you can use the body (e.g. Feet Seat Hands) or sounds as your anchor instead of the breath.

Making these kinds of choices is a skilful use of your toolkit. If you do want to try exploring the breath anchor, then we are just aiming to notice our breath without trying to change it, as best we can. With all of these activities we are simply setting our intention to explore something and then noticing how that works for us.

- In these later sessions it is helpful to keep reinforcing the idea that students already have some skills now that they can start to develop and apply.

Movement: Loosen Up

You can use some or all of these to help students loosen the body and open up the lungs a little.

- First get students to find a space to stand in.

- If space is too cramped, just use exercises 3 and 4 below.

- See video (www.mindwell-education.com/mtt-resources) for how to introduce these simple movements:

    1. One arm windmill - in-breath, out-breath.
    2. Other arm windmill - in-breath, out-breath.
    3. Both arms windmill - in-breath, out-breath.
    4. Arm swing - front and back, in-breath, out-breath.
    5. Natural stretch - *What does the body need right now?*
    6. Follow breath with hands - up and down (abdominal area).

 ## The Breath Practice

- Remind students about using an R&A posture to allow the breath to flow.

- Invite them to take three slow intentional breaths...

- Guide them to bring their spotlight of attention to FSH.

- Lightly scan up the body to include breath movement wherever they can notice it (unless they don't feel comfortable observing the breath, in which case remind them about the option to use other anchors instead).

- Remind students about the *quality* of attention we are trying to develop, i.e. attention that nurtures curiosity and kindness (not beating ourselves up!).

Explore any subtle movements of breath – e.g. back of chest, side of rib-cage, lower back.

Allowing the breath to come and go, and following it.

Noticing the in-breath, noticing the out-breath.

Notice how you feel... If your eyes are closed, allowing them to gently open... Notice how the room feels... Maybe stretching.

- You can follow this again with a **short Pair Share** on what they noticed, or go straight to a **Whole Group Inquiry (see Chapter 5 Top Teaching Tip 11)** and discussion on the breath. Keep an eye out for anyone who may really struggle with this, and if appropriate find a moment after the class to have a quiet check in with them.

It may be helpful to share some scientific evidence of the power of breath training. Here is a piece of research that was done in China:

Research Case Study: The Power of the Breath

Research on Breathing – Beijing, China

In 2017, Beijing Academy of Sciences, Beijing Normal University and Harvard Medical School worked on a joint experiment to examine 'The effect of diaphragmatic breathing in healthy adults' (Ma et al.). They trained a group of IT workers in a 'belly breathing' technique as a way of deepening their natural breath and found that, compared with a control group, they had:

- Significantly lower stress and anxiety.
- Significantly lower stress hormone (cortisol).
- Significantly higher sustained attention span.

When we do our seated practice and use the breath as an anchor we are simply following our natural breathing. We have been breathing this way since the moment we were born, so all we are doing is training ourselves to become

(Continued)

aware of our breath. But as humans we also have the ability to take conscious breaths and to breathe more deeply when we want to. Because the breath is connected to our body and our emotions, it is also possible to use the breath sometimes to help us deal with difficult moments, emotions and pain.

When we get a shock, we nearly always take an in-breath.

- Model a quick sharp intake of breath with a gasp, holding the breath in (this should make them jump a little!).

My breath came in fast and I am still holding it all up here (in the top part of the chest/neck). But what happens when we relax and sigh?

- Try to get them to do a couple with you.

Notice we are exhaling deeply.

So let's imagine you have something stressful to do that is making you a bit anxious.

What could do that to you? ...

How do you know you are stressed or anxious? ...

- Accept all offerings and emphasize those that describe physical sensations and reactions.

So, extending the out-breath can help the body's physical and emotional systems to calm a little. If you find yourself feeling stressed in this way, here is something you could try:

    ## Hot Chocolate Breath Practice

Imagine you have a cup of hot chocolate and it smells very good but it is too hot to drink.

As you hold it in your hands you can breathe in through your nose to smell it, and then blow very gently on it to cool it down. Careful not to splash it!

Just try that a few times now. Breathe in through the nose, and blow out gently through the mouth.

What did you notice?

What many people find with this type of breathing is that it calms their system down a little. You might not have noticed anything right now, but try practising this again sometime when you are already calm and see how it feels. Then you can use this breathing in moments when you are feeling anxious or upset.

TRY THIS OUT!

Practise the **Hot Chocolate Breath** a few times this week. Try it when you are calm, and also see if there are any stressful moments when you might have an opportunity to use it.

Dropping Anchor: Remember it's the anchoring practice that helps us really build our attention muscles. Try just sitting quietly for a few minutes (setting a timer usually helps) and choose an anchor: FSH, sounds, breath or a combination. Notice how it feels.

Session 4: Using the Tools

Intention:

- To reflect on the skills introduced and how they might be further developed and applied.

- To explore positive feelings and sensations whilst closing the course in a meaningful way.

Dropping Anchor Practice

- Settle and sit well.

- Guide from **FSH**, to **Breath** to **Sounds**.

- Invite them to choose an **Anchor**, setting an **Intention** to keep coming back to the anchor when they notice the mind has wandered off.

- Remind them to bring **Curiosity** and **Kindness** to their practice.

- Close the practice.

Pair Share: What Did You Notice? + Whole Group Discussion.

     ## Toolkit Activity

Imagine you have been asked to introduce some mindful awareness activities to children in the primary school or to a younger brother or sister.

List all the practices we have learnt that you can remember.

Compare your list with a partner.

Add any extra ones they have to your list.

(Continued)

Together, choose one practice that you would like to share with a younger child.

How can you best help them learn this? Take it in turns trying it out with each other.

See if you could explain how this could be helpful for them.

With the whole class you can list the practices they have chosen. This is their Toolkit! You can ask them to add any extras to their own lists and then have a second column where they can list possible situations where they might be able to apply these skills. This can also be done in pairs or small groups as a creative activity, using images and words to try to capture the key points and practices of the course.

You might consider actually having your students teach a practice to younger ones. You can also invite older student volunteers to come teach a practice to your group or talk to them about any positive experiences and challenges they may have had in using mindful awareness. Older students often enjoy doing this and younger students really listen to their elders!

Keeping it going:

- Discuss various ways they can continue to **practice and explore** if they want to.

- Maybe offer before/after school/lunch **drop-in sessions**.

- Describe **Seasoning Activities** (see below) that you will provide in your classes.

- Try to **apply skills** learned here in sports/exams/performances/relationships/ mental health, etc. (see Chapter 7).

- Is there a possibility to offer an **optional class?** (See below.)

Closing the course:

- Do a short, anonymous **Feedback Survey** (see www.mindwell-education. com/mtt-resources).

- Closing Activities and Practice, such as:

 ## Paper Clouds

- Give each student a blank sheet of paper and ask them to take a good look at it.

- Explain that the skills they have started to develop are not just for coping with difficulties and dealing with stress and worry, they can also be used to help notice and appreciate many enjoyable aspects of our lives.

- *Thich Nhat Hanh, a Vietnamese Zen monk, asks us to consider if we can 'see the universe in a piece of paper'. How could that be possible? Take some suggestions and ideas about where the paper came from and what it contains.*

Then ask:

If we removed the rain from this piece of paper, could it still exist?

If we removed the sunlight would it still be here?

Thich Nhat Hanh (1988) says, 'As thin as this sheet of paper is, it contains everything in the universe in it. There is a cloud floating in this sheet of paper. Without a cloud, there will be no rain; without rain, the trees cannot grow; and without trees, we cannot make paper. The cloud is essential for the paper to exist. If the cloud is not here, the sheet of paper cannot be here either'.

Our world is so interconnected, that even in a blank sheet of paper, if we look carefully, we can see the universe. There is so much around us in the world to appreciate. In our final practice together let's see if we can tune in to any positive feelings and sensations we might discover.

- Invite them to sit well and then take three slow breaths.

- Bringing attention to the Feet, and up to the Seat, and the Hands.

- Including any physical sensations of Breath moving in the body.

- Perhaps including Sounds that come to their attention.

Now turning to notice any pleasant sensations, and any positive feelings.

You can try allowing a slight smile at the corner of the mouth... and even around the eyes...

Noticing any feelings of warmth... perhaps exploring around the chest and heart area...

Just like the paper and the tree, you are also a natural part of the universe. Your body needs water, food, air and sunlight to grow. You are made of the same elements as other animals and plants and trees...

What sensations can you notice that tell you you are alive right now? ...

If you are noticing any positive feelings or pleasant sensations, try to stay with that for a few moments. Be curious: Where do you feel it? How does it feel?

If you are not able in this moment to locate any positive feelings, that is completely normal. You might like to try this again later and for now just keep coming back to your anchor, as best you can relaxing into the experience of sitting here breathing or listening...

(Continued)

Now seeing if you can just appreciate the opportunity to be sitting here quietly, breathing... sensing.

In a moment I will ring the chime bar to end this final practice...

So now just coming back to the whole body, sitting here, the sounds around us, gently opening the eyes if they are closed... stretching if you need to.

Whole Group: *How was that?* They may or may not feel like responding right now, and if not, that is fine, they can reflect in their journals and then you might mention that because of the way our body–mind systems are set up, it can be very helpful to sometime consciously choose to notice, even amplify, positive feelings. (See Happiness Habit, Chapter 4.)

TEACHING TIP

When exploring positive emotions such as gratitude it is natural that sometimes strong feelings might come up which may be quite poignant and even over-whelming. It is important to resource students so they feel able to choose to move away from strong feelings, connecting back with an anchor, as well as knowing how to gently explore them when that feels helpful. (See Strong Emotions, Chapter 4).

Closing Activity: Circle Up

There are many ways you can bring this course to a close. Here is one suggestion for a final activity:

- Bring everyone to stand in a circle. Take your time here to do this with care, creating a gentle atmosphere with your voice and pace.

- Bring attention to sensations of standing, the micro-movements in the feet... legs... arms.

- Ask them to look into the centre of the circle, on the floor (you could have a vase of flowers or another centrepiece) and then become aware in their peripheral vision of the others around them. *Becoming aware right now of the whole group, together in this moment.*

- Ask them to use their peripheral vision to stay tuned into *your* movements as they silently try to move in sync with you. Slowly move your hands forward and up into a slow-motion stretch. Do whatever movements you feel like doing, trying to keep the students in sync with you. (We sometimes make this fun by slowly moving a hand up to place a finger in your ear or turn slowly towards the person to one side and hover your hand above their head.)

- End by bringing the hands forward again and doing a single clap, with clear build up, seeing if you can do it in unison. Then continue and speed up until you end up with a round of applause.

Closure:

- Still in the circle, thank them all for participating; express your hope that they have learned something useful; remind them if they ever struggle with mental or emotional issues there are skills that can be learned to help them deal with difficulties. This type of training is available to young people and adults in all sorts of ways, and even if there are some things they have not found immediately useful, they may well find they come back to this at some point in the future.

- Wish them all well. From the heart.

Alternative Ending

  ## Savour and Share

You might create your own final ritual for your students. Sometimes, for example, we have been able to arrange pizza for the last session together. You can do a short final practice together and then ask students to just take a moment before they eat to notice any feelings of hunger or anticipation in the body. *How fortunate are we to be able to eat when we are hungry?* Note that there are children right now around the world who have these same feelings of hunger but are not able to eat today. Invite them to remain silent for a few moments while eating and savouring the first mouthfuls. Appreciate. Then have fun!

Some teachers like to close by offering each student something, perhaps a small chocolate, telling them something about their participation that they appreciated, and then giving them a second chocolate with the option that they can either enjoy it themselves, or give it in appreciation to a person who has been kind or helpful to them. This may help generate positive feelings and perhaps lead to conversations about their different experiences in the course.

Extension Activities and Practices

If you have space to offer your students a little more time for occasional mindful awareness activities, there are so many ways you can extend their experience. With students at the upper end of MYs, you might want to supplement the training with some thematic sessions from the Secondary Years chapter. With younger MYs students there are lots of great ideas you can adapt from the Primary Years Chapter 2.

(Continued)

Here are a few other examples.

  # Mindful Walking

Intention: To train students in bringing attention to everyday physical activities.

- At the end of a seated practice, or as an alternative, you can guide students to slowly stand, and without making eye contact, do a short, slow walk around the room with attention in the feet or hands, then slowly sit again.

  # Body Scan

This takes some organizing, but students often seem to enjoy this guided practice and it can be very helpful for relaxation and connecting mind and body (see Chapter 4).

  # Letting the Body Lead

Intention: To train students to move with awareness, 'listening' to the body.

- Start with students lying on their backs on the floor, noticing physical sensations...

- Roll onto one side... then slowly come to a sitting position, allowing the body to lead them in whatever way feels best (not interacting with or distracting anyone else!).

- Move slowly toward standing, again, moving however the body wants.

- Stay in a standing position; noticing...

- End here or allow the body to lead them into moving slowly around the room without interacting with others.

This activity could also be done in a gym or theatre alongside a Drama or PE teacher.

Activity licensed by the Presencing Institute – Otto Scharmer, under a CC-SA 3.0 license https://creativecommons.org/licenses/by-sa/3.0/

  # Guess Who?

Intention: To train students to use their senses and work together as a group in a mindful way without speaking.

You can use the Closing Activity in Session 4 as a basis for a mindful movement game. Once they get the hang of it, send one volunteer out of the room for a moment, choose a volunteer leader then invite the first volunteer back into the room and into the centre of the circle. The group has to use their peripheral vision to not look directly at the leader. The student in the centre has three guesses to try to find the leader.

 ### Sensory Safari

Intention: To provide a sensory experience for students where they will be able to use quiet observation skills, where possible connecting with nature.

- Explain everything in advance: You will be taking them out of the classroom on a special sensory safari to an open area where they will stay quiet, not speak and just observe and listen, even when walking. Acknowledge that you know this might be difficult to do. Don't over-enforce this at first, just encourage and remind them and then aim to have them quiet by the time you reach your destination.

- Get them to spread out, stand alone or sit if possible and just look silently at the world around them, using all of their senses. If you have access to nature nearby, it is well worth the effort.

- Stay long enough for them to settle a little and take it all in, but don't overstay.

- You can tell them when they hear the chime bar they should walk slowly, silently back to class.

- In class they can write or draw something they noticed or felt in a journal. This activity can be repeated as often as you like - each time they will have a different experience.

We have seen this Sensory Safari activity work well when lead by Art teachers, with students using sketch pads after some moments of contemplation. Many mindful awareness practices can be used across the curriculum in various ways. Let's now take a look at what can happen when one middle school Art teacher brings his mindfulness experience into his teaching:

Teacher Voice: Mindful Awareness in the Art Room

The Arts are a feast for the senses and the mindful Art teacher can facilitate engagement with materials in a way that instills wonder and calls attention to the sensory experience of mixing vibrant paint hues or shaping a lump of clay with the hands. Children are naturally drawn to these experiences, and by highlighting them, we can model and validate an attentive awareness and appreciation of our senses throughout life. The art room is a natural place to weave mindful awareness into the learning environment, for example:

(Continued)

- In contour line-drawing we might begin with a brief grounding practice to deepen awareness of the muscle movements and visual field with which we will be working.

- We might emphasize the mindful aspect of holding our visual attention on the contour of the object we are drawing.

- We might also emphasize the awareness aspect of noticing how our grip on the drawing material and the movements of the fingers, wrist, and arm affect the flow and quality of line.

- We may guide students to notice and let go of thoughts and emotions, such as self-criticism or fear, that can arise in the course of art-making.

The instinct to create is readily visible in the younger years, when art becomes an extension of the senses, a vital part of the process of inquiry and meaning-making. As students enter adolescence, many begin to disengage from artistic activity, seeing art as a set of skills or techniques to be mastered by those who possess the requisite abilities. The mindful Art teacher can guide adolescents to a deep and lasting connection to art-making by posing open-ended prompts, which invite students to contemplate their own experience as the seed of meaningful artistic imagery. Mindfulness practice can serve to create the space for this type of contemplation and reflection throughout the artistic process, cultivating a mindset of art as an integral part of life.

Michael Anderson - for more information on training with Michael on Mindfulness and Art, see https://onlineprograms.art-of-being.org/

Pause. Reflect. Plan

Having completed teaching your MAT sessions, where you go next depends on how much time and space you have available and also on your deeper intentions - **What do you really want for your students?**

This is a good time to pause and reflect again on where you are heading with this work and on how you can continue to sustain yourself on this journey.

To help you reflect on this, please turn now to the **'Teacher Reflection' on p. 45**.

Seasoning Activities

Once you have laid a foundation for mindful awareness practice and attention training you can build on this by introducing short Seasoning Activities to help students calm and refocus at any time during the school day. These brief exercises can be used at the beginning or end of a class; for a transition exercise between activities; or whenever you want the class to pause for a moment. By doing short movement activities with an awareness component you can also help students find ways to consciously self-calm. These simple activities can remind them of the benefits of self-care and present-moment awareness, and also that it can just feel good to be quiet together sometimes! In designing these seasoning moments, you can create short activities based on practices in the sessions above, and you will also find many more ideas that you can adapt to your class in the Seasoning Activities list in the Index.

Author Voice: Optional or Compulsory Classes?

Starting an awareness training course for students in the Middle School in Prague was actually quite simple – partly because I was the MS Principal but mainly because all teachers offered 12 week 'Exploratory' classes that students signed up for. The classes were part of the curriculum and in my case I started by co-teaching a course that combined Psychology with Philosophy. We called it What Do We Know and How Do We Know It? Later I changed to offering the Mindfulness in Schools Project's '.b' training course and that later evolved into '.b Plus' when we alternated mindfulness training sessions with yoga lessons taught by a specialist.

The fact that students could choose to sign up for the courses was, I feel, very helpful. I would give the whole Middle School an introduction in an assembly before students chose their options. Some students who teachers felt could perhaps benefit from improved emotional regulations skills were 'highly encouraged' to sign up but in general they all wanted to be there (and actually, those who were given a nudge to take the course often said they found it helpful). In the High School they decided to make this a compulsory course for 17-18 year olds. This had the benefit of ensuring that all students at this high pressure stage had a chance to be exposed to these skills, which was definitely an advantage, but it also meant that quite a few did not feel motivated to be there. Nevertheless, in feedback surveys the vast majority said they felt it should continue to be a compulsory course because they could see the benefit of the training. Even where the courses are compulsory, it is important that the tone is 'invitational', especially for those who for one reason or another may feel the need at least internally to 'opt out' at any particular moment.

Kevin

As you create various safe spaces for students to relax and share more openly you are again contributing to a gradual shift of culture in your school where practical, awareness-building methods, combined with embodied teaching, help knit a more closely connected community. The skills your students have been learning in this chapter can be enhanced and applied through various individual, pair and group work approaches across subject areas, for example employing mindful speaking and listening to deepen dialogue, learning and connection (see Chapter 7).

Hopefully you now feel better equipped to be able to play a larger role in introducing awareness-based wellbeing. As you continue this journey towards transforming learning in your classroom and your school, you will need the support of others within and beyond your community. It is so important to keep reminding ourselves there is no simple shortcut to delivering these learning opportunities for students. In this area, everything comes back to our embodied presence, so continue to devote time and energy to your own self-care and your personal mindfulness practice and seek out others who will become companions on this profound and transformational journey.

Chapter Summary

In this chapter we have:

- **Shown you how to get started on training mindful awareness to 11–13 year olds through a series of exemplar classes that focus on attention and anchoring skills.**

- **Explored ways to help students apply the skills they are learning in order to listen more deeply, to self-calm and to regulate their emotions.**

- **Shown you how to build on this foundation to embed mindful awareness into your teaching and your school day.**

Further Reading and Resources

Curriculum Training

'.b' Mindfulness in Schools Project – for ages 11–18, https://mindfulnessinschools.org/teach-dot-b/
Mindful Schools – for ages 11–18, www.mindfulschools.org/
Wake Up Schools – https://wakeupschools.org/

Books

Siegel, D. (2013) *Brainstorm: The Power and Purpose of the Teenage Brain.* New York: Penguin.
Srinivasan, M. (2014) *Teach, Breathe, Learn: Mindfulness In and Out of the Classroom.* Berkeley, CA: Parallax Press.

Apps

Inner Explorer – 90 days of short accessible audio sessions for MYs students (CASEL certified), https://innerexplorer.org/
My Life: Stop. Breathe. Think. (CASEL certified) – https://my.life/mylife-for-schools/

Movement

For ideas on simple movement exercises that go well with mindfulness training for students we recommend checking out Qi Gong by Lee Holden, www.holdenqigong.com/

4.
Mindful Awareness in the Secondary Years Classroom (14-18 year olds)

In this chapter we provide you with:

Mindful Awareness Training	Activities
Session 1: Mindfulness – Why Bother?!	Hand Heat Practice
	LeBron Breath
	How Well Are We?
Session 2: Managing Stress and Anxiety	Breath Breaks
	Soften and Support Practice
	Real World Soften and Support Practice
	Shakin' All Over
	Ground Down
	Walk This Way
Session 3: Dealing with Distraction	Pinging Practice
	Body Scan
	Just One Breath
Session 4: Working with Strong Emotions	Eliciting Emotions
	Ice, Ice Baby
	Caring Practice
	Happiness Habit

(Continued)

(Continued)

Mindful Awareness Training	Activities
Session 5: Meaning and Purpose	Contemplative Career Planning
	Intention Setting
	Future Chat
	Future Daydream
	Body Movin'
	Solo Sit
	Nature Nurture
Teacher Practices	Clarifying Your Intention
	My Tech Use
	Pause, Reflect, Plan

Working With This Age Group

Teenagers and young adults respond to being respected and valued. As with teaching any subject, it is vital when introducing Mindful Awareness Training (MAT) to this age group that you are not just a talking head, not just another adult telling them how things *should be*. If you can convey your enthusiasm and curiosity for the subject matter (whatever the course is!), it goes a long way towards piquing students' interest. Cultivating your own mindfulness and social and emotional skills before you embark on teaching this is essential as it will help inform your teaching and it will also ensure you are sharing from a place of authenticity. Teenagers can sense inauthenticity from a mile away!

Understanding how our mind, body and emotions work is not something we as adults have 'solved', or are 'experts' in, we just have a little more life experience than adolescents. When it comes to exploring the human condition we can invite students to join us on this journey, as their 'guide on the side' rather than as a 'sage on a stage'. Letting your students know a little about how this kind of work has contributed to your life may go a long way in helping them become interested themselves.

Author Voice: Being Human?

When I first started teaching it took me some time to find the balance of 'being Amy' and of also 'being Ms Burke'. When I was able to do so, my teaching became more connected and authentic. With mindfulness lessons in particular, I would sometimes share something personal with them like:

When I was your age I had a difficult time regulating my emotions. I could get angry SO quickly and often felt like I was being controlled by my emotions. I still get stressed pretty easily - many of us do! But mindfulness is one of the tools that has helped me to manage my emotions and stress levels better. It helps me to be aware of when I'm getting overwhelmed so I can care for myself, and it helps me to be nicer to myself, and others, as well.

My ability to connect with my students was the foundation of my educational philosophy, regardless of which subject I happened to be teaching, and as we know from social neuroscience and evolutionary psychology, young people are hard-wired to learn through relationships with adults. As you see, I don't get into specifics but I let them know that I am a human being who sometimes has difficulties being human. Don't we all!

Amy

Getting Started

A key factor in introducing MAT to teens is to avoid saying *This is something that you MUST do*, and rather present it to them as an offering, letting them know that it's a practical way to play an active role in their own mental health. Using real-life applications rather than abstract concepts also helps to make mindfulness more relevant for teenagers. The session themes in this chapter arise from what young people have told us is important to them. Depending on the age and interests of your class, you may want to consider:

- Teaching the five sessions as outlined below or splitting them into eight to ten shorter sessions.

- Using the four sessions from Middle Years (MYs) as a foundation and then moving on to the Secondary Years (SYs) sessions.

- Designing a 'Pick 'n Mix' from MYs and SYs based on the needs of your students and your context.

Clarifying Your Intention

Many adults come to mindfulness because they are looking for a way to alleviate some sort of suffering in themselves. This is not necessarily the case for young people, especially if it is a compulsory course at school! Our intentions for training in mindfulness may be vastly different than those of the young people we teach. It is important to continually check in with yourself about *why* you want to bring this to young people as you move through these sessions. Clarifying this intention will help guide your teaching and keep you focused on serving your students' needs. Before moving on, please turn to the **'Teacher Reflection' on p. 57**.

Session 1: Mindfulness – Why Bother?!

Intention:

- To pique students' interest and provide a clear rationale for why mindful awareness could be useful to young people.

- To provide students with an experiential understanding of mindful awareness.

Students are seldom given a reason for *why* they have to learn certain subjects – more often than not, it's just 'what's done'. But when teaching mindfulness to young people we like to provide them with a clear rationale for why they might want to learn this. In this introductory session we explore mindfulness as a skill that can help cultivate overall wellbeing. One way of starting might be to drop straight into the theme of busyness and mindfulness. There are some great memes you can use that capture the idea that just doing one thing like drinking coffee and not even looking at your phone or computer is psychopathic. Invariably this will get a few giggles and we explore the suggestion that it's 'crazy' to just be drinking coffee. *Why would it be weird to just sit there*? This can lead to a discussion about stillness and our inability to be still, our perpetual busyness and multi-tasking. *Have we lost the capacity to be comfortable with just doing one thing? This course is fundamentally about being present. But what does 'being present' actually mean?*

Modes of Mind: Thinking and Sensing

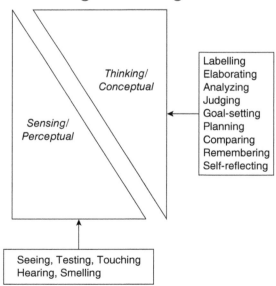

Figure 4.1 Modes of Mind (adapted from Williams, 2010)

Source: Williams, J. M. G. (2010) 'Mindfulness and psychological process'. *Emotion*, 10(1): 1–7. American Psychological Association. Adapted with permission.

Sample teacher scripts are provided throughout this chapter to help you get started, but we encourage you to make them your own, adapting them for your context and style.

The mind can be in the past, for example regretting something we did or didn't do, or it can be in the future worrying about something that hasn't happened yet, and all this mental activity can interfere with our connection with, and enjoyment of, the moment. The body, however, is always in the present moment. Even though mindfulness has to do with training the mind, it does so primarily by connecting with the body. We can train to use the breath, body sensations or sounds as anchors in the present moment. This can literally strengthen neural pathways in the brain that enable us to connect more easily with the body and the senses.

    ## Hand Heat Practice

So let's explore this connection with a short practice. Invite students to try this with you:

Rub your hands together vigorously.

Notice the heat building.

Stop and allow the hands to rest in your lap or on your desk.

Bringing your attention to the sensation in your hands ... what do they feel like? Is there any tingling or pulsing?

Are the sensations the same in both hands? ... Maybe there are no sensations and that's okay too. We are just beginning to explore using our Sensing Mode.

Noticing the sensations in the palms, the fingers. Are they fading? ...

- Draw the practice to a close by inviting them to wiggle their fingers, or shake them out.

- **Turn and Talk:** Find out from someone what that was like. What did they notice?

- **Inquiry** (see **Chapter 5 Top Teaching Tip 11**) + **Whole Group Discussion**.

The intention here is to bring their awareness into the body, dropping from Thinking into Sensing.

Of course, we intentionally created sensations in our hands for that practice but there are sensations happening all the time in our bodies. Can you notice anything even now if you put your attention back into your hands? ... We can use our awareness of these sensations to enhance our sensing capabilities and give our thinking mind a break. This is how the body can be used as an anchor in mindfulness practice.

(Continued)

It is important to make sure we don't give the impression that thinking is wrong! We are just introducing the idea of using sensing to bring some respite from our overly busy minds.

So What Is Mindfulness?

Offer the students this definition of mindfulness from the creator of the Stressed Teens program, Gina Biegel (2015):

> Mindfulness is noticing your thoughts, feelings and physical sensations in the present moment without judgement in as many moments of your life as possible.

So why would we want to notice these things? (Elicit responses.)

When we are aware of our thoughts and feelings and physical sensations in the moment, we are less likely to be driven by habitual patterns of thought or unconscious impulses which can cause undue stress or undermine our confidence.

With awareness comes the ability to choose how we want to respond to a particular situation rather than simply reacting - or overreacting! - automatically without consideration.

Practising curiosity and kindness in MAT helps us cultivate greater compassion towards ourselves and others.

It's one thing for me as an adult to stand here and tell you all these things, but it's probably more helpful to hear it from young people like yourselves who have done this type of training.

- Share with them the video, *Mindfulness: Youth Voices*, from Kelty Mental Health in Canada: www.youtube.com/watch?v=kk7lBwuhXWM&t=3s

- Or this short video of young people speaking about their experience on a five-day mindfulness retreat at Inward Bound Mindfulness Education, UK: https://ibme.org.uk/

Student Voices

I was a little bit skeptical. You know, I had that apprehension that 'Honestly, mindfulness, does that really work?' Turns out it does!

Karim, age 18

Mindfulness takes some time to get used to so don't dismiss it immediately. Give it some time. There are also different types of mindfulness practices you can do so try them all and see what works for you.

Ellie, age 14

> I began using mindfulness during school because I was constantly worried and stressed. With mindfulness, I was able to learn how to step back from thoughts and worries and be in the present moment. I now continue to use my mindfulness practice to feel more balanced, more creative, and to get more sleep. It has helped me to cope with changes, to deal with stress, and it has also allowed me to be more aware of my thinking and notice my surroundings to experience everyday life in a clearer way. I would recommend mindfulness to young people because it can help them feel less troubled and it can allow them to focus and feel more positive experiences in life.
>
> Jake, age 18

It can also sometimes be helpful to share examples of relevant research with your students:

Research Case Study: Mindfulness and the Adolescent Brain

While there is a lot of research on mindfulness with adults, school-based mindfulness research on adolescents is still in its early stages. Here are two studies with promising results that measured brain activity:

1. After an eight-week mindfulness training course students showed:

   - Better focus, less distraction.
   - Reduced self-critical thinking.

   (Sanger and Dorjee, 2016)

2. Mindfulness training helped students stay more resilient during challenging times (e.g. sitting exams). After training, compared with the control group, students had:

   - Fewer visits to the doctor due to mental health problems.
   - Improved empathy.
   - Maintained level of overall wellbeing.

   (Sanger et al., 2018)
   (See also Middle School Research study in Chapter 3)

Mindfulness at Large

Mindfulness has gained a lot of popularity over the last decade or so. It is used in medicine, treating people with chronic pain; many businesses use it to help their employees with stress management and many sports teams use MAT to help their

(Continued)

athletes focus and release tension during high-pressure situations. Even lots of celebrities practice mindfulness! For example, Jerome Flynn (actor in Game of Thrones) and LeBron James (American basketball player) are mindfulness practitioners.

  ## LeBron Breath Practice

Show this very short video of LeBron doing some deep breathing during a time-out in a very intense basketball game: www.youtube.com/watch?v=SCR7OfRuQd4 (YouTube search: 'LeBron's meditation during the time out').

- Prepare students by letting them know the clip is very short and to just notice what LeBron is doing. Play it a couple of times, perhaps once without sound.

- After the clip, ask them what they noticed about *how* he was breathing (in through the nose and out through the mouth).

- Invite them to practice a few **LeBron Breaths** right now. Model it by doing it yourself – the intention here is to 'slide into' this practice by not making a big deal out of it. There is no need to worry about posture. Some students will do it, some won't and that's okay. We are just establishing, in a very quick and seamless way, that this can be a normal thing to do in the classroom (and at home!).

LeBron trains in mindfulness and he knows that taking a few deep breaths can help him to refocus and calm his body down. Learning to work with your breath and body can help in various ways to regulate emotions and deal with challenging situations. In the next few sessions we are going to explore how mindfulness can contribute to certain areas of life like managing stress and anxiety, dealing with distractions and with strong emotions, and in finding meaning and purpose.

Alternative Framing Options

The 'Framing' from the MYs chapter also provides a helpful foundation that you could use as an alternative starting point for an introductory session. You can adapt it as you see fit and build on it according to your and your students' interests. For example you might consider adding more information about:

- Developments in **Neuroscience** that connect with understanding the brain as well as the growing research on school-based mindfulness (e.g. 'Mindfulness for students: Why is it important?' Greater Good in Education, 2019).

- Developments in **Psychology**, which has moved from focusing mainly on disease and mental illness to incorporating ways of cultivating positive mental health through the field of Positive Psychology, emphasizing a focus on human growth and flourishing (e.g. this four-minute video – 'Martin Seligman on Positive Psychology': www.youtube.com/watch?v=faT8jw17RHE).

Extension Activity: How Well Are We?

 (Soc-A) (Rel. Skills) (Resp. D-M)

You can use this exercise to conclude the session or it could be used at the beginning as a way to start a discussion on wellbeing.

- Put students into small groups and provide flip chart paper and a marker.
- Have them write their answers to the questions listed below:
    1. What does 'wellbeing' mean to you?
    2. What impacts your sense of wellbeing?
    3. What is already happening at school that helps promote wellbeing?
    4. What else is needed to help with wellbeing in school (and at home)?
- Return for a whole-class discussion and conclude with a definition of wellbeing. You can create a definition as a class or collaboratively compile a list entitled 'What helps with my wellbeing?'.
- Or, you can use this one from the New South Wales Government (2020) 'Wellbeing framework for schools':

In very broad terms, wellbeing can be described as the quality of a person's life. Wellbeing needs to be considered in relation to how we feel and function across several areas, including our cognitive, emotional, social, physical and spiritual wellbeing.

Session 2: Managing Stress and Anxiety

Intention:

- To explore our 'stress mindsets' and understand how stress appears in our body.
- To provide practices that can help us manage our stress.

Stress Mindset

It's pretty safe to say that all of us have experienced stress at some point in our lives and most of us would agree that it doesn't feel good to be stressed out! Even positive events like getting married or moving house can induce high levels of stress. We also know that too much stress can be disruptive and that prolonged stress can have damaging effects on our physiology and mental states. In this session, we are going to explore some practical ways to manage our stress.

(Continued)

So where do you usually feel stress in the body? (Encourage them to call it out or point to the area.) Familiarizing ourselves with our own stress - knowing the signs in our body and mind - can help us to take action to slow down and care for ourselves before becoming too overwhelmed.

One way to help ourselves is to change the way we think about stress. Most of us have a 'stress mindset' that says, 'Stress is bad and I shouldn't be feeling this way!' But when we are experiencing physical sensations of stress we can remind ourselves that this is the natural response of our body to challenging situations. MAT can help us be more aware of these sensations and notice if we are adding to our own stress by amplifying it with over-thinking. It can also help us take steps to alleviate the stress.

Our system has been developed to keep us safe from physical threat, releasing stress hormones cortisol and adrenaline into the body to give us the energy we need to fight or run away. However, much of our stress these days is more from psychological threats than physical ones - even a phone alert can set off our stress systems! Once those hormones get released in our bodies, our rational 'thinking' mind, the prefrontal cortex, can get hijacked by our stress reactions. That's why it's so hard to think straight when stressed. But we can cultivate the ability to intervene in our own physiology, for example, using our breath to help calm our system down.

(See Dr Daniel Siegel's two-minute YouTube video,
'Hand Model of the Brain', for a great way to explain why
and how we 'flip our lids!': www.youtube.com/watch?v=gm9CIJ74Oxw)

Autonomic Nervous System

The breath is closely related to our body's built-in Braking and Accelerating systems.

1. **The Sympathetic Nervous System (SNS)** *helps us when we need to expend energy. This is like our body's 'accelerator'.*

2. **The Parasympathetic Nervous System (PNS)** *helps restore and renew our energy. It's our 'braking system'.*

 ## Breath Breaks

In our busy world, so much of our time is spent with our 'foot on the gas pedal'. We can be expending energy even if we are sitting still if our mind is continually worried or caught in obsessive thinking. Taking a **Breath Break** *can help calm our mental and physical systems by engaging the PNS. Every time you breathe in*

your heart rate goes up very slightly and every time you breathe out, your heart rate goes down slightly. We can help calm our nervous systems by breathing more deeply and extending the exhale.

- Invite students to:
  - ○ Do a few **LeBron Breaths** together, or
  - ○ Guide them in some **Hot Chocolate Breaths** (see p. 74), or
  - ○ Try a few **Shhhhhh! Breaths:**

Inhale and on the exhale make the sound, 'Shhhhhhhh …'

Sense into the movement in the torso, notice how it feels.

Repeat a few times.

Longer mindfulness practices can also support engagement of the PNS, helping our bodies 'rest and digest'. So let's try one right now.

  ## Soften and Support Practice

Come to a Relaxed and Alert posture (see p. 66, Relaxed and Alert posture activity) allowing the gaze to soften or the eyes to close …

Taking a moment to sense the breath. Just noticing how it is right now … perhaps taking one or two intentional breaths, then letting the breath return to its natural rhythm …

Bringing your attention to the areas of the body where you are feeling supported (e.g. the feet on the ground, the body held by the chair, the spine supporting the body, etc. …)

Moving the attention to an area of tension or tightness or stress in the body. On each inhale bringing attention to that area and on each exhale allowing that area to soften a little bit …

Moving the attention away from that specific area … Sensing the whole of the body sitting here, softened and supported … breathing.

- Use some guidance to draw the practice to a close:

Wiggling fingers and toes, allowing the eyes to open slowly if they were closed, aware of the room and people around you …

- Turn and Talk + Inquiry + Whole Group Discussion.

(Continued)

TEACHING TIPS

- Try this out for yourself first using the audio at www.mindwell-education.com/mtt-resources

- If this is the first guided practice your students have experienced keep it fairly short, perhaps around five minutes.

- Use your own body awareness to sense into when to move on in each step of guidance. **See Chapter 5 Top Teaching Tip 4**.

- **For students who have experienced trauma, sitting in silence and/or focusing on the breath may be uncomfortable. See David Treleaven's advice on Trauma Sensitive Mindfulness teaching at the end of Chapter 5.**

So that was a more 'formal' mindfulness practice, but we can also incorporate 'informal' practices into our daily life:

Real World Soften and Support Practice

- This is an abbreviated version that can be applied in a stressful moment. Guide this practice with your students standing up to give it more of a 'real world' feel.

- Start by guiding them to imagine they are in a moderately stressful situation ... *How does it feel?* (Acknowledge that they may not feel stress at this particular time but that you are just practising for a 'real world' moment.)

Noticing any sensations of stress you may be feeling in the body ... naming for yourself what you are feeling (e.g. headache, tight shoulders, nauseous belly).

Acknowledge that your body is doing its job of notifying you of a challenging situation.

Standing and bending the knees slightly, feeling the pressure of the feet on the ground ... tuning into the breath.

Softening around the physical sensations, allowing them to be there as best you can instead of resisting them.

Noticing where you are being supported (through feet, legs, spine).

- Invite them to consider including a **Breath Break**.

- Remind them that the more they practice in a calm situation (like the earlier seated practice) the easier it will become to apply these skills in a stressful moment.

We can also release stress with physical movement, releasing the stress hormones to maintain optimum health. This is why, for many people, physical exercise is a great stress reliever. Sometimes, even a short vigorous physical activity can make a difference!

 ## Shakin' All Over

This is a quick way to transform stress energy into helpful energy:

Stand up and bring the attention to the sense of the feet on the ground.

Start with loose shaking of the wrists, arms and each leg just like athletes do before a big moment.

Then move to a more vigorous shaking of the arms and hands, counting down from ten, shaking harder as you go.

Stop and notice how the body/mind feel, taking a moment to really sense into what is happening.

Anxiety

Anxiety and stress are closely related and share some similar characteristics. In general, stress is a response to external factors but anxiety is more about our reaction to stress and can keep us in a perpetual state of alarm which can be debilitating. We can talk about 'feeling anxious' and that may not be very different from being worried about something that hasn't yet happened. But when we talk about someone 'having anxiety' as a medical condition, that is quite different. This may mean that someone is suffering from long-term bouts of anxiety that aren't going away. In these cases, we need specialist help. Chronic anxiety is a condition that is very common in the world these days, especially amongst young people. However, there is much that can be done to help people deal with it.

Expert Voice: Hacking Our Brains

Anxiety is defined as 'a feeling of worry, nervousness or unease, typically about an imminent event or something with an uncertain outcome'. We get anxious when our prefrontal cortexes don't have enough information to accurately predict the future. Without accurate information, it is easy for our brains to spin stories of fear and worry. When we can't control our anxiety, it can spill over into panic (sudden uncontrollable fear or anxiety, often causing wildly unthinking behavior).

(Continued)

So how do we not panic?

To hack our brains and break the anxiety cycle, we need to become aware of two things: *that* we are getting anxious or panicking; and *what* the result of this is. This helps us see if our behavior is actually helping us survive, or in fact moving us in the opposite direction towards panic that can lead to impulsive behaviours that are dangerous. Mindfulness training can help us develop this awareness of what is happening in our body (sensations) and our mind (thoughts) and with practice we learn to self-calm so we can start to see straight again.

Judson Brewer MD, PhD - Associate Professor, Director of Research and Innovation, Mindfulness Center, Department of Behavioral and Social Sciences Brown University School of Public Health

(For more information see Brewer's (2021) *Unwinding Anxiety: New Science Shows How to Break the Cycles of Worry and Fear to Heal Your Mind*. New York: Avery/Penguin.)

Mindful awareness can be very helpful for managing stress and anxiety. Just learning how to not add to our suffering is a huge part of this. We know that with our thoughts we can sometimes make mountains out of mole-hills. Quite often, things we spend a lot of time and energy worrying about don't actually happen. Just thinking something doesn't mean it's necessarily true. All thoughts are not facts! Much of our stress or anxiety can be fuelled by our own thinking when it becomes circular or obsessive. A good regular preventative practice is to help ground ourselves in our body, learning to calm our physical, mental and emotional systems. We spend so much time 'in our heads' thinking about the past or the future, that it can be very helpful to bring our attention down through the body into the feet. Dropping out of the head and into the body is like earthing electricity through the ground.

Ground Down

This is a simple practice that can be done at any time, but here we are also using it as a setup for the following practice, Walk This Way (Mindful Walking). Included here are brief bullet points upon which you can elaborate as you see fit.

- Have students stand with a slight bend in the knees to bring the weight more fully into the feet.

  Gently lean forward - notice how the toes grip the ground like fingers:

  o *Do all toes touch the ground evenly?*

  o *Which one takes the most weight?*

Gently lean backwards - bring attention to the pressure in the heels:

○   *Does the whole heel take the weight?*

○   *Does it gather to a single point of pressure?*

Lean from side to side:

○   *Notice the pressure on the outside of the left, then the right foot.*

Come back to the centre.

• Invite stillness, sensing into being held to the earth by gravity, and tune in to the breath.

• Turn and Talk + Inquiry + Whole Group Discussion.

Walk This Way (Mindful Walking)

Intention:

• To bring the attention to the physical sensations of walking, connecting to the body, using this as an anchor for a wandering mind.

• To practise bringing mindful awareness to everyday movement.

It could be helpful to do this in an area with more space, but it is also possible to do this in your classroom. Start with a short **Ground Down** then offer the following instructions:

The sensation of our feet on the floor is another anchor, so we can bring our wandering mind back to this as we walk slowly around the room.

Bring attention to the pressure of the feet on the ground and sensations as we start to slowly move each foot.

• Vary the pace and invite them to notice at which point they lose attention most easily - this can be done with a light and humourous touch as mindful walking can sometimes feel very serious!

• Turn and Talk + Inquiry + Whole Group Discussion.
(Consider having students journal responses sometimes.)

For formal walking practice, encourage students to choose a short stretch to walk back and forth on reminding them of the intention. For informal practice, they can just try to bring awareness to walking at any point during their day.

(Continued)

Extension Activity: Consider doing **Water Walking** from Chapter 2. It works well with this age group too!

You can use the shorter practices we have started to learn here to try to calm your system down a little in moments of stress. Practising in the longer term can change your general stress response so circumstances don't get to you so much, or the stressful reactions don't last so long.

TRY THIS OUT!

Take a **Breath Break** when you wake up in the morning before getting out of bed.

Try a **Soften and Support Practice** at home when you feel calm.

If you become aware of stress arising in the body during the week, try a **Real World Soften and Support**.

Session 3: Dealing with Distraction

Intention:

- To normalize the struggle with distraction as one that impacts all of us.
- To provide practices that help us to be aware of and manage our impulses and reactivity.

What the Heck, Tech?

Many teachers and parents ask how we can use MAT to help with screen and social media addiction. It's important to say that mindfulness is not a simple fix for this extremely complex problem. Our intention is to help young people (and ourselves!) understand the dynamics of what is happening in the brain when we are compulsively pulled to our screens and to provide practical exercises that can help support us as we try to cultivate a more balanced relationship with our devices. It is helpful to approach this topic with young people by getting alongside them, perhaps by sharing a personal story about your own relationship with tech, rather than simply being an adult telling them what they *should* do. So let's start with a reflection on our own tech use.

Teacher Reflection: My Tech Use

How do I feel about my relationship with technology?

What do I enjoy about my connectivity?

What do I find frustrating about it?

Start this session with the same reflection for your students – in a Pair Share (or Journaling) + Whole Group Discussion. At this point you can also share your own personal story about your relationship with tech.

Why Are We So Connected to Our Devices?

1. Dopamine

There is a reason why Unboxing videos are so popular. Their success relies on a basic function of the brain, the release of dopamine in order to form habits. Dopamine is a 'feel-good' chemical that is released when we anticipate or receive a reward. It's why opening presents is so exciting, and this 'dopamine hit' can also occur when we receive a 'like' or any notification from our apps. We are unconsciously seeking that shot of habit-forming dopamine because it feels good in a very literal sense!

2. Attachment

One teacher in Denmark we worked with told us about an experiment he did with his students: they all agreed to give him their phones to keep for 24 hours to see what that experience would feel like. After two hours, one student came and begged him to be able to see his phone. He was distraught. He didn't ask to use it, he just needed to see it, then he was OK! We can create attachments to objects in the same way as we create attachments to other human beings.

3. Avoidance

Sometimes we turn to social media for distraction when we are bored or when there are other emotions or states that we may not want to be feeling. Developing an awareness and curiosity about why we are reaching for our devices can help us understand more about our patterns of behaviour. Building awareness of our impulses gives us the possibility of choosing our responses, rather than being driven by unconscious urges.

Attachment to our devices is not 'all your fault'. A lot of very clever research has gone into understanding how the brain works in order to get us all hooked into adverts, Snapchat, Instagram, 'Like' buttons, etc. so that we will be clicking and scrolling away and spending much more time on-screen than we intended. Our attention is actually what a lot of commercial companies are working very hard to attract.

Show the following video as a catalyst for in-class discussion and reflection about this: 'This Panda Is Dancing – Time Well Spent' is a four-minute video that looks at the commodification of our attention: www.youtube.com/watch?v= tf9ZhU7zF8s&t=10s

After this, consider showing Dr Judson Brewer's TED Talk, 'A Simple Way to Break a Bad Habit', where he explains that using mindfulness practice – specifically getting curious about what is happening in our experience – is a very effective way of changing habitual behaviour: www.ted.com/talks/judson_ brewer_a_simple_way_to_break_a_bad_habit?language=en

Research Case Study: It Ain't All Bad ...

Contrary to common adult belief, not all screen time is 'bad' and many teens report high levels of satisfaction from their phones. The amount of time spent on the app, as well as the specific app it is spent on, are determining factors in this satisfaction. However, there is also evidence that 'Teens with low social and emotional wellbeing experience more of the negative effects of social media than kids with high social and emotional wellbeing' (Common Sense Media, 2018), so developing SEL in young people is a key factor in supporting a healthy relationship with their devices.

Extension Activity: Consider screening the documentary LIKE, from the IndieFlix Foundation (www.thelikemovie.com/about/). It's a compelling documentary that explores the impact of social media on our lives with expert advice and adolescent perspectives.

Pinging Practice

Intention:

- To begin to cultivate the ability to notice how phone and screen notifications impact us, especially noticing physical responses in the body.

(Share this intention after the practice rather than before so there is an element of surprise when you play the notifications.)

We can understand intellectually that we may want to pull away from the screen but it's quite another thing to actually do this – to integrate our knowing into action. Cultivating awareness of bodily sensations and curiosity about our reactions can be a first step towards a healthier relationship with our device. With awareness comes choice!

- Lead students in a short sounds practice (see p. 44).

- Let them know you will introduce other sounds and they are to notice what impact those sounds have on the body and mind (if any).

- Play a medley of notification sounds and ringtones from social media. (Compilations can be found on YouTube.)

- Bring their attention back to grounding in the breath and body, aware of any effects on the body/mind.

- Turn and Talk + Inquiry + Whole Group Discussion.

Student Voice: Taking a Tech Break

I took a break from socials [social media] because I felt addicted to my phone, like I was always needing to look at it and my mood was affected by it too. After about eight months away from it, I went back. I am conscious of how much I am on it now. I was probably on it eight hours a day before I took the break and now it's about three to four hours. My mindfulness practice has helped me notice that I want to look at my phone when I'm bored or as soon as I hear the 'ding', so I try to turn off the phone sometimes or put it on silent so I don't feel like I have to look immediately. Because of my mindfulness practice, it's much easier to notice when I'm becoming too attached to it or spending too much time on it, and it's easier to put it down now too. I still try not to be on it all the time, and 'Look up' more often. I try to do healthier things like golfing or spending time with my family, and when I really want to talk to my friends, I try to call them or FaceTime instead. I wouldn't tell other teens to get off of socials because that's a decision they have to make on their own, but I would suggest they try it for a week and see how they feel. For me, I felt freer, healthier, and more in the present. I think there will be times when I deliberately take a break again from socials. I'll probably go back and forth, depending on what's going on in my life. I like not being addicted to looking at my phone because that's when I'm actually more connected to people.

Adam Avin - 16 years old, Creator, Wuf Shanti
Children's Wellness Foundation and Mindful Kids Peace Summit

See Adam's TEDx Talk 'Mindfulness in education to lower stress and violence': www.ted.com/talks/adam_avin_ mindfulness_in_education_to_lower_stress_and_violence

Body Scan

The Body Scan practice is the foundational mindfulness practice in adult Mindfulness-Based Stress Reduction courses, useful for both stress management as well as cultivating deeper connections with the body. While the intention is to stay alert and relaxed, many people, and especially teens, use body scans to relax and to fall asleep, and we all know that our teens need more sleep!

Try the short seated body scan on the Inner Explorer App or one from the Mindfulness in Schools Project (MiSP) who provide a free teen-oriented body scan on YouTube called *Beditation*: www.youtube.com/watch?v=T5ut2NYdAEQ&t=239s

Do them yourself first to get a feel for them and then try them in class or guide your own.

Include Turn and Talk + Inquiry as in other practices.

(Continued)

TEACHING TIP

In our experience Body Scans are a hit with teenagers but there are many consid-erations in preparing to lead this practice in the classroom. Lying on the ground at school can feel awkward, so ensuring that all students feel safe and secure is impor-tant. A seated body scan is also a viable option. Either way, make sure they have their own safe space (e.g. not near the door or anyone else). Keep your eyes open as you lead this practice. Consider having all legs pointing to a wall (in case someone is wearing a skirt!), or using a larger space in the school with yoga mats and/or blankets if available.

Just One Breath

*I'm not saying that we all need to go on a digital detox but perhaps consider taking **Just One Breath** before picking up your device as a mini-practice. Notice the urge to pick up your phone and be curious about the physical and emotional pulls. Try putting your phone in a different room when you are watching TV, spending time with friends or family. It's not about NOT having a device, it's about develop-ing awareness and not being driven so much by unconscious habits.*

TRY THIS OUT!

Any time you hear *any* bell – from your phone, the school bell, someone's alarm – use that as a reminder and opportunity to take a few deep breaths.

Consider **turning off your notifications** for an hour, a day or an evening and notice how that feels.

Try the **Body Scan** practice on the Inner Explorer App or from MiSP on YouTube called *Beditation*: www.youtube.com/watch?v=T5ut2NYdAEQ&t=239s

Session 4: Working with Strong Emotions

Intention:

*   To recognize, respect and work with strong emotions.

In our sessions we have been cultivating the capacity to notice what is happening in our bodies and minds because when we can notice what is happening, we have a better chance of being able to respond to a particular situation rather than react automatically or unconsciously. This is particularly helpful when dealing with strong emotions. Our awareness of how emotions impact our body and mind is what gives us the choice to act in the way that we want, expressing our emotions in healthy and appropriate ways.

R.E.S.P.E.C.T.

*In Session 2 we explored the idea of having a more positive mindset in relation to our body and its stress response, and we can bring a similar philosophy to our emotions. Emotions are neither 'good' nor 'bad', rather they are pleasant or unpleasant. Knowing their purpose can help us to learn to respect **all** emotions – even the ones that don't feel so great. Emotions give us important information about our environment that can help protect us. They motivate us to act in certain ways and also help us to connect with others. Take anger for example – it can be very useful because it gives us the physical energy we need to take action. However, anger is also tricky because it can come on very quickly with a lot of energy that can cause us to act in unskilful ways.*

All emotions have a physical component and being able to recognize that we are experiencing an emotion is the first step in helping to regulate it. Regulating doesn't mean controlling or suppressing emotions, it's about being able to express emotions in an appropriate way.

So let's practise recognizing emotions right now. Being able to name the emotion that you are having, 'labelling' it, activates a linguistic part of the brain which can help to take away some of its power. If you can name it, you can tame it!

Eliciting Emotions Practice

Intention:

- To notice how emotions impact the body and practise identifying the specific emotion.

Tell students that you will play three pieces of music and invite them to notice how the music impacts their body. Choose three different pieces – consider a wide range of expressive music, from ballads to techno/rock/jazz or heavy metal.

- Start with a basic anchoring, then as you play the pieces encourage them to notice any sensations, feelings or thoughts that arise.

- End by allowing a moment to come back to the body and breath and to notice any 'echoes' of the songs' impact.

- Consider journaling before the Turn and Talk + Inquiry + Whole Group Discussion.

(Continued)

Alternative Sounds: Instead of music play a medley of sounds, such as a baby crying, glass smashing, loud traffic noises, soothing babbling brook, etc.

*Most of the time it's not the actual emotion itself that is a problem but the way we **relate** to the emotion. If we encounter something uncomfortable, of course we want it to stop. This is basic human nature. However, sometimes our resistance can amplify the difficult emotion and uncomfortable feelings. We can amplify the disturbance by adding our stories to it, our worries, our re-playing and our judgements (Hawkins, 2017: 94-8). So the invitation is to notice the physicality of the emotion, and allow it to be there, with curiosity and kindness rather than getting hooked into the storyline.*

Let's practise this by working with unpleasant sensations.

     ## Ice, Ice, Baby Practice

This activity takes some preparation. Ensure that you have at least two ice cubes (always helpful to have extra) per student as well as paper towels to wipe up the melting water!

Intention:

- To notice physical reactions to (safe) unpleasant stimuli so we can familiarize ourselves with the body's emotional response and practise 'being with' challenging emotions as they arise.

- To practise working with choice points, deciding when to explore the sensations more closely by turning towards them, and when to turn away if it becomes too much.

Encourage students to approach this as scientists - to really observe and explore with curiosity what their experience is like. With this practice they can apply the skills they have been learning, building their mindfulness toolkit.

- Start with an anchoring practice (see Chapter 3). Be deliberate about guiding them to the anchors of breath and body, in particular 'feeling your feet' as we did in the **Ground Down** practice. Then encourage students to connect with the anchor that works best for them and which they will be able to return to whenever they need to during this practice.

Notice any thoughts or sensations that may be arising ... Now pick up the ice and let it rest in the palm of one hand.

Notice the sensations of the ice ... How does it feel? Fresh? Pleasant? Unpleasant? Is the sensation changing? What does it feel like now?

Notice your reactions ... do you want to drop it? Move it? Maybe you are enjoying it?

Are any emotions arising? Any thoughts or concerns? What are they?

Remember, if you are finding it challenging, you can use your anchors, come back to the breath or to grounding through the feet, moving your attention away from the ice sensations. Take a breath, knowing that this sensation is temporary. It will pass.

Consider turning towards the sensations. Be curious about how it really feels as opposed to any 'story' about the discomfort.

*You can also decide, if it becomes too much, to move it to the other hand or let go of the ice cube altogether and take a break. When you reach this point, consider taking **Just One Breath** before you let go and perhaps choosing to pick it back up when you want to.*

- Turn and Talk + Inquiry + Whole Group Discussion.

The ability to be in discomfort, within reason, can help us to cultivate the capacity to work with strong emotions. As we practise in these ways we are cultivating our emotional intelligence, which contributes to healthy relationships with ourselves and with others.

Caring Practice

Intention:

- To help students feel cared for and nourished after the Ice, Ice Baby practice.

- To help them cultivate the ability to connect with their own hearts and offer themselves care during or after difficult moments.

It can be helpful to tap into your natural sense of care for your students as you lead this. We provide just basic bullets here so you can use the language that works best for your students and your context.

- Short anchoring, calming.

- Bring attention to the heart area, notice the heart beating. Perhaps put a hand on the heart, or cross hands to opposite shoulders as a gentle hug.

- Sense into the warmth, the front and back of the heart, aware of the blood being pumped throughout the body to nourish it.

- Bring awareness to the breath, nourishing on the inhale, relaxing on the exhale.

- Remind them that at any time they can tune into the heart and to the breath as ways to offer themselves care.

(Continued)

Caring for Our Emotions

Thich Nhat Hanh, a Vietnamese Zen monk, has a great visual metaphor to explain how to manage difficult emotions, which you might want to share with your students.

- *Make a fist with one hand - this represents the strong emotion, anger for example.*

- *Use the other open hand to gently cover that 'fist of anger'.*

This doesn't mean the anger goes away - but when it arises, you can bring something else to it - the caring awareness cultivated through mindfulness training. You can take care of your own anger perhaps in the same way a parent might take care of a toddler who is upset, by being present without judgement. You can bring this same kind of care to any strong emotion that you may encounter.

Another way of caring for ourselves and enhancing wellbeing is to sense into pleasant emotions. Our brains have a built-in 'negativity bias' - based on our physiological survival system - so we notice and remember negative feelings and sensations more easily than positive ones. Therefore it can be very helpful to practise noticing and even amplifying our more pleasant emotions.

Happiness Habit

- Guide students to ground through the body and/or breath.

- Invite them to remember a happy experience. Give time for one to arise, offering possibilities for them to choose from (a time with friends ... or family ... with a pet ... etc.).

Bring that memory alive by mentally replaying the details - what does it feel like?

- Acknowledge that it may not be easy to think of a happy time on the spot. Reassure students that it can be a very small thing, and if nothing is coming to mind, invite them to see if they can just appreciate the feeling of sitting here, breathing ...

Really absorbing the feeling of happiness as best you can, like a sponge. What does 'happy' feel like in the body?

- Give time for this to settle in, then gently close the practice and share as usual.

TRY THIS OUT!

This week, if you sense an unpleasant emotion occurring, connect to the lower half of the body with a short **Ground Down** practice and do your best to **observe** the emotion with curiosity. If you notice wanting to 'leave' by distracting yourself, take **Just One Breath** before you 'go'.

Try amplifying your **Happiness Habit** the next time you sense a pleasant emotion.

If you don't catch the pleasant emotion at the time, take time at the end of the day to reflect and remember a positive moment and how it made you feel.

Session 5: Meaning and Purpose

Intention:

- To encourage young people to trust their ability to make healthy decisions by listening to themselves and to provide practices and exercises that cultivate this ability.

This session has an introductory foundation and then offers suggestions of various contemplative practices for your students that you can choose from.

Rachael Kessler (2000) said that, developmentally, adolescents are inclined to seek answers to profound questions like *Why do I feel scared and confused about becoming an adult?*, *What kind of life do I wish to have?*, *What is my purpose in life?* How can we expect our students to answer these questions - questions that require a deep inner knowing - when we have never taught them the skills or even the value of listening to one's own self? Contemplative practices like mindfulness, journaling, stillness, silence, and being in nature are a few ways of cultivating this ability to access our deeper knowledge (Burke, 2019). We are allowing the opportunity for insight to arise when we are not distracting ourselves with external stimuli. This ability to be in connection with one's self, and value the messages from the body, mind and heart, is crucial in developing discernment and reflective decision-making skills. It's like having an inner compass we can keep coming back to, one that helps us to navigate our way through our lives.

Having a sense of purpose contributes to greater wellbeing, but finding that purpose isn't always easy. In this session we are not so much looking to find the meaning *of* life as to find meaning *in* one's life. Though purpose isn't always aligned with one's job, career planning can be a good place for students to start honing the skill of listening to themselves and trusting their choices. Schools aren't necessarily very adept at helping students figure this out, even though

(Continued)

it's one of their primary aims. Schools (and parents!) put too much pressure on young people to decide what they want to do with their lives at such a young age. Most don't even know what they want to do that evening, let alone five years from now! At its core, career planning is about the ability to make sound decisions. Rather than telling young people what to do or what to think, we want to encourage them to cultivate the ability to discern – to make healthy choices based on their own values.

Contemplative Career Planning:

Mindful awareness and contemplative practices can support the cultivation of self-awareness and help foster the ability to tolerate ambiguity, deal with confusion and be okay with 'not knowing', all of which may be part of developing a career path. Augmenting your school's career-planning tools with contemplative practices enlivens this exploration by cultivating the ability for young people to listen to themselves to support healthy decision making. In our approach to this work with students, we combine some activities from *Designing Your Life* (Burnett and Evans, 2016) with MAT and other contemplative practices (see Tree of Contemplative Practices below) to help young people honour their *inner* knowledge as a valid form of knowing.

You can find more information here: www.mindwell-education.com/contemplative-career-counseling.

Intention Setting

A very practical skill that can help cultivate inner awareness is to set intentions for how we want to be. Intentions can be anything you want – smiling more often, taking a breath every hour, listening well, not reacting to your little sister when she gets on your nerves ...

Intentions help remind us what we aspire to. You can set a daily intention before you get out of bed. Or you can set one for just the morning or even for a particular class or specific conversation. Intentions are flexible and forgiving. You can adjust them as you move through your day. Let's take a moment to check in with a personal intention with a very short practice.

Settling into your seat, adopting the R&A position.

Notice the breath moving in and out of your body, feeling supported by the chair.

See what arises to this question: 'What is your intention for this class?' Take a moment to see what arises ... it is private and you don't have to share it ...

Have the students check in with themselves before they leave your class and reflect on how that intention went. They might have even forgotten about it! No problem. Encourage them to reset the same intention (or maybe change it) for their next class.

Writing

Creative writing can be used as a contemplative practice to support career planning. Begin and end each of the following writing exercises with mindful moments of grounding and anchoring through the body and breath.

Future Chat

Use your imagination. Have a conversation with your future – you can even give it a name. Tell your future how you are feeling these days. Ask it questions. Is there anything you want to know? Anything you are worried about? Excited about?

Sample script format:

Amy: Hey Super Future. What's up?

Future: Not much Amy. I'm just hanging out here, waiting to happen. What about you?

Amy: I'm feeling a little concerned because I'm really interested in graphic design but I'm also into fashion. So I don't know what I should do ...

[Continue the written dialogue for a ten-minute timed write]

Future Daydream

Lead students in a short sitting practice before guiding them through this visualization, which will be about imagining an ideal workday five years from now. Invite them to have paper and a pen ready for journaling after the reflection.

Use the points below as signposts; no need to repeat them exactly as they are here. Try to use words that connect with the senses as you move them through this exercise, noticing details about their future work day.

... Now imagine that it is five years from now. It is a weekday and you have just woken up for work ... What time is it? Look around your bedroom. What colours are the walls? Are there curtains? Blinds? Can you tell what the weather is outside?

Imagine yourself getting ready for work. What clothes do you find to wear? What do you make yourself for breakfast?

(Continued)

What is your commute like? Do you travel by bike? Public transportation? Or maybe you work from home? How do you feel as you go to work?

• Continue moving through this imaginary day, providing guiding questions up until bedtime, then guide them gently out of the practice and invite them to write about the details of their Future Daydream. Then Pair Share or share in small groups. In all of these activities we are not expecting direct answers or that this 'daydream' will come true. We are just practising different ways of accessing inner awareness and of sensing into the future.

Contemplative Practices

As you see in the tree below, there are many other ways to access inner knowing. Choose some you feel may work best for your context. In addition to journaling, we have found that movement and nature practices work well with SYs students.

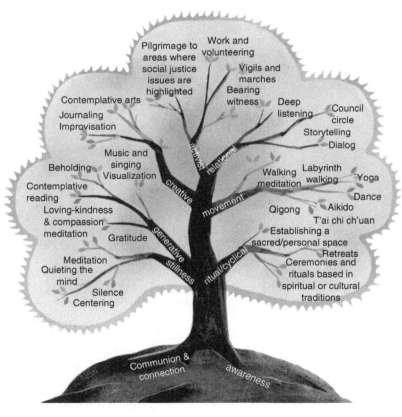

Figure 4.2   The Contemplative Tree

Source: CMind (2014). The Tree of Comtemplative Practices [illustration]. The Center for Contemplative Mind in Society. https://www.contemplativemind.org/practices/tree. Reprinted with permission.

Movement

     Simple Stretch: Body Movin'

Stand and ground through the feet, sensing the connection to the ground.

Come to stillness and close the eyes or lower your gaze.

Move and stretch in whatever way the body wants to; 'listen' to where it wants to go.

- Model this for students as you stretch yourself. You can offer a couple of verbal suggestions at the beginning and then slowly taper off as you invite students to 'listen' to their own bodies to see where and how they want to move next.

- **Extension Activity:** To explore this further, see Letting the Body Lead in Chapter 3 and Lee Holden's short Qi-Gong exercises: https://7mins.holdenqigong.com/video-practice

Nature Practices

Research suggests that being in nature contributes to overall wellbeing (White et al., 2019). Spending time in nature is also a helpful way to connect to our inner knowledge by limiting distraction and noise and taking time to just 'be'.

Solo Sit

If you have green space near your school, invite students on a Solo Sit. Consider combining it with a Sensory Safari (Chapter 3) and/or Nature Nurture (below).

- Find a quiet space to sit or lie down.

- Set a time (e.g. ten minutes) and let your students know when it begins and ends, perhaps with a chime bar.

- Invite students to notice what it feels like to 'do nothing' in nature. Remind them to open their senses and connect with their anchors if they want to.

- Journal + Pair Share + Whole Group Discussion.

(Continued)

Nature Nurture

- Encourage students to find an element of nature (flower, weed, branch, bark, rock, etc.) and spend five minutes 'with it' by looking at it, feeling it, observing it.
- Remind them to be curious, and when their attention wanders, to bring it back to seeing and experiencing this particular element of nature, noticing details in the object as well as any reactions, thoughts, sensations, feelings.
- Journal (Journal Prompt *'What message did you receive?'*) + Pair Share + Whole Group Discussion.

It's not always easy to incorporate contemplative practices into our lives, but even a few minutes here and there can help support our ability to trust our own decisions and deepen our sense of purpose. Through developing connections with our inner experiences and our natural intelligence we can learn how to access a different way of knowing that can help us on our path of determining who we are and how we want to be.

Student Voice: Making a Difference

To people who have not practised mindfulness it can perhaps appear somewhat self-centred and passive, but in fact, mindfulness gives us more of an understanding about how our own minds, bodies and emotions work, and this then builds empathy for others and often leads to compassionate action.

When **Leandro Johner** was 12 years old, he was the youngest person to be trained as a teacher of MiSP's '.b' curriculum. A few years later he used this training to provide support for an underserved community of young people in Colombia.

In August 2015, I arrived in Cazucá to teach a Spanish-adapted mindfulness course to 15 teenagers from both sides of the guerilla war conflict selected by community leaders for their leadership potential. After two intensive mindfulness and compassion meditation courses followed by weekly online meetings, their feedback was incredibly encouraging. They felt better able to regulate their anger and anxiety. Their mindfulness experience enabled them to spread their knowledge to others and has given them the tools to come together in the hopes of finding a constructive and peaceful solution to the violence ravaging their community.

Author Voice: Are They Really Listening?

I once taught three one-hour mindfulness sessions for 17-18 year olds. At the end of the three sessions, one of the students said, *I wish I had spent that time studying.* I was frustrated and disappointed but this helped to remind me that not all young people are interested in mindfulness. We can't *make* all young people like it. But we can see it as an offering of a skill and way of being that they might return to at some point in their lives. As with so much of our teaching, we may never see the benefits or the impact on our students in the future. I have been fortunate enough to hear from past students every now and then and this feedback has confirmed my hope that they find this training useful at some point in their lives! A few years ago, I received this email from a former student, **Maike Wagner**:

I'm not quite sure whether you remember me but I was a student of yours in 2013. After graduating I started medical school. I have one more year of intern-ing but last week I wrote my final exams. Those exams were very hard and intense and many people go a little crazy while preparing for them – as did I! I especially had trouble sleeping and became so frustrated because during such a long period of hard studying the most important thing for me is to get a good night's sleep. And then I remembered all the things you taught us about mindfulness and started to do a short session of mindfulness every night before I went to sleep. That really helped! All of a sudden I fell asleep quickly again and slept through the night which really helped my mood as well as my con-centration. I even did mindfulness during the exams last week; I just took a few seconds, closed my eyes and focused on myself and my body – and I could re-focus on my exam. I just wanted to thank you for introducing mindfulness to me back in high school. It really helped me throughout the last couple of months and brought me through my exams successfully!

These emails always make me emotional. To hear that these young people felt able to access mindfulness now, when they needed it, *because* they had been introduced to it in school warms my heart and inspires me to continue this work.

Amy

Pause. Reflect. Plan

This is a good time to pause and reflect again on where you are heading with this work and on how you can continue to sustain yourself on this journey. To help you reflect on this, please turn now to the **'Teacher Reflection' on p. 45**.

Now that you have shared these sessions with your students, you can continue to invite mindful moments into the classroom, seasoning the day with moments of peace, calm and reflection (see Seasoning the day in the Index). You can revisit some of the practices, choosing the ones that fit best at the time. For those stu-dents who are interested in continuing their mindful awareness training, you can recommend some apps (see below) and you might also consider forming voluntary mindfulness sessions at lunch or after school. These can be open to both staff and students, helping to build a community of care as you continue your journey of bringing awareness-based wellbeing to your school.

Chapter Summary

In this chapter we have:

- Shown you how to get started on training mindful awareness to 14–18 year olds through a series of exemplar classes that focus on cultivating awareness of mind, body and emotions.

- Explored ways to help students apply the skills they are learning to manage stress, anxiety and distraction, regulate their emotions, and develop their capacity for discernment.

Further Reading and Resources

Curriculum Training

'.b' (Mindfulness in Schools Project) – for ages 11-18, https://mindfulnessinschools.org/
iBme Mindfulness Teacher Training Program – https://ibme.com/mindfulness-teacher-training/
MBSR for Teens – by Gina Biegel, www.stressedteens.com
Mindfulness Without Borders – https://mindfulnesswithoutborders.org/

Books

Broderick, T. (2021) *Learning to Breathe: A Mindfulness Curriculum for Adolescents to Cultivate Emotion Regulation, Attention and Performance.* 2nd edn. Oakland, CA: New Harbinger Publications.

Rogers, H. and Maytan, M. (2019) *Mindfulness for the Next Generation.* 2nd edn. Oxford: Oxford University Press.

Vo, Dzung X. (2015) *The Mindful Teen: Powerful Skills to Help You Handle Stress One Moment at a Time.* Oakland, CA: Instant Help Books.

Willard, C. (2014) *Mindfulness for Teen Anxiety: A Workbook for Overcoming Anxiety at Home, at School and Everywhere Else.* Oakland, CA: Instant Help Books.

Retreats for Young People

iBme – Inward Bound Mindfulness Education, https://ibme.com/ in the USA and https://ibme.org.uk/ in the UK

Apps

Calm – https://app.www.calm.com/meditate
Headspace – www.headspace.com/

Inner Explorer – 90 days of short accessible audio sessions for SYs students (CASEL certified), https://innerexplorer.org/
My Life: Stop. Breathe. Think. (CASEL certified) – https://my.life/mylife-for-schools/
Smiling Mind – www.smilingmind.com.au/smiling-mind-app

Video

Jill Bolte-Taylor, TEDx Talk, *The Neuroanatomical Transformation of the Teenage Brain*, www.youtube.com/watch?v=PzT_SBl31-s

5.
Top Teaching Tips

Throughout Section I we have included Teaching Tips within each age band, and in this chapter we pull together some more general guidance that applies to most age groups. If you are a class or subject teacher, it has been our experience that the areas teachers struggle most with initially are the new skills of guiding practices and leading inquiry after practices. If you are a mindfulness teacher looking to offer training to schools as a visiting expert then you may need to concentrate on establishing effective classroom management techniques in addition to your mindfulness skills. You will find advice for both areas in the tips in this chapter.

TOP TEACHING TIP 1: EMBODIED PRESENCE

Some teachers we have worked with have commented that it can be challenging to be both a classroom teacher *and* a mindfulness teacher, as if there was a special distinction between the two. In fact, when you are teaching mindfulness to students you still need to draw on all of the skills of a classroom teacher. Many teachers actually find that teaching more mindfully enables them to be more authentically themselves, 'more embodied', whatever they are teaching. The number one tip that we have for anyone looking to teach mindfulness to young people is to be cultivating your own practice. This will benefit your teaching on so many different levels, such as:

- Providing an experiential understanding of what you are asking of your students.

- Cultivating responsiveness as opposed to reactivity, supporting classroom management by not escalating situations.

- Fostering patience, empathy and compassion.

- Supporting your ability to embody what you are teaching.

The more we develop our own mindful awareness, the more embodied – present in mind, body and heart – we become. When we are more embodied we have a more tangible, relational presence that enhances the authentic connection between ourselves and our students. We

(Continued)

are the unspoken example of how mindfulness practice manifests in a person in a very real way.

How we teach is just as important as *what* we teach.

How we *are* is the strongest message we can give our students about being mindful.

TOP TEACHING TIP 2: PRACTICE WHAT YOU PREACH

Make sure to try out any activities and practices yourself before you introduce them to students. This will support your ability to guide the practice as well as have an experiential understanding of what they might be experiencing.

TOP TEACHING TIP 3: WHAT IF THEY MISBEHAVE?

This is a fundamental worry for many new teachers, regardless of what they are teaching, and experienced teachers may also feel vulnerable when starting to introduce Mindful Awareness Training (MAT) to their students. The basis of successful classroom management is building strong relationships between teacher and students and this can take time to nurture. Respecting students, honouring their developmental stage and setting clear boundaries are integral to teaching any subject matter and no less so in MAT. It is important to remember that aspects of these classes such as sharing silence or talking about subjective experience can be uncomfortable for some students. Giggling and messing about might be natural reactions to avoid this discomfort. Many teachers agree group norms with student input when they start teaching mindfulness. These can be posted in the classroom and are helpful to refer back to in order to support and guide behaviour.

Of course there are also times when the practices will go awry and may fall apart and stopping the lesson is the only option. Maintaining a sense of humour about it all can be very helpful – though admittedly it's not always easy to do! Don't feel you made a mistake if for some reason you can't complete a practice. When it feels right, exploring the reasons for this with the students may lead to some helpful learning opportunities even if it didn't go the way you expected.

If you find yourself getting frazzled during these activities or perhaps triggered by student behaviour, keep coming back to your practice – this is why we do it!

Take a look at Setting the Weather in Chapter 1 and learn to make use of the restoring, calming practice 'Relax, Release, Return' on p. 29.

Checking in with your intention, *Why you want to bring this to young people*, can help to guide your own behaviour and responses in some of these challenging situations. Remember, mindfulness is not something we 'give' students, it's an innate human quality that can be explored and nurtured. Try to take the pressure off yourself to 'make' your students be mindful!

If you remind yourself of this, and that what you are providing is an offering rather than a curriculum to be learned, you may find it easier to approach and they might feel less pressure.

Author Voice: Getting the Giggles

Once I was leading a seated mindfulness practice to teenagers and a few of them couldn't stop giggling. It was frustrating but I let it continue and I even started giggling myself. After the laughter subsided I said, 'Notice what the body feels like now, after the laughing fit. Is there any lightness? Warmth?' I was able to build in a small awareness practice even amidst the disruption. Then we had an open discussion about why there was giggling and we were able to acknowledge that, yes, it can be difficult at first to practise mindfulness in a room full of people.

Amy

TOP TEACHING TIP 4: LENGTH AND PACE OF PRACTICES

The length of each practice will depend on the age of the students, their previous experience, and the intention of the particular practice. Of course younger students should not be expected to sit for long stretches of silence, but this could be appropriate for older students who are cultivating attention training. Over time you will develop a feel for the length of pauses and longer silences. You can often feel from the class atmosphere when to end practices.

When guiding try to do the practice yourself at the same time, keeping some awareness inward and some outward. For example, if you invite students to 'feel their feet', then you can also bring your attention to *your* feet. This, combined with your outer awareness, will help you with pacing.

TOP TEACHING TIP 5: THE EYES HAVE IT

For the Teacher

Keep your eyes open as you lead practices. This is not only for safeguarding but also to help you get a sense for how your students are experiencing the practice. Of course

(Continued)

we can never really know what is going on inside them, but students' fidgeting and facial expressions can tell us a lot. Use your tone of voice and eye contact, if necessary, to guide behaviour.

For the Student

We never force young people to close their eyes during practices. One teacher told us that he had his primary students face the wall if they didn't close their eyes! This can feel punitive, which can potentially turn young people off of mindfulness. Keeping the language invitational and providing choice can help engage students more. For example, you can say something like, '*Perhaps closing the eyes if that feels comfortable … or keeping them open but softening and lowering the gaze, looking a few feet ahead of you on the floor or desk*'. We are trying to make sure that students aren't looking *directly* down with a bent neck which may compromise their breathing or level of alertness.

TOP TEACHING TIP 6: NO BELL BANGING PLEASE!

Whether or not to use bells is really up to you. Sometimes a meditation bell might be seen as a religious object so we often use chime bars, vibra-tones or musical instruments. Many people use these sounds to signal the beginning and end of practices, which can work quite well, but you can also use your voice and language to accomplish the same thing. Chimes can be used effectively as a listening focus when doing a Sounds Practice.

We discourage teachers from using the bell as a control method to get their students' attention or to make them be quiet. We have seen some teachers 'bang the bell' in not a very mindful way! When the bell is used as a silencing tool, we can give the wrong message. Of course, you can use the bell to *invite* students to silence and stillness when things get too hectic in class, but this works only when you have taken the time to train students in mindful awareness so they know what the bell represents – an invitation to come back to the breath or body to reset.

TOP TEACHING TIP 7: WHAT IF THE TERM 'MINDFULNESS' GETS IN THE WAY?

Depending on your context it can sometimes be more powerful to consider letting go of the label 'mindfulness' and focusing on the established scientific understandings and benefits of approaches and exercises that help promote wellbeing through building attention, awareness and emotional regulation. Some schools have developed this type of approach to mental and emotional wellbeing using terminology from neuroscience as a basis for this work. Instead of talking about 'mindful moments' it might, for example, be more meaningful to talk to students about taking time to 'reset' or 'reboot' because we know from the research that this is helpful to our mental health and ability to focus. This is not about putting a spin on things. It is about framing this new and, for many schools, somewhat unusual topic in ways that make sense to you and your school community. By taking time and care over the way you frame MAT in your school you are revisiting the essence of what you want to convey and formulating it in a way that will be most accessible to your students.

TOP TEACHING TIP 8: SILENCE IN THE CLASSROOM

If you see a photo of a group of students meditating it may look lovely and peaceful, but unless you have actually tried it for yourself, you may not know that those students could be feeling a full range of emotions and sensations, some of which might be quite uncomfortable. We have heard of enthusiastic leaders who arranged for a whole school weekly silence without any explanation or training for the students, and though the intention may have been good, the result was confusion and disinterest for many students. One of the key outcomes of mindfulness training is that many students will discover that sitting quietly together in a safe environment for a few minutes – a rare experience for most – can actually feel very pleasant and nourishing. But this is not a given. Not all students like silence. Start with short moments of silence that can be gradually extended as your students become more comfortable. Offer various attention anchors (see Chapter 3) and options such as keeping eyes open, etc. As always, your own mindfulness practice will support you in holding this space for your students with compassion.

TOP TEACHING TIP 9: SLIDING INTO A PRACTICE

You can introduce practices in a non-threatening way by 'sliding into' them. While it can be absolutely fine to say *Now we will do a practice*, it can sometimes feel more natural to seamlessly weave it into what you are saying. You can use the tone of your voice and cadence to lead students directly into a practice. See LeBron Breath in Chapter 4 for an example of sliding into a practice.

TOP TEACHING TIP 10: INVITATIONAL TONE AND LANGUAGE

One of the keys to successful MAT with teens is to always allow the practices to be – or at least, feel – optional. It may be that your school has a compulsory mindfulness course, but even within that, if the language you use is invitational and you offer options and choices during the guidance, it will help create a gentler atmosphere, reducing the likelihood of inner (or outer!) rebellion.

Examples of invitational, rather than instructional language may be:

- *... perhaps noticing the sensations in your feet, as best you can ...*

- *... and then choosing whichever anchor feels most accessible to you right now ...*

- *... if you notice you are feeling tired today and maybe don't feel like doing this, can you still turn your attention to sense what tiredness feels like in your body? ... How do you know you are tired?*

TOP TEACHING TIP 11: INQUIRING MINDS

Much of the learning points come when you inquire into the students' experiences after leading them in a practice. It is entirely possible with older students that when you ask how the experience was, you get the dreaded 'tumbleweeds' – vacant expressions, lack of eye contact and a sense of the wind sweeping down a deserted, dusty road! Young people may be used to you asking them questions in school but these are generally of an objective nature, about their studies. It is often a new experience for teens to be asked about their subjective experiences. For many this may feel uncomfortable, and sharing in front of their peers even more so.

Depending on your class dynamics, it may sometimes be more effective to invite students to journal or do a quick Pair Share or Turn and Talk after the practice. *Find out from another person what that practice was like for them,* before asking for volunteers to reflect to the whole class. It is entirely possible that there will be lots of discussion in the Pair Share and then no responses when you open it up to the whole class. If nothing arises, it is possible to provide some content for them. For example, by saying something like *When I first tried to keep my attention on my breath, I noticed my mind wandering almost ALL THE TIME! Did anybody else have that experience? ... I see a few heads nodding....* This questioning is an example of 'horizontal' inquiry, where you spread some responses across the group rather than putting an individual on the spot in front of their peers.

Vertical inquiry is between the teacher and one student. This is used often in adult mindfulness classes but it needs to be used sparingly and with sensitivity in schools. It allows for going a little deeper but we would advise really knowing your students well. If you drill down too much on one student and it makes them uncomfortable, they may never answer again – this is training not therapy! And some other students may be too nervous to answer if they expect to get the same attention.

Some questions for vertical inquiry include:

- *And then what happened?*

- *And then what did you notice?*

- *Would you like to say a little bit more about that?*

Horizontal inquiry invites the whole group to answer and we recommend it more often with students than vertical inquiry. It is less daunting because they can also respond by nodding or raising a hand:

- *Show of hands – How many people also felt tired?*

- *Did others notice …?*

- *How many of you …?*

TOP TEACHING TIP 12: DON'T TAKE IT PERSONALLY!

For some students a course in mindfulness may be highly useful or inspiring. For others it might feel really boring. Not all students will be in a space where they can really relate to it at this moment. But don't take teenage reactions too personally. You never know what seeds you may be planting. It can be enough for some young people to learn that this type of training is available and that if they struggle at some point with mental or emotional health issues there are ways to get help.

Author Voice: Eye Rolling

Students could choose to sign up for my middle school Exploratory courses in mindfulness, but some were 'strongly encouraged' by their teachers, or parents, to do so. In one course I had a group of girls who were quite lively and one in particular who never held back her feelings and was keen to give me critical feedback, including frequent bored sighs and rolling of the eyes. Two years later she was in High School and one day we came out of the doors at the end of school at the same time.

'Hi Mr Hawkins. You still teaching that mindfulness stuff then?'

(Continued)

'Yes', I sighed, 'Still teaching it'. Then I asked her, 'Tell me the truth, did you ever really get anything out of any of those classes?'.

'You're joking! It's one of the best things I did. I still use it everyday!'

Now this doesn't mean of course that all students who rolled their eyes in my classes were actually really learning something! But it does mean that we should never make judgements based on body language alone – especially from teenagers.

Kevin

TOP TEACHING TIP 13: TRAUMA AWARENESS – PROVIDING CHOICE

In Top Tip 10, we underlined the importance of making mindfulness in the classroom feel invitational. This is especially true because of the very real possibility that some of our students may have suffered some form of trauma. One way to support our students is by offering a few choice points within any practice and showing them from the beginning that they can find various ways to resource themselves if they experience discomfort. For example, sometimes choosing *not* to continue with a practice can be a form of self-care. Let students know they can keep their eyes open if that feels safer or they can use a different anchor if, for example, focusing on the breath provokes any anxiety. They don't always have to follow your guidance! It is all about making conscious decisions to support themselves.

Expert Voice: Sensitivity to Trauma

David Treleaven, PhD, is an international speaker and teacher whose work focuses on the relationship between mindfulness and trauma. Here he offers us his advice on developing greater sensitivity to trauma in our teaching of mindfulness.

Over the past decade, mindfulness has exploded in popularity. At the same time, the prevalence of trauma is extraordinarily high. The majority of us will be exposed to at least some type of traumatic event in our lifetime, and a smaller percentage of us (research suggests 10–12%) will develop debilitating symptoms in its aftermath. What this means is that in any environment where mindfulness is being practiced, there's a high likelihood that someone will be struggling with traumatic stress.

Trauma-sensitive, or trauma-informed, practice means that we have a basic understanding of trauma in the context of our work. A trauma-informed physician can ask a patient's permission before touching them, for example. Or a trauma-informed school counselor might ask a student whether they want the door open or closed during a session and inquire about a comfortable sitting distance. With trauma-sensitive mindfulness, we apply this concept to mindfulness instruction. As teachers, or as an organization, we commit to recognizing trauma, responding to it skillfully, and taking preemptive steps to ensure that people aren't retraumatizing themselves under our watch.

Educators are often well aware of the high prevalence rates of trauma in their classrooms, and the importance of adopting trauma-informed care. But the question inevitably comes: Why would students run into trouble inside of mindfulness practice?

One important reason is that trauma often lives on inside the body – often out of view of others. Traumatic events persist in the form of petrifying sensations, emotions, and intrusive thoughts. Consider, then, what it means to pay mindful attention to one's internal experience if someone is struggling with trauma.

This isn't automatically a bad thing. Mindfulness can help us get a bit of distance from these experiences and manage them more effectively. When left to our own devices, we'll tend to over-attend to stimuli that suggest we're in danger or not okay. By paying mindful attention to what's predominant in their field of awareness, people struggling with trauma will naturally latch on to remnants of the trauma: upsetting flashbacks, for example, or particular sensations that connect to survival-based responses like fight or flight. It's hard to resist paying attention to these kinds of intense stimuli.

To manage traumatic symptoms, people experiencing post-traumatic stress require more than basic mindfulness instructions to thrive. They need specific modifications to their mindfulness practice. They require tools to help them feel safe, stable, and have the ability to self-regulate.

David's advice is highly relevant to any teacher seeking to bring MAT to their students. By creating a safe space in school for students and paying attention to social-emotional aspects of their experience we are opening the possibility, especially in moments of silence, for strong emotions to arise. This is not necessarily a bad thing and for some it can be very helpful, but it is also important to be aware that some individuals with a history of trauma or mental illness may need extra vigilance on our part. We are not therapists and we need to know how to respond in the moment and how to arrange for follow-up support if necessary. For further information and training courses, see David's book *Trauma-Sensitive Mindfulness: Practices for Safe and Transformative Healing* (Treleaven, 2018), and his website: www.davidtreleaven.com

Section II

Embedding Mindful Awareness

Once you have established your personal mindfulness practice and begun to explore delivering various aspects of Mindful Awareness Training (MAT) to your students, the question will naturally arise: How can we begin to embed awareness-based wellbeing into our school processes, culture and other curriculum areas?

- In Chapters 6 and 7 we explore, on a practical level, how schools can tap into this broader potential of applying MAT to a range of curriculum areas and activities.

- In Chapter 8 we look at a series of questions and issues that schools often face around implementation and coherent culture change.

6.
Mindful Awareness in Sports and Performance

In this chapter we provide you with:

- Examples of how Mindful Awareness skills can be applied and extended through both individual and team sports.

- An extended case study of school sports coaching in action, with a variety of practical activities.

- Ways of applying this awareness and the transferable skills learned through sports to other areas of life and learning, within and beyond school.

In any subject area, finding opportunities for students to try out and apply the skills they are learning reinforces and deepens understanding and competence. If students learn mindful awareness or emotional intelligence skills in a discrete course, this can certainly be helpful to them, but how much more powerful is it if, for example, they learn their MA skills with one teacher and then, a few days later, their PE/Sports teacher/coach says something like:

> I hear you have been learning about mental focusing in your mindfulness classes. That's really helpful because in sports, many athletes train in mental fitness skills these days. So, let's see if we can use some of your focusing and body awareness skills in our warm-up activities this morning and then we will reflect on how you are doing with emotional regulation after our five-a-side soccer matches.

Here the PE teacher is providing opportunities for students to explore and apply their recently learned skills in 'real world' contexts. The same could of course happen in a Drama, Art or Speech and Debate class – or wherever some type of individual or team presentation or 'performance' is required. You can help your students make the connection between learning mindful awareness skills, applying them in one area and transferring those same skills to any other performance area – even to exam taking!

So, what might 'doing warm-ups with awareness' in PE look like?

Warm Up Wonderings

Connection with the body is a foundational practice in Mindful Awareness Training (MAT) so warm-ups provide a great opportunity for students to apply their mindfulness skills. Instead of going through the motions on autopilot they can bring present-moment awareness to the movements and sensations of the warm-ups. Curiosity is a helpful quality in making this come alive:

What does the stretch in your calf (neck rotation, triceps stretch, etc.) actually feel like?

Is it pointy? Smooth? Jagged? Pleasant? Unpleasant?

Notice any changes that take place as we tense and relax our muscles ...

... Just tuning in now to how the whole body is feeling ...

Taking Your Emotional Pulse

This can be done at any time during the PE class but may be better suited to a post-game reflection. You can also consider stopping the match/game part way through to do a quick 'Pulse Check'.

How do I feel right now? How do I know that I feel that way?

Am I frustrated at myself or my teammates? Am I enjoying myself?

Name the emotion as precisely as you can.

Notice if you feel this anywhere in the body and breathe with whatever you notice, just allowing the sensations to be there.

The intention is to help young people become accustomed to checking in with themselves, noticing and acknowledging what is happening for them in the moment. This can be especially useful if things are beginning to become heated or intensified during the game.

In Chapter 3 you will find other suggestions on using sports as one way of framing an introduction to MAT. In this chapter we provide more detail in this area that you can draw examples from. First we will look at individual sports (in this case tennis) because here we can see more clearly the link between physical achievement and mental fitness. We then go on to examine team sports, using basketball as an example. Finally in this chapter we offer an extended case study of the approach of a school coach who uses mindfulness awareness in her training. Our intention here is to show how practical these MA skills can be in any performance area. If you are a Sports/PE teacher or coach, we aim to give you here an initial framework that you could develop and apply in your own work with students.

Performance Nerves

You can show students how awareness and social-emotional skills are being used and applied in professional areas. We may train our bodies to compete in sports or play a musical instrument; we may train our minds to be able to debate, speak in public or act on stage; but even with these skills in place we can sometimes still fail to perform well because of nerves, lapse of concentration, or perhaps self-critical thinking undermining our confidence.

- If you are introducing this area to students, you could start by showing them this short clip of Jordan Speith in the final round of a US Masters golf tournament. He goes from a commanding lead to a trailing position within a few moments, and with hindsight he realizes he crucially forgot to pause and take a breath in the midst of his meltdown: www.youtube.com/watch?v=PPLsVVEWXhY

- You could then go on to explore how these days, many athletes, coaches and sports psychologists are using the same kind of training your students have done in MAT, applying *Understanding how our minds, bodies and emotions work and how they can sometimes trip us up* to a sporting context.

Individual Sports

Author Voice: Mind Coach

In June 2015, leading British female tennis player Johanna Konta was ranked 147th in the world. Many observers (and Konta herself) attribute a large part of her success in overcoming on-court anxiety and becoming a top 10 professional by 2016 to her 'mind coach', Juan Coto. In 2016, I was presenting at a conference on mindfulness in education in London along with Juan. I was curious about his work and attended his workshop on mindfulness in sports in which he explained his approach to working with young athletes and professionals. Before his untimely death later that same year, Juan generously helped me prepare for a training course on mindfulness for PE teachers. His approach resonated with a lot of teachers and school coaches, and although Juan never published his work he shared with me some of his materials and ideas, excerpts from which we reproduce here with kind permission from his wife, Julia Coto.

Kevin

Mental Toughness

Juan Coto combined **mindfulness training** with **visualisation techniques** and **positive psychology** to help train the sports quality known as 'Mental Toughness', which he defined as 'The ability to work with one's thoughts, emotions and energy in order to achieve and maintain states that support peak performance in a demanding environment'.

Juan referred to the performance concept developed by Tim Gallwey (who wrote the seminal sports psychology book, *The Inner Game of Tennis* (Gallwey, 1997)) whereby Performance is described as a formula:

$$P = P - I$$

Performance = Potential - Interference

Coto saw the job of a coach as helping to reduce that interference. His approach with Johanna Konta, and with the budding young athletes he coached, was to find ways to relax the mind, even in exceedingly challenging situations. He applied this approach not just in sports coaching but also in his 'day job', which was coaching business leaders.

Coto's Coaching Approach

Philosophy: Focus on Process not on Outcome

- Focus on the things you *can* control. Release pressure on what you can't.
- Place attention on 'Effort and Attitude' rather than 'Ranking and Winning'.

Primary Tools: Mindful Awareness + Breath + Visualisation

- Build awareness and understanding of mental interference. Replace negative thoughts with positive trigger words.
- Use breath techniques and body awareness to relax body and mind.
- Visualize game strategy using small intentions and positive outcomes.

Training Principle: Alternate mental stress and recovery (as with physical muscle building).

The Wheel of Emotion

Coto explained to young athletes the importance of giving attention and time to awareness training. He would ask them how highly they rated the importance of the mental side of the game. Most would say 70% or more. Then he would ask them how much practice time they allocated to mental training. There was always an obvious deficit. Juan talked about the fact that just knowing about mindfulness is not enough; you need to practice. In a challenging situation, he would say that the untrained mind starts thinking about the future: *I need to win. I don't want to make a mistake. What if I lose? What will my coach say?* When you think about the future you become anxious and your system fires the fight or flight response. You tense up, your heart rate increases and you start making errors. Then the untrained mind starts dwelling on those mistakes and generates emotions such as anger or frustration. This becomes a **wheel of emotion**.

Coto used MAT to help players recognize how mental processing can interfere with peak performance and to understand why it is necessary to practice working with this

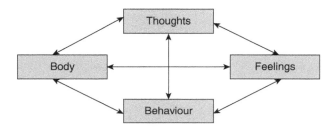

Figure 6.1   A Cognitive Behaviour Model

Source: Adapted from Factors Involved within the Cognitive Behavioural Therapy Model (Fig.3) Beck, A. T. (1976) *Cognitive Therapy and the Emotional Disorders*. International Universities Press. Figure reproduced with permission under CC BY-SA 3.0 license https://creativecommons.org/licenses/by-sa/3.0/deed.en

This diagram from Cognitive Behaviour Therapy can be helpful in illustrating the interconnected nature of our **thoughts**, **feelings**, **actions/impulses** and our **behaviour**.

Coto used a similar diagram to exemplify the 'Wheel of Emotion' in a tennis situation. When beginning a match a player may feel **nervous**, which can lead to a **tight physical state**, which will impact **behaviour**. Or when serving for the match, **thoughts** about what might happen in the future or what has happened in similar situations in the past can impact **feelings** perhaps in feeling **angry/sad/frustrated**, resulting in **physical states** that might be, respectively, **jerky/heavy/slow**, again impacting **behaviour (performance)**.

If you are a PE teacher or sports coach with personal experience of mindfulness practice, you could try adapting Coto's training approach and try this out in a Sports/PE session. He shows us how to escape the wheel of emotion by using mindful awareness to *Get Present*.

(Continued)

Get Present!

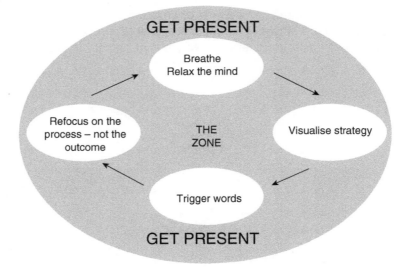

Figure 6.2 Get Present!

Source: © Juan Coto. Reprinted with permission.

- Breathe, Relax the Mind and Body:

  Take three deep diaphragmatic breaths.

  Environmental scan. Be aware of your surroundings. Focus on the texture of the court, or the colour of the sky.

  Progressive relaxation. Lightly scan through the body, tensing and releasing some major muscle groups.

- Visualise Strategy:

  Bring to mind your tactical strategy.

  Don't dwell on the past. Even Novak Djokovic makes errors. Don't beat yourself up if you make a mistake.

- Trigger Words:

  Be Positive. Tell yourself it's OK.

  Use trigger words. *Keep fighting. That point doesn't matter. I can do it.*

- Refocus on the *process* not the outcome:

  Don't think about the outcome. Focus on what you *can* control, such as making your first serve or targeting your opponent's backhand.

Adapted from Juan Coto

Coto said that if you focus on the outcome, i.e. winning, then you are focusing on something that you cannot control, which creates anxiety. He referred to Carol Dweck's 'growth mindsets' (Dweck, 2006) and John Wooden's definition of success:

> Success is the peace of mind that comes as a direct result of knowing that you put your best effort into becoming the best that you are capable of being. (Wooden, 1997: 174)

Coto explained that by focusing on the process, you open yourself up to your full potential, 'It's not about winning. It's all about growth' (Hawkins, 2016). Konta is not the only top tennis player who has drawn support from mindfulness. Amongst others, Novak Djokovic has described how mindfulness has helped him on court, especially in dealing with negative thinking after making mistakes, using present-moment awareness to let go and refocus.

The Gratitude Switch

Coto helped players harness positive emotions such as gratitude to help them deal with fluctuating feelings during matches. 'When a player feels gratitude, they feel positive about what is happening instead of seeing it as a threat' (Hawkins, 2016). This type of thinking can harness the Wheel of Emotion to your advantage as you work creatively with your own physiology to shift out of fight/flight-triggered narrow thinking and contracted states into a more expansive, open awareness. You can actually train your students to use gratitude, almost like a switch that can lift them out of a mental slump when they notice the undermining nature of habitual negative thought processes in the moment. For example, you might say:

> If you notice during the match today you are getting down on yourself or frustrated, you might try using gratitude to just appreciate the moment and the opportunity. 'OK, I see I am beating myself up here and it's not helping. What can I be grateful for in this moment? (The sun is shining; I am with my teammates, playing a game; I have a healthy body; I am not sitting an exam right now! etc.). How lucky am I? Let's enjoy this before the match ends.'

This is also something students can use in non-sport situations. In fact, all of these lessons learned from sports and performance can be applied to many other areas of life. Johanna Konta acknowledged that Coto's approach impacted her far beyond the tennis court, providing her with skills and habits that continue to influence her daily life.

Sitting Exams – Performance Anxiety

> When the mind is fastened to the rhythm of breathing, it tends to become absorbed and calm. Whether on or off the court, I know of no better way to begin to deal with anxiety than to place the mind on one's breathing process. (Gallwey, 1997: 140)

Our students experience a lot of pressure to perform well on exams. Obviously, this stress and anxiety can impede their level of success. Similar to a sports performance, in the challenging situation of a 'make or break' exam, students can get lost in the Wheel of Emotion, worrying about the outcome. 'I need to get a good mark', 'I don't want to make a mistake', 'What if I fail?' 'What will my parents say?'

When we are stressed, the amygdala is activated, which engages the fight, flight or freeze response. Many students may feel they can't recall answers because of the freeze response, not because they didn't study. Their amygdala is in the driver's seat while the pre-frontal cortex (the 'thinking' brain) is a passive passenger. Many mistakes are made by students trying to rush through the question 'before I forget everything' and some may even read the question wrong because of this panic.

When students have been trained in mindful awareness, they can use their toolkit to help them reset in these moments of stress. Some schools now incorporate mindful moments or short guided breathing practices a few minutes before the exam starts to help students relax and focus. Of course, this is only effective if students have received MAT *before* the exam – it could be very off-putting for students if their first introduction to it was during their exam block!

Team Sports

Many professionals in team sports are also trained in sports psychology, which will sometimes include this combination of mindfulness, visualization and positive psychology. In team sports there can still be significant stress on individual players. There are plenty of individual moments that require the same kind of mental calming and focusing as in individual sports, and then there is the added factor of interpersonal relationships.

With students it's often easier to start by focusing on preparing themselves for these 'individual moments' before moving on to the relationship aspects of team sports. In rugby and soccer for example, a lot of mental training goes into preparing for the moment when an individual steps up to take a penalty on behalf of the team. And in basketball there is that free throw moment when players have to detach themselves from the team and perform in isolation, scrutinized by teammates, opposition and onlookers. A true moment of performance testing!

Author Voice: Magic Hawkins?

In one of my Middle School mindfulness courses I had a number of students who were on the school basketball team and so I used sports as a way of making connections for them to the training. Having sold them the idea, they kept pushing me to take them out during a lesson and try applying their skills on the court. I know soccer pretty well as a player and school coach, but I had no idea about basketball, so I was a little reluctant at first. They kept on though, and one day, despite a light drizzle of rain, we all went out to the playground with basketballs and started doing some warm-up exercises, linking breathing with passing. The test was then to see if they could apply the breathing techniques we had learned in class to a free throw situation.

First, I let everyone have one go without any special preparation and then we all crowded around the free throw line to put added pressure on the shooter, who used a simple extended out-breath routine whilst preparing. On the actual free throw they had to try to allow the breath to be fully exhaled as they let go of the ball. To my amazement 12 out of the 13 scored the basket on their first try using the technique. It felt quite spooky to watch this happen, one after another and the students got very excited. From them on they were hooked, and often when I was on lunch playground duty some other students would come up and ask me to show them the magic free throw technique they had heard about!

There's More to Basketball than Basketball …

Let's take a look now at some people who really *do* know something about basketball and about applying mindfulness and emotional intelligence training to the game. You can use these examples or find some of your own to help students make the connection between MA skills and sportsmen and women that they relate to.

Phil Jackson is one of the most successful NBA basketball coaches of all time, with a record 11 Championship wins. An early adapter of meditation in sports, Jackson explored combining mindfulness with Native American spiritual practices in his own career as a player, and later as a coach with the Chicago Bulls and the LA Lakers. In the 1990s Jackson hired George Mumford, ex-basketball player, ex-heroin addict and professional mindfulness instructor, to train his teams. Mumford taught Jackson's players a simple approach to anchoring attention in the breath and noticing the wandering mind. Many of Jackson's players took very positively to the training and understood the practical benefits of being able to step out of overthinking during a game. The late Kobe Bryant, for example, one of the greatest all-time NBA players, used Mumford's training in the 'art of mindfulness' to great effect in helping him be fully present during matches and B.J. Armstrong found he was able to simply 'go with the flow' in high-speed games and not get wrapped up in thinking.

Emotional Regulation and Teamwork

Mindfulness may seem like an individual endeavour, but when practised together it strengthens community. Like Coto, Jackson combined MAT with visualization and also applied his deep understanding of teamwork. Jackson observed that when his squad started to meditate quietly together the cohesiveness of the team began to increase.

Perhaps the most significant impact of Jackson's leadership and of Mumford's training was in the team's ability to work together and to learn to regulate their emotional reactivity. They had plenty of opportunities to practise self-calming in the face of obstruction during highly charged moments on their journeys to becoming NBA Champions!

Jackson understood that mental 'toughness' does not equate with reacting from a place of hatred or violence. He taught his teams the difference between reacting with negative aggression and learning to harness aggression without anger. This was especially notable in the Chicago Bulls' high stakes games with old rivals the Detroit Pistons, as they learned how to disarm their opponents by simply not hitting back when provoked. Understanding that most times anger just breeds more anger is a valuable life lesson for us all:

Author Voices: Emotional Regulation — Learning Life Lessons from Sports

I was an athlete in high school and played on sports teams all year round. I got fouled out of most of my basketball games because I couldn't control my anger. Even during practice I could get very aggressive. Once, when I had overreacted during practice, my coach told me to go stand in the corner. This didn't go over well - as you can imagine - and I stormed out. I don't recall ever resolving this. It was a missed opportunity for the coach to help me learn about emotional regulation. I knew that I didn't want to act this way but I had no idea how to control my volatile emotions. As the quarterback and captain of the girls' football team, my intensity and expectations of perfection from all my team members resulted in a tense atmosphere. I wish I had learned how to manage my emotions so I could have been a better teammate and leader.

Amy

I saw some students use their MA training in very practical ways through sports. One middle school student who had taken a course with me in Prague told me that he played football (soccer) for a Czech team and had decided to use the mindfulness skills he was learning to try to deal with his anger, which often flared up during matches. He never told anyone what he was doing but at the end of the season his coach said 'This is the best season you have had with us, well done!'

Kevin

Embodiment

Phil Jackson is a powerful example for us as mindful educators, not just because he was a successful coach but also because he really embodied the values he believed in and continued to develop in himself. His efforts to pass some of his understandings on to his players would not have had the impact they did if he hadn't been able to 'walk the talk' through his own bearing and character. From his own account and from the way others perceived him, we can see that Jackson developed a leadership style that personified his commitment to compassion, values, and respect for all. This emphasis on self- and peer respect, and the way he modelled kindness, curiosity and the ability to really listen, all helped build cohesive teams even in a profession where strong egos frequently clash and struggle for control. Jackson had learned to trust his 'inner knowing' and this helped him make decisions and solve problems in the moment. By developing our personal practice and beginning to teach more mindfully, we can also bring a greater depth of embodiment into our work and our classrooms.

As we use these examples from sports or from other performance areas to help ourselves and our students understand the full potential of mindful awareness and emotional intelligence to impact our work, our studies and our lives, we can see more clearly the importance of persistence with practice in really making these deeper qualities a part of our unfolding character. Sport is a powerful example and metaphor for the wider application of these qualities, so let's continue to explore this by looking in detail at a case study of how one educator with a background in mindfulness has been able to use her training, experience and practice to develop mindful awareness and emotional intelligence in her students through coaching team sports.

Case Study: Mental Toughness in School Sports and Performance

By Lina Paumgarten

Over the course of my time as a coach I have worked with hundreds of young athletes in school sports and have developed an approach to training them in **'Mental Toughness'** that many have found very helpful in supporting not only their performance on the court but also in life. At its foundation are mindful awareness and SEL, though I rarely use the term 'mindfulness' as I find student athletes generally relate better to the idea of developing 'mental toughness' in sports. My personal development of these mindfulness skills has informed the way that I coach.

My coaching style is more strategic than tactical. This means that I am looking at a bigger picture when I coach, rather than just wanting my teams to win at all costs. Of course I definitely still fight for a win, however I focus on process rather than outcome and put strategies in place that hopefully help all team members cope with the challenges that come with training and performing. I sometimes see student athletes in a tournament shut down in a close game because they get frightened of losing. They might be thinking, *What if I'm the one that makes the last mistake?* Their mind is racing into the future, so we practice staying grounded even in high pressure situations. For example, sometimes I deliberately put them in uncomfortable situations. For my volleyball team, I might purposely book the outdoor area where it's cold and windy and they can't dive properly on the ground. Or in a practice match if a team is

(Continued)

winning 20–15, I might switch the points around and say, *Okay now you guys have 15 and the others have 20.* Of course they say, *That's not fair!* and they get annoyed. I tell them that they have to adjust. *In the tournament there's no 'But why …?', so try to notice what's happening in your body and your mind. You have to be able to accept it and switch back into the present moment.*

Afterwards we reflect about it and they complain, *Why did you do that? It really pushed my buttons?!* I explain this is preparation for when things go badly, for example when a referee's decision goes against them and they don't like it, so they need to know how it feels, and how to respond. In all these ways I am trying to help them learn to be comfortable with discomfort.

The following is a simplified outline of my Mental Toughness program as applied to a girls volleyball team. To find out more about the program go to: www.mindwell-education.com/lina-paumgarten

Part 1: Building a Foundation

Mind–Body–Heart Connection

Objectives:

- Building self-awareness as athletes and as humans, as well as awareness of others, including teammates, coaches, opponents, etc.
- Connecting teambuilding with deeper meaning and values we have as individuals, coaches and athletes.

Everything in the program is related to developing **connection**. Connection to ourselves, our teammates, our coaches, our performance. At the start of any season, it is important to create a foundation of Mind–Body–Heart awareness from which all other strategic coaching and performance aspects are built. The key training elements of the program are:

- Breathwork.
- Focus and Attention.
- Self-Reflection.
- Performance Mindset.

Breathwork

Objectives:

- Understand how to use the breath to connect with body and mind, to calm or energize.

We can use the way we breathe to support our mental state, which in turn affects our bodies. For example, when we extend our exhale, we start to reset or balance our central nervous system and induce a more relaxed state. The breath slows down, the mind calms, and the body opens and releases. In a performance situation, this means we can be more present, without letting our minds run to 'what ifs' or our bodies clench up in fear.

Our breath is also like a barometer that tells us how we are doing. When we are anxious, nervous, or fearful, we might notice that our breath becomes jagged, short, and high in the chest. This can be a cue to use the breath to reset ourselves (as above). When we are relaxed, we might notice that our breath feels smoother, deeper, and more even. There is no one way to be in a performance situation: sometimes it is very useful to be fully relaxed with slow, deep breathing. Other times it can help to quicken the breath, increasing the rate of oxygen to the brain, heart and lungs. The important point is the ability to **notice** the breath and to be able to work with it to support each performance situation.

> I usually take my time and breathe before entering the court. While being off-court, I usually focus on the game and on my breathing to stay present and not start getting lost with my thoughts.
>
> Simone, age 16

Focus and Attention Training

Objectives:

- Build awareness of thoughts, emotions, impulses, sensations in the moment.
- Focus on helpful aspects of performance.

Attention lies at the center of any mindfulness-based practice, and in performance situations we need to learn how and where to place our attention. This is key to honing our focus in a whole game situation, a specific moment such as an important serve, or an attitude that we want to embody.

Here is an example of how to guide athletes through recognizing what is happening in their mind and body on court:

In the middle of a drill, call out:

- *Freeze! Stay in your current posture, and don't move.*
- *Bring your attention to your body. Notice what sensations are there.*
- *Is your heart beating faster or slower than you thought it would?*
- *How is your breathing connected to your heartbeat?*
- *What sensations do you feel in your legs and arms? We are not practicing judging what we find, we are training our minds to notice things without judgment, in fact with curiosity and kindness.*

(Continued)

- *Now, shift your attention to what thoughts might be popping into your mind right now. Notice if they are judging thoughts about this drill, about this exercise, about yourself or another teammate.*

- *Now slowly move into a more comfortable position and close your eyes and notice what emotions are there. Do you feel excitement, annoyance, nervousness, frustration, ambition, competitiveness? What is there?*

- *There is no right and no wrong. What's important is your ability to drop into your body, mind, and heart and notice what's there. You can choose your action based on what you find. Do you want to act in anger, in kindness, with compassion, with impatience? How would you like to take your next action step?*

- *Remember that our emotions, our physical sensations, our thoughts and our actions are all connected and feed off each other. With awareness we can help redirect ourselves if we are spiraling in a direction that is not valuable or helpful.*

- *With the teammate closest to you share what you noticed and how you can use that to your benefit in a situation on or off the court.*

Self–Reflection

Objectives:

- Learning how to receive honest feedback/criticism that is sometimes hard to hear.
- Practicing internalizing these messages into setting meaningful intentions.
- Creating self-awareness of an athlete's impact on and off the court and within a team.

Performance Moments are not as time-bound and closed as one might think; in the case of athletes, the performance begins far before and ends long after a game situation. The mindful athlete develops the ability to reflect – individually and with the team – after each game in order to continually learn and grow in his or her game. In the Mental Toughness program we engage in varied moments for reflection as a tool to pause and build greater self and team awareness (see 'After Performance' activities in Part 2).

Performance Mindset

Objectives:

- Building a growth mindset of non-judgment, curiosity, and courageous open-heartedness.
- Becoming comfortable with compassion, empathy and strong vulnerability to help with the inner self-critic as well as the outer critic.
- Embracing both humility and confidence.

A Performance Mindset includes important attitudinal qualities such as empathy, compassion and seeing vulnerability as a strength. As a competitive athlete, this can easily be misunderstood as weakness, laziness, or the opposite of resilience; it is very easy to turn off the button of vulnerability to try to be strong. However, what we are trying to role-model and guide our athletes to explore and ultimately find is the athlete within them that is strong, vulnerable, and connected. This takes practice and work.

We train to bring our awareness to strong and challenging emotions, body sensations or thought processes. It is important to have open conversations about our own vulnerability as a coach/person and to model that it is okay to be fearful, angry, jealous, frustrated, etc. As a team, we need to work through these emotions (sometimes alone, sometimes together) to help us then focus that energy into our performance.

> From the position of captain, I would excuse my bad performances in a game because of my injuries. I would give myself a safety net before the game and think, 'You will try your best but if you don't have a good game it's because you are injured and you have not had much time to practice'. Having this kind of narrative in my head really held me back. I felt a lot of pressure to be the best one on the team and would compare myself to others, so that is why I needed excuses to fall back on. But then I realized that when my co-captains had a bad game that never affected the way I saw them as captains, so I decided to apply the same idea to me. In the following two years, I let those excuses go, and thought to myself: 'I am going to do my best and fight until the end'. When I let go of my safety net I really started to grow as a player. I stopped making excuses, took criticism better, and had a more positive outlook on improving my skills.
>
> Yixin, age 19

Part 2: A Strategic Approach to Peak Performance

I include here a few training examples that might be used **Before**, **During** or **After** Performance.

Before Performance

Preparing for performance starts at the beginning of a season. Creating rituals, traditions, and routines is vital in helping athletes find calm and intensity for their performance.

Visualization

Objective:

• Developing agility and resilience through mental preparation.

(Continued)

Our volleyball team had a trainer who coached us through the mental portion of the game. Dave taught us how to visualize the game before we got on the court. My team would always arrive at our games extra early to spend a few minutes visualizing ourselves and the gameplay both playing well and making mistakes. It really helped us feel confident in our skills and not get frustrated when things went wrong.

Amberly, age 15

Intention Setting

Objective:

- Setting a realistic intention for performance that is 'process'- rather than 'outcome'-based.

The difference between a goal (which you achieve) and an intention (a way in which you value responding to a situation) is vital. It is not about WHAT we do as much as HOW we do it. If an athlete sets a goal to win and they lose, they will focus on the failure (outcome). If they set an intention to stay focused throughout the game, every time their attention sways, they have learned tools to bring themselves back (process). It is something they can be more in control of than the score itself. It empowers athletes to feel confident to deal with any situation, win or lose.

Before a game, even in practice, you might ask all athletes to huddle together:

We are going to take a moment to set an intention before our performance moment.

First, connect with your center, your breath, your belly, your chest.

Now take a moment to observe who you want to be in the game.

When you make a mistake, how do you want to respond?

When you do something well, how do you want to respond?

When you see a teammate struggling, how do you want to respond?

When you are struggling, how do you want to respond?

Pick one word, an action or a focus or an adjective that will drive you today.

'I want to be ... (fill in the blank)'.

Keep repeating this phrase as you inhale and exhale. This is your intention for today.

Today you will choose to respond, act, play, support, cheer and fight with this intention as your driving force.

Take a moment to share each of your intentions, so you can keep each other accountable and support each other in the game.

This last piece is extremely important for the athletes to support each other and their intentions. At the beginning, your role is to help redirect if an intention is too goal-oriented. With time, athletes can do this process without you there, as they take ownership and become more independent in their game preparation.

Attention Training

Objective:

- Training attention to prepare for getting into the zone.

Training our attention and focus is an important aspect for a performance situation. An example of how we can do this in volleyball training is with an activity called Pressure Serves. The athlete must serve three serves perfectly in a row (no mistakes); she can choose her level of risk and intensity, and she will be distracted by all her teammates surrounding her within a 1.5 meter distance creating chaos, noise, negative 'trash talk' and visual distractions. We are simultaneously training our serves for a game, as well as our attention and focus in preparation for the one action we have 100% control over.

> I remember Pressure Serves forced me to control my mind, to focus solely on my serve, my hand movement, my feet, and to concentrate on my game rather than the noise. I realized that it's in my hands whether or not I can get distracted. It is all up to me. And although it was a tough exercise, I started to train my mind to concentrate on what I wanted.
>
> Isabela, age 17

During Performance

During training, there are ample opportunities to stop and correct a situation and model the type of response we want to have in a performance situation.

Sensing Mode – The Way into the Zone

Objective:

- Using our sensing mode of mind as we train our attention to be present and with practice, to slip into 'the zone'.

Most professional athletes and amateur athletes will speak of 'being in the zone' as an important aspect of their performance. Musicians, actors, singers and other individuals in performance situations also talk about this state of mind where they are able to focus in an effortless way. However, once they start thinking about this state of mind, they are in danger of losing it. What our experience shows us is that being present allows us to slip into the zone where we feel the

(Continued)

sweet spot of performance. During training we learn that our Thinking/Doing Mind will not allow us to play as well as when we are in our Being/Sensing Mind, which is more directly located in the present moment. Athletes may use a grounding or centering strategy related to their feet or their breath, or other parts of their body and physical sensations, as they move away from thinking/doing and towards sensing and being.

- *Let's slip into this space by becoming aware of our breathing - extending our exhale to find focus, centering and grounding.*

- *Reconnect with your physical sensations of right here and right now by touching something; maybe your hair, or the ground, or swiping your hands.*

- *Whatever you choose to do, do so in a way that is very connected to the actual physical sensation.*

- *Notice what it feels like, feel your fingertips touching, tickling, scratching.*

- *Notice surfaces that are hard, soft, bumpy, wet, anything you may notice.*

- *Come back to this space whenever you feel your thoughts, worries, anxieties pull you away from your performance.*

Mindset

Objective:

- Building resilience by learning to draw on compassion and vulnerability when pushing through discomfort and difficulty.

Resilience is the ability to bounce back after a difficult experience, whether that be physical pain (like an injury), a loss (in an important game), or a personal disappointing experience (like a disagreement with a coach or teammate). We access this quality more deeply with compassion and vulnerability than with hardness and anger. When athletes understand that pushing through tough moments using compassion and vulnerability builds deeper resilience, they start to see the long-term value of incorporating this mindset into their game.

You can show athletes how to notice and be with real discomfort of the body and mind during, for example, a plank exercise (Noticing, Identifying, and Breathing with the discomfort) and then using those same awareness skills when working through challenges during a performance.

You can train your body to control discomfort and even come to enjoy it. When I give up, it is because I am not comfortable or feel I cannot do something. Working out at home is difficult because I find myself doubting my ability to do certain exercises. As soon as I have the smallest amount of doubt in my mind, I quickly convince myself that I cannot do something. This is why I am convinced that the most important part of becoming comfortable with being uncomfortable is having a growth mindset. If you tell yourself that you can do something, you will find yourself able to do it. With the right mindset and determination, the connotation of discomfort can be positive instead of negative.

Amberly, age 15

After Performance

Team-Talks can be one of the most important rituals and expectations you can set for athletes at the end of each performance, whether big or small. Some of the main aspects are summarized below, but should not be limited to these. Creating your own genuine after-performance ritual is important for mind training.

Mind–Body–Heart Recovery

Objective:

*   Connecting Minds, Bodies and Hearts after a performance through body scans, stretching, self-reflection and/or sharing.

When we take part in a performance situation, something in our mind and body changes. Our heart rate may spike during performance and adrenaline may remain in the body for quite some time so we want to intentionally signal to our nervous system that we are ready to begin our reboot and cool-down. We do this through breathing, stretching, eating, and other physical and emotional recovery strategies. We even make taking off the jerseys after a game a ritual, signaling the body to come back down to balance again.

During a Team-Talk, athletes reflect on their own experience, and most importantly, they eat, drink and relax together. Depending on the intensity of a performance it may be appropriate to do a more formalized version of this, for example through a body scan (see Chapter 4) checking in with mind and heart after performance. The length and focus of a body/heart/mind scan would depend on how the game went and how hard they pushed themselves. This is a nervous system reboot opportunity, before we go into the reflection on the performance itself.

Mindset

Objective:

*   Reframing the performance experience.

*   Expressing gratitude through appreciations for self and others.

*   Creating an attitude of compassion for failures of self/teammates/opponents.

We begin this process not with *what could we have done better* but instead with *shoutouts, appreciations, who stood out, who was amazing and when*. By focusing

(Continued)

on the positives, regardless of how hard the loss may have been, we are then coming from a more positive perspective when we want to focus on areas of improvement. Every performance is an opportunity to grow confidence, trust and connection first and skills and areas of improvement second. Many ups and downs happen in a single set, in a single game, in a single tournament, in a single season. Taking time to reframe experiences at the end of a game is important for the athlete to be able to walk away with a feeling of accomplishment for the game itself and also with the possibility of life lessons beyond the game.

Although very ignorant to its effects in the beginning, Mental Toughness has played a crucial role in the advancement of my athletic skills, and consequently, on me as a person. Simple exercises, like visualization, breathing, and being aware of my surroundings have made me a much more humble player, but at the same time a much 'smarter' player. I have realized that I have the ability to control my emotions and my actions which has made me realize the power that I, as a person, have in my ability to play. Mental Toughness has taught me that everything that is going on, or that can happen to me, is up to me. Either I can have a good perspective and learn from my mistakes, or I can instantly get mad and stop my growth, but both are in my control.

Isabela, age 17

Lina Paumgarten - Wellness Coordinator, High School Counsellor and Coach at The International School Nido de Aguilas, Chile

Chapter Summary

In this chapter we have:

- Used the example of Sports (professional and school; individual and team) to demonstrate how mindful awareness can be trained and applied in highly practical situations.

- Highlighted ways of transferring these awareness skills to any performance area or event.

- Showed how professionals and students alike are able to learn life lessons and skills from such training and experience.

Further Reading and Resources

Curriculum Training

Online Coaching for Athletes and Sports Coaches - by Todd Corbin, www.toddcorbin.com/pages/athletes-sports-coaches

Still Quiet Place for Athletes and Coaches – by Dr Amy Saltzman, www.stillquietplace.com/still-quiet-place-athletes/

The Mindful Athlete Course – by George Mumford, https://georgemumford.com/the-mindful-athlete-course/

Books

Biegel, G. and Corbin, T. (2018) *Mindfulness for Student Athletes: A Workbook to Help Teens Reduce Stress and Enhance Performance*. Oakland, CA: New Harbinger Publications.

Education 4 Peace (2013) Football – A Path to Self-Awareness: Becoming Master of Your Emotions (Sport-Attitude). www.education4peace.org/

Jackson, P. (2006) *Sacred Hoops: Spiritual Lessons of a Hardwood Warrior*. New York: Hyperion.

Mumford, G. (2015) *The Mindful Athlete: Secrets to Pure Performance*. Berkeley, CA: Parallax Press.

Saltzman, A. (2018) *A Still Quiet Place for Athletes: Mindfulness Skills for Achieving Peak Performance and Finding Flow in Sports and Life*. Oakland, CA: New Harbinger Publications.

Apps

Calm – Train Your Mind with LeBron James, https://app.www.calm.com/meditate

Headspace – Meditation for Sports, www.headspace.com/meditation/sport

My Life – Stop. Breath. Think. – https://my.life/mylife-for-schools/

Smiling Mind – Sports Program, www.smilingmind.com.au/smiling-mind-app

Videos

George Mumford, *The Sports World's Mindfulness Whisperer*, www.youtube.com/watch?v=WVplE1WoA1E

Headspace, *How Mindfulness Helped a Young Basketball Player*, www.youtube.com/watch?v=09Fd-H6akUk

7.
Mindful Awareness Across the School

In this chapter we look at how:

- Mindful Awareness Training (MAT) can enhance the acquisition and application of social-emotional skills taught in a range of classes such as Health Education and Life Skills or in Advisory and Tutor Groups.

- MAT can support the work of SEN teachers, School Counsellors and any specialist staff designated to student care and wellbeing.

- Developing an overall framework for wellbeing, and making connections with existing frameworks, can enhance the coherence of efforts to embed Awareness-based Wellbeing (ABW) in school culture and practice.

Embedding Mindful Awareness and Social–Emotional Learning

Mindful awareness training really comes into its own in this area of supporting and enriching the acquisition and application of key social-emotional competencies. In very practical ways students and teachers can begin to see how these skills can be applied in various situations in school, as well as in their relationships in general. In this way we help to cultivate more mindful ways of interacting that contribute to the development of wellbeing in ourselves and in our school communities.

What We Want for Our Children We Need for Ourselves

These developments towards embedded wellbeing approaches and practices in our schools can only happen in meaningful ways if we, as educators and parents, are also stepping out on this journey towards greater self-understanding and greater valuing of the development of social and emotional capacities in ourselves. It's our embodiment of these qualities that drives home the learning we want for our students. Would you really listen to, or respect, a leader or a teacher who tells you how you should be, but who doesn't exemplify this in their own actions and character?

It is encouraging to see in the USA whole educational districts, such as the Oakland Unified School District, that have adopted social-emotional standards that are 'K-Adult', i.e. for everyone over 5 years old (OUSD, 2015). How cool is that! In setting out aspirational qualities for our students, it is fully appropriate that those same standards apply to all adults in the school community. Everything we have been learning in this book so far, the principles as well as the practical activities and the practices, applies to us, as adults. In learning how to deal with the stress of teaching – collaborating in mature, healthy ways with colleagues, leaders and parents whilst connecting in meaningful ways with our students – we need all these skills just as much as our students do.

As we continue to focus on this area the combination of MAT with personal growth and the development of social-emotional competencies begins to bear fruit and find expression in our work and relationships. For students and teachers alike, MAT supports the development of our social-emotional 'toolkits':

- Mindfulness training helps strengthen our attention skills and increases our capacity to sustain curiosity about emotional, physical and mental events and processes, even when situations become difficult or challenging.

- The breathing and grounding techniques we practise can help us to calm and centre ourselves, giving us just a little more space and time in which we can choose to respond rather than react when the going gets tough.

- Heightened awareness of physical, emotional and mental events can increase our self-knowledge, for example in noticing what nourishes us, as well as in becoming aware of the recurring, self-critical thought patterns and habits that can undermine us or drive our behaviour in directions we really don't want to take.

- This growing self-awareness combined with the fostering of kindness to self and others helps build empathy and connection. As we understand more about ourselves we can also relate more to what others are dealing with.

- Empathy and understanding can develop into self-compassion and compassion for others, which can motivate us to take action for those who are suffering or less well off.

These examples of deep, meaningful growth in our lives illustrate the potential for awareness-based processes to significantly increase our wellbeing and contribute to healthier school and social environments. Of course, we can't necessarily expect to see such deep-seated change in our students just because they have done a short course in mindfulness or SEL. However, over time, as we spiral practice and opportunities for the application and transfer of social-emotional skills throughout our schools we gradually begin to shift the culture of our communities, which in turn will impact the everyday experience of our students as they grow and develop in an evolving institution committed to truly fostering human development.

Finding Time and Space for MAT/SEL Classes

If it is not traditional in your school or national culture to focus on social and emotional aspects of learning, it can be challenging to know where to start when trying to open up this door within our school curricula. Although our intention is to provide ABW for all as a universal offering rather than an individual intervention, sometimes we just have to start where we are. Some school systems already have well-developed SEL programmes and time devoted to this in the schedule, while many others have not yet given much recognition to this area. Often, 'Student Wellbeing' refers to working with a group of students who are 'not doing well', but some schools have managed to overhaul their Student Wellbeing departments and broaden their role to focus on the fostering of wellbeing for *all* students. Many schools are now creating or augmenting existing organizational structures to include Directors of Student Wellbeing in order to give a higher profile to this area.

If your school already has staff dedicated to Student Wellbeing and classes that can be used for this subject then you are in a good position to build on this and develop it further. Many schools now include courses on mindfulness and SEL in classes such as Health Education, PSHE (Personal Social/Health Education), Life Skills, Citizenship, Ethics, etc. With the increased concern surrounding student mental health, some countries are beginning to require that such classes include elements of social-emotional and mental health skill development.

Another possible area to consider is whether your school has provision for 'Pastoral Care' or 'Affective Education'. In some school systems this may be a 'Tutor', 'Mentoring' or 'Advisory' system that provides regular small group meetings with a teacher facilitator. Here the emphasis may be on relationships and other social issues, although in practice these groups can often get diverted to dealing with information dissemination and other year group administrative issues that detract from the social-emotional focus. If so, there needs to be a review of how these valuable sessions are used and a prioritization of SEL and relationship building. School leaders need to be persuaded of the need to allocate significant scheduling time to these classes in order to provide a greater balance. Some understanding of the research in this area may be helpful, for example:

Research Case Study: SEL and Achievement

A significant study (Durlak et al., 2011) into the impact of SEL programmes in schools (USA) found that when we pay attention to the social and emotional aspects of learning, academic standards are raised:

- In addition to increased social-emotional skills, the meta-analysis showed that those students who attended schools with SEL programmes on average scored **11 percentile points higher** on standardized tests compared with control groups.

(Continued)

In 2017 a follow-up study, Taylor et al. (2017) demonstrated the long-term benefits of universal SEL interventions. This meta-analysis tracked nearly 100,000 students who had been in those schools with SEL programmes over the next three to five years and found:

- **Academic performance** was 13 percentile points higher than their peers.

- High School and College **graduation rates** were higher (6% and 11%).

- There were significantly lower rates of **behavioural issues**, unsafe sexual behaviour and drug use.

- Higher **social-emotional skills** and positive attitudes to self, others and school.

Post-intervention social-emotional skill development was the strongest predictor of well-being at follow-up. Participants fared significantly better than controls in social-emotional skills, attitudes, and indicators of well-being. Benefits were similar regardless of students' race, socioeconomic background, or school location (p. 1).

A Practical Application of MAT/SEL in Schools

It can be difficult for new initiatives like MAT to gain traction in schools, so aligning with what is already happening, or with a thread that all stakeholders can support, can ease some of the tensions that inevitably arise with change. What if, instead of trying to *add* something new, a school just focuses on something that they are already doing, and apply MAT to that particular skill?

A Mindful School = A Listening School

As we saw in Chapter 3, awareness training can build from establishing the foundations of attention anchoring, to deep listening practices, and then on to structured activities that help develop applied listening skills in pair or group work in any subject area. Listening skills are fundamental to teaching and learning but, in many instances, they are *assessed* whilst not necessarily *taught*. When we look at listening through an SEL/mindfulness lens, we begin to see the potential for a focus on this skill to actually become a core attribute and unifying theme of a school culture.

The five core SEL competencies can all be cultivated through the development of this one powerful skill in any and all subject areas, for example:

- **Self-awareness:** How am I listening? Where is my attention?

- **Self-management:** Can I hold back where appropriate and not interrupt?

- **Social awareness:** Do I value other people's opinions and voices?

- **Relationship skills:** Can I use my listening skills to help build teamwork?

- **Responsible decision-making:** Can I listen to myself and act from a place of kindness and care for others, with curiosity and open-mindedness?

Reflection on Listening

This can be a way of opening up a discussion about the importance of listening and can be used with students, colleagues or parents.

Set up a structure - pairs or groups* - to discuss the following questions:

Can you think of a time when you really wanted to share something with somebody and they didn't listen to you? What did it feel like to not be listened to?

Can you think of a time when you really wanted to share something with somebody and they did listen to you? What did it feel like to really be listened to?

What gets in the way of listening? What can make it hard to really listen to someone? (It can be helpful to list these as a whole class.)

Listening is not easy! But we can develop this skill in very practical ways. What gets in the way of listening is really the same as what gets in the way of being present. We can use our mindful awareness to help us develop our capacity to listen. The next time you are listening to someone, see if you can notice any of your habitual tendencies - do you have the impulse to interrupt? Or to try to solve their problem? Consider using your mindfulness practice to ground yourself through the body and, when your mind wanders, coming back to just listening to the person as directly as you can.

*Consider using the Pairs Whispering approach from Chapter 3 as a format for this reflection. In doing so, you are creating an experiential opportunity for the concept of 'listening mindfully'. We often start this with a short Sounds Practice (p. 44).

Council Practice

Another way of using and developing mindful listening skills in classroom contexts is through Council Practice. Council is a form of communicating which has its roots in indigenous communities and wisdom traditions from around the world. The four intentions of Council, as stated by the Ojai Foundation, are:

1. Speaking from the heart.

2. Listening from the heart.

3. Speaking spontaneously.

4. Speaking leanly.

These intentions shape the experience and offer a safe container where both children and adults alike can feel supported to share openly within a group.

Educator Voice: Permission to be Heard

I first introduced Council to the faculty in my school and it had a profound impact. Their ability to truly listen, to suspend judgement, and to speak from their heart cultivated a powerful sense of community. I then brought Council to all homeroom and advisory classes, where they would practise once per week, from Grade 1 to Grade 12.

When introducing Council, it is best to introduce it with inviting, simple prompts such as sharing a 'rose, thorn, and bud' or a fun question like 'Would you rather fly or be invisible? Why?' After the group develops trust in the process and with each other, you can offer prompts that may elicit deeper responses. Sometimes the prompts can seem light but may end up taking the Council into more emotional territory. While leading a Council with a Grade 8 group, I started us off with the prompt, 'Tell about a journey that changed your life'. Little did I know how profound this prompt would get, especially as students felt so comfortable with sharing all types of journeys, both literal and metaphorical. With this deeper sharing in mind, it is critically important that teachers experience Council for themselves first and foremost. In order to know how to hold the group, teachers must experience for themselves the permission that Council gives; permission to feel, permission to be heard, permission to be seen, permission to be human. This is emotional intelligence training of the highest order.

Krysten Fort-Catanese - Founding Director of Mindfulness and SEL at UWC Thailand (formerly Phuket International Academy).

Further information on Council can be found at https://waysofcouncil.net/

We have used the Council approach with teachers and students in many different contexts and always found it a valuable process. You can explore combining mindful awareness with any structured speaking and listening approaches and protocols you already employ in your schools, such as Literature Circles, Harkness Method, Restorative Circles, Adaptive Schools, etc.

Metacognition – Learning to Learn

Understanding our strengths and challenges as learners is key to growth and development in education. It is highly valuable for students to build their awareness of their individual learning styles and, especially in this age of distraction, to notice what leads them to procrastinate and where their attention is being pulled to (see 'Dealing with Distraction' in Chapter 4). Developing this understanding and familiarity with oneself as a learner, being able to be honest with yourself about what you know and what you don't know, is really what helps us 'learn how to learn'. In this way, a personal 'Learning Profile' becomes an increasingly important aspect of a student's skill set as they progress through the education system.

Knowing When I Have Not Been Paying Attention Is a Valuable Piece of Information...

'Meta' + 'Cognition' means being able to step back and have the awareness to see beyond our habitual thought processes. An important aspect of metacognitive abilities is to be able to monitor and direct attention. When you read a passage of a text book and then realize that most of the time you were actually thinking about something else when reading, that is a moment of metacognition – when you become aware of your own cognitive processes and can bring yourself back, acknowledge that you didn't really read that page and can then choose to have another go at it if necessary.

MAT can support the development of metacognitive skills in our students as they grow to understand more about themselves as reflective learners. It can be helpful if teachers first develop metacognitive awareness about their own learning styles and then engage students in discussions about what works best for them and what sometimes gets in the way of studying and learning. One way to start such a discussion could be with this reflection activity, adapted for your age group:

My Learning Profile – Reflection

Do you easily get distracted or sometimes rush your studying? Or do you have trouble getting started?

Do you notice any strong positive or negative responses to any specific subjects or to areas within some subjects?

Do you find it easy to read fiction and understand characters but struggle with abstract ideas such as in mathematics or sciences? Or maybe it's the other way around for you?

What conditions work best for you when studying?

Do you know how to draw on your mindful awareness training to refocus, take a breath, ground yourself or just slow down a little?

If you are trying too hard to work out a mental problem and are going around in circles can you notice this and use a breathing practice to step back and let it go for a while?

(Continued)

We can also help students develop metacognitive awareness when working with others, for example in understanding how they function in collaborative teamwork:

Are you a good listener?

Do you dominate groups?

Students can learn to apply awareness skills and self-regulation in group work, for example, pulling back if speaking too much or encouraging themselves to speak up sometimes even when they are feeling timid.

Some general research on metacognition in education (Quigley et al., 2018) has suggested that students learn to apply metacognitive study skills most effectively when taught them within each subject area, rather than in a discrete course, because then they have practical opportunities to apply their growing awareness within that context. We believe that MAT can support this by providing practical skills for students to draw on, playing a significant role in the development of more self-regulated learners.

Bringing Mindful Awareness to Special Educational Needs Students

Please note that many of the areas outlined below apply to students whether or not they have a Special Needs diagnosis.

Perhaps the single most important development for a student with learning needs is when they begin to understand, own and consciously work with their particular challenges to learning. MAT can support the effective development of such metacognitive skills in our students as they grow to understand more about themselves as learners.

Many students with learning needs benefit from training that improves their executive functioning, because this has significance for their ability to:

- Focus
- Organize
- Plan
- Manage time

MAT in essence helps develop three core areas – attention, self-awareness and emotional regulation – so we can see the potential here for improving skills in some of the key areas in which our SEN students may be challenged.

These are students that have severe issues with regulating their emotions – for a lot of our kids, this is the crux of their issues. Mindfulness gives them a self-esteem boost because they have a strategy to use to control their emotions – it helps them stay focused and stay calm. That's huge for a kid who may have a lot of issues with that. (Thomas, 2016)

Research Case Study: Mindful Awareness and Executive Function

Numerous research studies and anecdotal articles have demonstrated the impact of mindfulness on executive function and emotional regulation (Fuster and Scholar, 2009). Some studies have directly explored the use of mindfulness in SEN classes (Frank et al., 2013), although in general there has still been little research directly into this area. One study that looked at using Mindful Awareness Practices (MAPs) with 7–9 year olds found that '...those children starting out with poor Executive Function who went through the MAPs training showed gains in behavioral regulation, metacognition, and overall global executive control' (Magaldi and Park-Taylor, 2016).

There is growing evidence that mindful attention training can increase the ability to focus and to be able to filter out distracting stimuli. A number of studies have looked at the use of MAT with students with ADHD. For example van de Weijer-Bergsma et al. (2012: 775) focused on adolescents and found that '...after mindfulness training, adolescents' attention and behavior problems reduced, while their executive functioning improved'.

MAT is thus a universal intervention that can be particularly helpful to students with special needs, especially where there is a need to strengthen executive functioning, attention and emotional regulation. But it is not a magic pill that fixes everything. In the final study above (van de Weijer-Bergsma et al., 2012), the researchers also commented that 'Effects of mindfulness training became stronger at 8-week follow-up, but waned at 16-week follow-up'. This underlines the importance of providing regular ongoing opportunities to practise and apply learned mindfulness and social-emotional skills. Eventually, these altered states of mind can become traits (Goleman and Davidson, 2017), but in the short term we just need to keep practising.

Parent Voice: Mindfulness and Autism

Jake was diagnosed with Autism at age 4, and we had many coping strategies in place to get through each day, especially in his younger years. His main challenges were sensory overload, transition and inability to communicate. We found strategies that helped

(Continued)

support him but he had a pretty rocky transition from Primary to Secondary School and it took him the whole of Year 7 (Grade 6) to settle into his new environment.

In Year 8, a new lunchtime Mindfulness Club started at his school on Tuesdays. Jake attended and from day one he connected with it. Normally after a full day at school he would come home and just want total quiet. On a Tuesday he seemed different. He would come home happier, have a better evening with the family and his anxiety and stress levels were noticeably lower.

Mindfulness has given Jake control of how to cope with his anxiety, and it has helped him with many aspects of day-to-day life, as well as taking exams, participating in activities and social events and being able to attend college independently.

As parents, we are so grateful that Jake has found a tool that he can use himself on a daily basis that supports his mental health. I would suggest it to other parents who have a child experiencing anxiety or poor mental health, and would encourage parents to actively participate with them, as you can share the experience together, have discussions around mindfulness and encourage each other to practise.

Jake's mindfulness teacher, Sarah Gotting, literally changed life for our whole family by introducing him to mindfulness. We are so grateful!

Kat Holgate - Parent, The King's School, Devon, UK

One of our colleagues, an experienced SEN teacher, says that she uses her mindfulness training to help establish a warm, relaxed environment in her classes and to help her students to centre, ground, refresh and feel nourished: 'I often begin sessions with a focused breathing activity to "slow down the wigglies and squigglies". Students really value it because it supports their transition, giving them space and time to adjust.' By learning to use simple calming and focusing activities within our classes we can help our students – and ourselves – find moments of calm within a busy and demanding school day.

Case Studies: Special Education

Clare Winter is a leader in a setting for students in the UK who have been, or are, at risk of permanent exclusion. She has worked in Special Education for 15 years:

Working with the most distressed young people brings both benefits and demands to us as teachers and practitioners. While working in a regular school setting usually entails conscript audiences, young people with SEMH (social, emotional and mental health needs) can throw up additional challenges. The young people who frequently communicate their needs with the most socially inappropriate behaviour can benefit immensely from the compassionate approach of an experienced mindfulness teacher. They are also the learners who may need the most support with directing their attention in a positive way and sitting with the internal noise that silence may reveal.

You may experience negative feedback at first – many students will find silence intrusive and will have difficulty with focus. Keep practices short and simple to start with. When practising together it can also be useful to take into account the following considerations:

- **Relationships:** Learners who have experienced traumatic life events or are disenfranchised need to know that they can trust you. It really helps to have a positive rapport. Find out if there are any past traumas or difficult experiences that may impact on your students' practice.

- **Silence:** Many young people in this demographic experience chaotic lives where quiet time is unusual. Some of them feel the need to fill any gaps with noise. Reassure students that silence need not be uncomfortable and expect to make modest steps of progress. Praise any small victories and accept students just being silent or still for a moment as a starting point.

- **Safety:** Some students will feel uncomfortable or even unsafe with eyes closed or in a prone position. Being trauma-sensitive is important here too. Allow them to sit in a comfortable position with gaze lowered. Blankets can be useful to avoid feelings of being too exposed when lying down. Students may find it very difficult to remain in their own space. It can be useful to place chairs facing away from each other. This can be done before learners enter the class to avoid resistance.

- **Start with the Feet:** With so much buzzing around inside their minds it is advisable to move awareness as far away from the head as possible. Start with practices that move focus to the feet. Perhaps encourage students to remove shoes or socks to increase sensitivity in this area. This will be easier for lots of young people as this area is more concrete and obvious than the breath. Also, focusing on the breath can bring feelings of discomfort or reminders of stressful situations when their breathing was heightened.

- **Movement is Key:** Take advantage of many students' compulsion to move by doing short movement practices. Move between slow and fast at regular intervals. Using simple workout exercises such as running on the spot or slow push-ups can help engage teenage audiences. Working with groups can be a good time to do activities that involve focused teamwork. For example, passing an increasingly full cup of water around a circle of students can bring awareness to movement, balance and proximity to others.

- **Connect with the Senses:** Go outside and bring awareness to the movement of the clouds, the wind or sun through the trees, the sound of the wind or the birds.

- **Consistency:** Incorporate practice into every day. Make it an expectation and a regular occurrence.

- **Neuro-education:** Students love finding out about how they tick. Teach them about their plastic brains and what happens when their emotions push the neocortex 'offline'.

(Continued)

- **Personal responsibility:** Be mindful of your own life experiences and what your students may bring up in you. Seek support where necessary and, where possible, access supervision with an experienced, accredited teacher of mindfulness.

- **Celebrate:** Congratulate yourself and your young people regularly on any progress, however small!

Terry Taylor was previously the Principal of Hopetown School for Specific Purposes in Australia, which services the needs of students ages 5-18 who are classified as having Emotional Disturbance.

Hopetown's students struggle with a wide range of mental health issues including anxiety, depression, aggression, histories of abuse and neglect in their early years. Several years ago, we introduced a Mindfulness programme based on '.b' (Mindfulness in Schools Project, UK) and elements of Acceptance and Commitment Therapy. Lessons were taught to small groups by dedicated mindfulness teachers and principles of trauma-informed practice were employed. The success of the programme came down mainly to creating an environment of safety, trust and acceptance by teachers who embodied the essential qualities they were promoting, such as empathy, compassion and curiosity. One challenge though was achieving 'buy in' by all staff. There was no opposition but there were varying levels of interest and confidence in implementing mindfulness practice. With hindsight, voluntary staff participation would probably be a better way to go. It is crucial for the trainers to be properly prepared and competent in safely allowing a student to 'sit with' any intense or unnerving thoughts and emotions which may arise during a session.

Self-Care

As specialist teachers who often bear a heavy load supporting students for whom school can be a major challenge, it is vital that we also take time to focus on ourselves and our own ability to be present, well-regulated and calm under pressure. In fact, the real power of mindfulness often becomes apparent when the adults in the building begin to apply these skills to themselves. Most of the benefits we have listed in this section can be just as helpful for adults as they are for children. Developing greater self-awareness can transform our daily experience as adults in a demanding social environment and help us to work more effectively with students and parents, whilst sustaining our energy in advocating for our students with colleagues. As Special Education teacher Jada Thomas (2016) says:

You know, for most teachers, self-care really isn't on the list because there's just no time for it. It's the nature of our profession - you're giving and giving and you're never replenishing anything. But, when you sit down to practice mindfulness, that's a moment that you're taking for yourself to help replenish everything you give.

Bringing Mindful Awareness to Counselling and Student Support Services

Different countries and education systems have different ways of organizing support for students with academic issues, mental health concerns, and college/career planning. Some countries may have Educational Psychologists who can support schools, some have School Social Workers and some may have School Counsellors. In this section we will refer in general to support as 'counselling support', but we realize that many schools have to cope without these specialist positions and have to delegate the various responsibilities as best they can, often to overworked teachers, deputy heads and assistant principals. School counsellors often prove an invaluable asset to a school community, and when well organized and -staffed we can even see their roles as being at 'the heart of the school' because of their expertise and because they bring an organizational focus on emotional health and wellbeing.

As well as providing emotional, academic and career support for students, counsellors often support teachers' mental and emotional health and are usually tuned in to wellbeing issues in the whole school community in general. In some schools the university application and academic timetabling issues dominate, so there is little space left for the emotional aspects of counselling. It is important that school leaders protect these aspects of the counsellor's work because they provide such crucial support to students and teachers.

Many School Counsellors are beginning to incorporate mindful awareness in various ways in their work:

Educator Voice: School Counsellor's Perspective

As a school counsellor, I can see the positive impact of mindfulness on my students' mental and physical health, as well as the growth of their social and emotional skills and overall wellbeing. This might, for example, take the form of learning how to respond to and cope with challenging experiences in the moment. A simple mindfulness tool that I use nearly every day in my work to help with this is the 'mindful pause' followed by conscious breathing. Afterwards we reflect on the experience together and explore how this can be empowering for the student.

I highly recommend the **International School Counselor Association's** 'Core Counseling Curriculum Scope and Sequence' (iscainfo.com) because it's a model that guides counselors in the domains of academic, personal, social, career, and global perspectives. Mindfulness supports the competencies of self-awareness and self-management that can be used from early childhood to Grade 12.

Cultivating my personal mindfulness practice continually supports my ability to meet my students where they are at and has helped me with my own emotional regulation and self-care.

Chrystal Kelly - School Counsellor, The American International School of Muscat

---

As Chrystal illustrates, when you have your own mindfulness practice it becomes easier to draw from it in supporting others in the moment:

Author Voice: Emotional First Aid...

One day, I was counselling a young girl who was dealing with anxiety and depression and we were exploring practical ways she could support herself in moments where she felt overwhelmed. I spontaneously suggested the following activity to her and have continued to share it with students and teachers:

       # Finger Press + Self Pep Talk

If you notice yourself getting overwhelmed or undermined with strong thoughts or emotions, you can try this:

- On your desk, press each of your fingers down one at a time, moving from one hand to the other, and internally recite, one word per finger:

- 'I. Am. Doing. The. Best. That. I. Can. Right. Now'.

- (Or you can choose any ten words that suit you at any given time.)

- Fingers can be resting on your legs or you can even have your arms crossed or in any position really - no one will know you are doing it!

- Even doing it without the words can sometimes help open up a moment of physical connection and a lessening of tension and overthinking.

A small activity like this is obviously not a simple solution to the difficulties this young woman was grappling with, but, as a practical exercise, she did find it useful and empowering and practised it many times throughout the day.

Amy

Frameworks for Wellbeing

Embedding Awareness-based Wellbeing across the whole school starts to have a more coherent impact when we begin to include Wellbeing, MAT and SEL within our curricula frameworks and mission statements. We look in more detail at questions of coherence and implementation in the following chapter and here share a few examples of schools that have already gone some way in developing or adapting their frameworks, statements and curriculum content.

Don't Recreate the Wheel!

All schools have some form of charter or mission statement that helps to guide their community, and some already have social and emotional competencies built in. It is also possible to adapt approaches that you already have in place. For example,

Phuket International Academy (now UWC Thailand) adapted the International Baccalaureate Learner Profile to incorporate social-emotional aspects that could be promoted through regular curriculum work:

Case Study: Embedded Wellbeing in Action

Since our school was founded on SEL and Mindfulness, we wanted our application of the IB Learner Profile to reflect these values and qualities. With this in mind, our school treated the IB LP as it was intended to be – a working document – and created the 'IB Learner Profile through an SEL Lens' in 2010–2011:

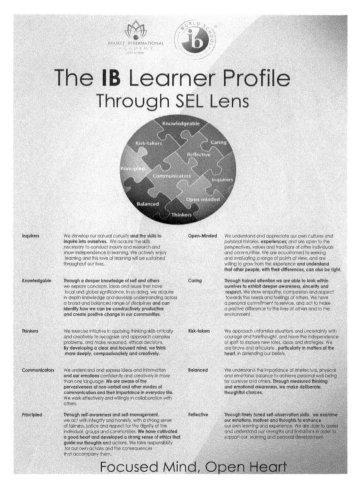

Figure 7.1   IB Learner Profile through an SEL Lens

Source: Created by Krysten Fort-Catanese

A pdf version of this document is available at www.mindwell-education.com/mtt-resources

(Continued)

To assist us in embedding these qualities into our school day, we created 'Time-In', which provided a daily quiet time for students and teachers to engage in mindful awareness practices that encourage Movement, Stillness, and Reflection. This was an opportunity for children and adults to calm and ground their minds and bodies, shifting out of 'thinking mode' into a 'sensing mode' of mind and establishing greater balance between 'doing' and 'being'. This sensory mode of inquiry enhances our ability to engage – with a calmer, clearer perspective – with what's happening within us, to us, and around us. Time-In ends with setting an intention for the day. Eventually students, even as young as 5 years old, learned to lead some of the practices. Having these times for stillness and reflection each morning changes the tone and climate of the classroom to help everyone feel less frazzled from their busy start to the day and to feel more grounded and resourced for the day ahead.

Figure 7.2   'Time-In' Activity Pouches

Source: Created by Krysten Fort-Catanese

As we weave these standards and skills into our curriculum frameworks and school days, we begin to find practical ways of making these deeper qualities a natural part of our students' everyday experiences at school. This process may be somewhat easier if you are ever fortunate enough to be part of planning a school's vision from scratch:

Educator Voice: Be Open, Be Curious, Be Kind

I had the opportunity to be the principal of a new school and I was very fortunate to be able to help create our focus on mental and emotional wellbeing from the start. The work of implementing mindfulness and SEL in the school began with the development of our school vision and motto statement: 'Be Open, Be Curious, Be Kind'. That was the beginning. This motto is the foundation for our school and it is fostered through our mindfulness practices. It has allowed us to move forward in ways that I never expected. Those teachers who were trained in mindfulness started to notice differences within themselves. They were calmer in the classroom and were pleasantly surprised that the 'core breathing moments' actually helped them as well as their students. Every student, parent, staff member, and anyone who comes into the building is aware of our motto because we live and breathe it in everything that we do and say.

Pauline McKenna - Principal, Kanata Highlands Public School, Ottawa, Canada

More often though, you are likely to be working in a school or educational system that is more resistant to change. We will explore this further in the following chapter, but it can be helpful to see examples of school communities that have done pioneering work in this area and also to note the impact this can have on students.

Case Study: A School's Wellbeing Journey

Like many schools, the American School of The Hague (ASH) has, for many years, been on a journey towards supporting wellbeing and resilience for all learners. Like many schools, we too sometimes focus so much on the destination (i.e. a holistic wellbeing program) that we forget to celebrate the successes we already encountered along the way. Through a number of initiatives over the past few years, we are slowly but surely reaching a critical mass of adult advocates for a holistic approach to wellbeing. Some of these initiatives for staff have included:

- Visiting trainers and active sharing of research and classroom materials.
- Staff signing up for personal mindfulness apps.
- Regularly having a few minutes of mindfulness at the start of a meeting.
- Professional Development support for staff on a continuum from 'being mindful' to 'teaching mindfully' and eventually 'teaching mindfulness'.

(Continued)

As a result, we have also seen an increased number of initiatives for students, including:

- Mindfulness courses for all Grade 6 and 8 students.

- The creation of a student-led yoga club.

- Personal wellbeing sessions built into High School Advisory.

- Guided breathing exercises at the start of some classes as well as at the start of every International Baccalaureate and Advanced Placement exam.

At the same time, as we continue our journey towards designing a holistic wellbeing program we have worked with parent and student representatives to try to outline more specifically what such a program might look like in our school and to begin to draft an outline framework that we have called 'Being Well, Doing Well'. To support this, ASH just became the first school in Europe to start a three-year partnership with Dr Lea Waters and her Visible Wellbeing program from Australia.

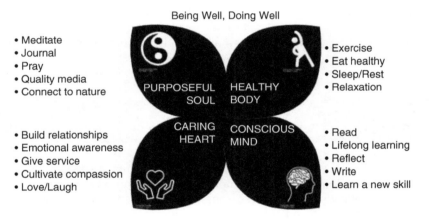

Figure 7.3   A Wellbeing Framework

Source: Credit to ASH Being Well, Doing Well Team

Bart Dankaerts - CAS and Service Learning
Co-ordinator, American School of The Hague

Let's close this chapter with a personal perspective on the wellbeing work at ASH from a parent who has seen first-hand the benefits of the school's commitment to student wellbeing and the introduction of mindfulness into the school community:

Parent Voice: A Parent Perspective on Mindfulness in Education

In 2011–12, **Kara Smith's** middle school children were introduced to mindfulness at ASH. Her daughter took an eight-week course that ran as part of Grade 8 PE/Health class, and her son followed an innovative, customized unit that integrated mindfulness practices into a unit on Chinese culture in Grade 6 Social Studies.

I knew right away that something was wrong when I saw that my 12 year old was calling: he should have been in class at his new school, but instead he was phoning from the washroom, in a total panic.

For what felt like an eternity, I listened to the sound of the rapid, jagged breathing high in his chest, and the quivering sound of his broken words as he struggled to articulate the situation that had triggered such anxiety. I felt like I could practically see the tears welling up in his eyes as he fought to stay brave... looking for a lifeline while spinning and tumbling around in a sea of his fearful emotions, exhaustion, and distress.

I felt utterly helpless: the worst feeling as a parent is when your child is not well. My mind searched for 'solutions' to help him, but I didn't know anyone at school and I was far away on a business trip.

And then – almost out of desperation – I stepped way back, against my instincts to jump in and 'fix;' I remembered the mindfulness lessons he learned at his old school. 'Let's stop talking, let's do nothing now but 7-11 breathing', I suggested. 'Let's not wonder or worry, only breathe for two minutes'.

I will never forget the sound of his breath gradually changing as we inhaled and exhaled together across the miles. I actually heard it slow down and take on a deep, steady rhythm, until he was able to explain the situation much more clearly.

And I noticed that I also shifted from a panicky 'What do I do to help him?!?' to a more settled, centred perspective where we could talk through next steps. In his words 'I could think more clearly about what was really wrong, or not, and figure out how to deal with it after [the breathing]'.

I had always been a big supporter of the mindfulness lessons my children had learned the prior school year; I understood the evidence base and admired the school for equipping students – along with parents and teachers – with such practical approaches to wellbeing. But until then, I had not really experienced the palpable, measurable impact they can have at unexpected moments.

On this day, the techniques we learned almost a year earlier truly came to the rescue for both of us. Everyone in my family has called upon the school mindfulness lessons many more times since then – sometimes for pivotal moments like before an exam or big match, and other times just to reset at the end of a busy day or to help facilitate a conversation. I have watched my children adapt and implement these tools as they work with their own unique stress points, fears, and anxieties.

Although they are now young adults, in some ways little has changed for my son and daughter since they were little. As the saying goes: small children, small problems...

(Continued)

> big children, big problems. Though very different, they each carry the same fears and sources of anxiety or stress, as well as elemental strengths and worldviews, as when they were young. And while the pressure moments don't necessarily go away, my children's ability to respond from a place of mindful awareness when they do happen has transformed their life experiences for the better.

Chapter Summary

In this chapter we have:

- Seen how the deeper potential of MAT becomes more apparent and engaged when combined with social-emotional programmes and initiatives across the curriculum.

- Considered the benefits for students of developing metacognitive and attention skills through awareness training, especially for those with Special Educational Needs.

- Looked at some examples of initiatives in schools aimed at embedding ABW more coherently into their curricula and culture.

Further Reading and Resources

Curriculum Training

Sea Change Mentoring – Relationship-based learning and wellbeing, https://seachangementoring.com/

SEE Learning – Social, Emotional and Ethical Learning for Early Elementary, Late Elementary, Middle School, and High School, https://seelearning.emory.edu/

SEL Everyday Online Courses – for educators and school leaders, by Meena Srinivasan, www.meenasrinivasan.com/

Take in the Good with Mindfulness – Mindfulness-centred SEL curriculum, by Gina Biegel, www.stressedteens.com/all-school-program

Books

Hawkins, K. (2017) *Mindful Teacher, Mindful School: Improving Wellbeing in Teaching and Learning*. London: SAGE.

Ribas, W. B., Brady, D. A., and Hardin, J. (2017) *Social-Emotional Learning in the Classroom: Practical Guide for Integrating All SEL Skills into Instruction and Classroom Management*. Norwood, MA: Ribas Publications.

Srinivasan, M. (2019) *SEL Every Day: Integrating Social and Emotional Learning with Instruction in Secondary Classrooms*. New York: W.W. Norton & Company.

Websites

CASEL – The Collaborative for Academic and Social and Emotional Learning, https://casel.org/

Edutopia – www.edutopia.org/social-emotional-learning

8.
Developing a Coherent Approach: Implementation Q&A

In this chapter, we explore:

- Common questions and challenges that need to be answered and overcome if we are to transition from individual, pioneering approaches to embedded, system-wide change.

- How the work we are all doing can contribute to an essential shift of focus in our schools towards incorporating student growth and wellbeing, alongside academic achievement, as central components of our educational systems.

One of the most frequent questions we are asked in diverse educational settings around the world is, *How do I bring this to my school in a way that will make it sustainable?* Our immediate response might often be, *It depends on your context.* This may not be a very satisfying answer, but the reality is that it *does* depend on a range of factors that are particular to your school community. All schools are not created equal – and of course this kind of work is likely to be easier in schools with more money and space to try new initiatives. So much depends on budget and opportunity, as well as leadership and community support. In this chapter we have compiled some of the key questions educators and parents ask about wellbeing and we hope that some of the responses, along with the personal stories and expert advice, will help clarify your own ideas about these issues and provide practical guidance when pursuing next steps in your school.

Questions in Part 1 deal with organizational issues, while Part 2 covers other commonly raised questions.

Part 1: Organizational Issues

Q1: How can I start to promote and develop Awareness-based Wellbeing (ABW) in my school?

- You might be a **class, subject or specialist teacher** already exploring mindfulness-based wellbeing with your students and wondering how best to enlist the support of sympathetic colleagues and leaders.

- You might be a **school leader** wanting to bring a greater emphasis on wellbeing to your school community.

- Or you might be a **parent** wanting to support this type of development in your child's school.

So where *do* you start?

Start where you are ...

There is no one-size-fits-all approach and each school operates within a different environment. An important part of our journey is to learn to step back and try to understand the interaction of complex factors that impact wellbeing in our school communities. Combining this cognitive ability to 'see the system' for what it actually is, with a more embodied presence rooted in your personal practice, is a powerful way to begin to effect change in our schools.

As a teacher, it is your embodiment of ABW that helps create stronger relationships with students, along with perhaps a greater sense of calm in your classroom. This can then begin to impact student learning and draw potentially interested colleagues to you.

If you are a school leader who has teachers in your school who are informed and passionate about this area, and who embody a mindful approach to wellbeing, then these are the people to work with (see Q2).

If you are a school parent, you can support your child's health and wellbeing along with whole school developments by aligning yourself with teachers and leaders in the school who are beginning to explore and promote this work.

Good intentions and better connections are not, however, in themselves sufficient to stimulate change. Systems Thinking has shown that even a group of well-intentioned individuals working in a flawed system can actually harm some of those they intend to help. What we know from the limited research on the implementation of mindfulness in education is that to move from explorative efforts by individual teachers to a more embedded, whole-school approach to wellbeing is neither a smooth nor a straightforward process. From our experiences of working with schools and teachers around the world for the last decade, and from the research so far available on successful implementation, we have learned that:

1. A top-down approach to implementing ABW has so far not proved effective.

2. Individual teachers working in isolation in this area have not generally been able to promote school or system-wide changes.

3.   (And now, the good news ...) A combination of 'bottom-up' pioneering work with 'top-down' support and resourcing can help embed real change in educational communities.

'Champion' teachers, supported by visionary leaders who appreciate the value of fostering teacher self-care and of developing a more balanced approach to student achievement and wellbeing have demonstrated that this formula helps drive successful implementation in schools. (Wilde et al., 2018)

Based on what we have experienced and observed, and on what other schools have told us about what works and what doesn't, we have developed the **MindWell Pathways** framework (see www.mindwell-education.com/mtt-resources). Bearing in mind the importance of understanding local contexts, this framework sets out a broad pattern that we have identified for schools wanting to build greater coherence into their approach to developing ABW.

Q2: How do we engage school leaders in this work?

Unless a school leader already has some intrinsic interest in the areas of personal growth, wellbeing or mindfulness, this can be a tough sell. For many reasons it is not easy for most administrators to grasp this nettle. Even if they recognize there is a need to deal with aspects of student mental health or teacher wellbeing, the demands on curriculum time are just too intense and the demands on their own time often prevent them from seriously considering making space for personal reflection and growth. Many of us fail to make space for self-care until compelled to do so by illness or burnout. In some cases, schools have been forced to come to terms with levels of student anxiety and depression because of a tragic incident of self-harm or suicide. Whilst we can never fully prevent such tragedies from occurring, it is incumbent upon school leaders, aware of this current trend around the world in educational systems, to be more proactive in making efforts to address student mental health more directly. The disruption triggered by the COVID-19 global pandemic and the accompanying threats to physical, social, emotional and mental health for students, teachers and families brought home to many schools and school leaders the crucial need to prioritize health and wellbeing in education.

When interested leaders come across teachers in their schools who are actively promoting and exemplifying wellbeing, self-care and mindful awareness in themselves and their classrooms, this can be one of the best ways of engaging their interest. By listening to teachers who have had some success in working in this area for their own self-care and with their students, leaders can learn a lot about the benefits and challenges of this collective journey towards greater wellbeing. By observing, listening to and connecting with these 'Champion Teachers', you are showing them that you value their efforts and are interested in the potential benefits such approaches can help foster in your school community.

Sometimes it can also be helpful to bring in an outside trainer to reinforce what is beginning to happen in the school and to introduce the topic to the full faculty in a common-sense and experiential way. Drawing on relevant research and good practice, such introductions can help build interest, and when leaders notice other teachers getting involved, they begin to take more notice. The research link-ing student achievement with social-emotional interventions can be important here (see Chapter 7, p. 158) as well as evidence on Mindful Awareness Training (MAT) for attention, emotional regulation and self-awareness (see Chapter 4, p. 93). It is also important that leaders hear positive stories from their peers in other schools about efforts to tackle mental health and to focus on social and emotional aspects of learning, and so networking between schools can be very helpful in this regard.

Mindful leadership and wellbeing at work are hot topics these days in indus-try and management and there are many programmes and conferences on the subject.

Some examples include:

- Institute for Mindful Leadership – https://instituteformindfulleadership.org/

- Search Inside Yourself Leadership Institute – https://siyli.org/

- Inner MBA – https://innermba.soundstrue.com/

If schools can send leaders and aspiring leaders on these kinds of courses or even on specific training programmes on wellbeing for school leaders in particu-lar, this can also be highly beneficial, both for opening up their understanding of the importance of wellbeing for their school communities as well as for their own sustainability in a demanding career. This is still an emerging area, but current examples of these courses include:

- Transformative Educational Leadership: Transformative Leadership, Equity, SEL, Mindfulness – www.teleadership.org/

- CARE (Cultivating Awareness and Resilience in Education): Training for Principals – https://createforeducation.org/

- Passageworks: Transformational Leadership for Educators – https://passage works.org/our-programs/

- Mindfulness in Schools Project: School Mindfulness Lead Training – https://mindfulnessinschools.org/school-mindfulness-lead/

- MindWell Education – Cultivating Mindful Leadership in Education: Training for Leaders and Aspiring School Leaders – www.mindwell-education.com/

We often advise leaders that getting teachers to take an eight-week mindful awareness course for their own wellbeing can be one of the most effective forms of professional development. Who wouldn't want their teachers to be more sen-sitive to students and colleagues? To be calmer in challenging situations and more present in their teaching? In schools where there are a significant number of teachers taking mindful awareness courses, members of the leadership team often sign up themselves. This sets a powerful example to teachers and to other leaders in the school.

Educator Voice: A Principal's Perspective

I took an eight-week Mindfulness-Based Stress Reduction course and was pleasantly surprised by the effects. I noticed my sleeping improved, I was more attentive to listening and was aware of my thoughts. When in a discussion with a staff member or parent, I noticed an increased focus on listening to understand rather than planning what my response would be. I was more present for discussions. I had an increased awareness of my body and mind. This awareness allowed me to notice where the stress was showing up in my body and what I needed to do to work through it. I am better able to let go of things that I used to obsess about and remind myself to 'let go, let go, let go'. I am just more comfortable with who I am. The more I practice the more I have seen positive changes in myself and my leadership. We all need to improve our self-awareness and self-regulation! If I, as the principal, make it a priority then staff will make it a priority too.

Pauline McKenna - Principal, Kanata Highlands Public School, Ottawa, Canada

The Lens of Wellbeing

What really seems to make a difference in the schools we have worked with is when a number of teachers and school leaders start to look at their school community through a 'Lens of Wellbeing'. When setting out on this journey, more important than creating a new strategic plan or a list of agreed objectives is to spend time reflecting at 'the bottom of the curve' (see Conclusion). Really being present with the problems, exploring them together and sharing openly with each other can have a powerful influence on developing sustainable solutions. We recommend using structured approaches to deepening the dialogue that create a safe space and support mindful speaking and listening (see Chapter 7). When a growing body of people in a school community, including parents and students as well as teachers and leaders, begins to operate from this deeper place, connecting the deeper purpose of schooling with the real human needs of society, then we can gain the space to really re-envision our schools as places where we want young people to learn, grow and achieve whilst being healthy and well in the process. Once people start to see through this lens of wellbeing, possibilities begin to open up, even within the very real constraints of restricted time and money.

Q3: When and how do we include parents?

This is a vital component of any successful school initiative. We need to get beyond the 'us vs them' mentality that sometimes exists between schools and parents and re-emphasize the communal aspects of education. In deepening the dialogue about What Really Matters in education, the intent is for both groups to be united in their quest to support young people in their growth and wellbeing. We have seen schools begin this process by inviting all interested parties to a 'round table' discussion. This can include teachers, parents, students and administrators so that all are encouraged to share their perspectives and have a say in how the process develops. Keeping all parties informed is key, so information sessions for parents are essential in garnering support for this important work. We are often asked by schools to present to parent groups as well as teachers, and many schools are now providing mindfulness classes (and sometimes mindful parenting classes) for their parent community.

It is important to take your time with these initial phases. By focusing on *What do we really want for our children?* – from the *heart* as well as the *head* – we usually find much more common ground than division. It is on this common ground, through respectful, honest and attentive speaking and listening, that a community foundation for Awareness-based Wellbeing is built.

Sometimes it may be more practical to support the pioneering work by lead teachers in the school before involving parents. Focusing first on teacher self-care and then training to prepare other teachers to use Seasoning Activities with students in their classes can create an effective starting point. Quite often when this approach has started in schools, a significant section of engaged parents start to say they want more. For example, in one school we worked with, the main initiative had begun in the Primary School, but then the High School parents became very vocal in expressing their need for their children to also get increased support in mental health and wellbeing. Our experience in our own schools and those we have worked with is that parents are very interested in this area. They are often stressed themselves and many are keen to learn about stress management, and they also want to know how best to support their children who may be dealing with anxiety, depression or other mental health issues.

Q4: What if all this emphasis on social and emotional skills and wellbeing takes up too much curricular time and budget?

Demands on individual teachers, on leaders and on schools, are, in general, overly burdensome. Pressures on school schedules can be intense and teachers sometimes feel obliged to campaign for more minutes in their subject in order to be able to prepare their students properly for exams. Challenging behaviour and mental health issues increase demands on classroom management. Budgets are constrained, and finding the financial resources as well as time in the schedule for new initiatives, no matter how important we might feel they are, is highly challenging.

We used to hear these types of concerns more often than we do these days, which is indicative of the fact that many schools are now accepting the need and seeing the value of this kind of work. Precisely because of all these factors and pressures, it is vital for teachers, leaders, schools and educational systems to carve out space for reflection. To begin to talk openly with each other about How Well Are We? To revisit our deeper intentions in becoming educators. To take some precious time to focus on our own wellbeing. To find ways to support ourselves and each other in order to be able to do the best we can for our students and the future of our schools. As we have seen, when teachers are well, it can have a tangible impact on the wellbeing of their students. Most school leaders these days understand the importance of wellbeing. They recognize that mental and physical health are the basis for learning and development. They know that developing emotional skills can make a vital difference to the future growth, both personal and professional, of the young people in their care.

In terms of time, it depends what exactly you are trying to make time for. A concrete wellbeing/mindfulness/SEL curriculum does require a certain amount of hours per week, depending on the type of programme your school chooses. Many schools have been able to embed such courses into existing PSHE (Personal Social/Health Education), Advisory, Pastoral or Health time slots. However, even without teaching a specific curriculum many teachers are able to 'Season the Day' with brief moments of calm and re-energize their students in ways that support both learning and wellbeing, without taking up too much time. It just becomes a normal part of the school day.

When schools do take the time to focus on social and emotional factors in learning, the impact on academic achievement can be impressive (see 'SEL and Achievement' research, Chapter 7). We are not saying that we should teach mindfulness and SEL skills so students can do better on tests, just as we are not saying if you train teachers in self-care they can take on more work. It is helpful though to have high-quality research evidence to show busy educational leaders what we already know instinctively – that when we are not well, we do not learn well.

Q5: How sustainable is Awareness-based Wellbeing? What if our 'Champion Teachers' move on to another school?

This is a valid concern that many school leaders have in relation to any specialist training, not just wellbeing and mindfulness. When strong teachers with particular expertise leave a school, it inevitably creates a gap. There can be even more of a challenge with replacing SEL and mindfulness practitioners because this training depends so much on personal qualities that have been trained and enhanced. That is why we say this is 'not your average professional development'. The standard model for most PD in schools is for the teacher who has been trained in a new skill set to come back and train colleagues right away. However, it just does not work effectively for a teacher who has taken an in-depth training in mindful awareness to come back to school and train up other teachers. To do so requires a higher level of specialized preparation and training, so we have to look at alternative models in order to be able to sustain mindfulness initiatives.

Some schools have managed to develop in-house training through supporting lead teachers to get certification, for example in delivering eight-week personal mindfulness courses for their colleagues. One school we worked with required new teachers to take an eight-week mindfulness programme as well as attend a weekend retreat for educators – both of which were provided in-house. This might not be an achievable option for many schools, but in terms of sustainability what can be very helpful is to connect with a local or online mindfulness trainer who can provide programming for your teachers.

Some schools now hire teachers with wellbeing in mind, thus ensuring that new teachers are aligned with the school's values. We have also found that, given the increased worldwide interest in mental health and wellbeing, schools that begin to commit to development in this area attract teachers with skills and/or interest in wellbeing and mindfulness.

As wellbeing becomes a more foundational component of a school's mission and approach, leadership needs to commit time and resources for further development. The message here is not so much that school leaders need to feel responsible for taking direct care of all their teachers, but more that school leaders should recognize the value of teacher self-care and articulate this both verbally and in the resourcing they begin to provide for wellbeing.

Q6: We already have Mindfulness and Wellbeing initiatives in our school but they are isolated and patchy. How do we embed it more holistically and make our approach and delivery more coherent?

With this question (and the one following) we come to the core issue of the current work in this area and the major focus of attention for the development of ABW in education. As you will have gathered from the practical examples and encouragement offered in these pages, this question also speaks to the essence of our book. So many of the schools that we have worked with have been asking this question, either directly or implicitly in their requests for outside help. This should not surprise us, given that mindfulness in education is still a very recent development with few established models to work from.

Patchy development is, in itself, not a problem. In fact, it is symptomatic of the way this work seems to unfold, with individual teachers first trying it out for themselves and then in their classes. The next stage though is where it can get messy. Colleagues may know about what you are doing in your classes and want to try something similar. Leadership may have heard of other schools teaching mindfulness or focusing on social and emotional learning and they may then want to initiate this in their own schools. These intentions of colleagues and leaders are positive and understandable – they see the need and they have heard about possible interventions and so they want to take action. It's logical right? On the one hand we have a lot of anxious or stressed students and on the other we have mindfulness or SEL programmes designed to help mental and emotional health. Just put the two together, and problem solved! Except, of course it isn't. In this key area of our mental health and wellbeing, students learn at least as much from copying and modelling themselves on the adults around them as they do from being taught a programme. It is essential that the adults in the building take time to reflect on their own wellbeing and their own mental health and social and emotional competencies before trying to tell young people how to work with theirs.

As our colleague Chris Willard says, 'The best way to create stressed-out kids is to surround them with stressed-out adults. But of course, the opposite is also true. The best way to create mindful, compassionate kids is to surround them with kind, caring, compassionate adults'.

Although it goes against the normal 'push-through' pattern of strategic planning in schools, if we are to embed a more grounded, holistic approach to fostering wellbeing alongside achievement in our schools, then we have to take the time to step back, look at what has already been achieved, and be prepared to slow things down so that we can understand more clearly what needs to happen next in order to organize a more coherent approach to sustainable growth.

Q7: What is the best way of organizing oversight of wellbeing in our school?

We recommend that schools consider carrying out a wide-ranging Wellbeing Survey, if possible linking it with a holistic curriculum review of the areas of Health Education/Physical Education/Advisory-Pastoral/PSHE. If feasible, engage an outside agency to come and survey the whole school community and interview focus groups of teachers, parents, leaders, and of course, especially, students. Results can be fed back to the school community and then representatives from each sector can work committee style, with the engagement and support of leadership, to carry the work forward. The processes we employ for this work should reflect the holistic and humanistic values we are seeking to instill and embed in our curriculum approaches and in our students and teachers (see the Amsterdam Case Study in the Conclusion).

School leadership needs to openly value these qualitatively different approaches as well as those individuals involved in leading this work: the champion teachers, champion parents and even champion students. For successful and sustainable implementation it is vital at this stage that schools redirect time and resources to this important work. We need to keep highlighting good practice and articulating the benefits of this **shift in focus** for the whole school community. It can be very helpful here to link up with some like-minded schools and, if possible, include one or two who are a little further along in this work than your own.

The move to embed sustainable approaches to wellbeing is a major shift for schools, so remember you don't have to do the whole thing in one go! It's more important to get used to pausing and reflecting, taking the time to reach agreement on a common direction and then taking small steps. But don't allow this major shift to be trivialized – for example expecting that a *Staff Wellbeing Quiz Night* or *Mindful Mondays* will solve teacher retention and student stress issues. These might be helpful initiatives but they do not reflect the core of what we are talking about here. Likewise, a focus on teacher self-care and stress management should not deflect us from facing head-on challenges such as excessive teacher scrutiny and workloads. A shift to ABW in schools necessitates a full and honest appraisal of all the factors and processes that lead to student and teacher overload and distress. Through understanding the central importance of wellbeing in education we can begin to change those systems that reinforce approaches to learning that actually undermine our deeper aims and values.

Those with oversight of wellbeing need to establish clear and open communication networks where they can provide supportive, engaged leadership. If you become part of such a group you will also need to be able to:

- Represent the whole school community, not just the like-minded.

- Think holistically, about people and about programmes, not just about creating add-on classes but also about finding opportunities to transfer and apply skills in a range of subject areas, extra-curricular activities and school events.

- Develop a vocabulary and ways of communicating that make sense to your community.

- Keep refreshing your ideas, revisiting the essence of what it is you are trying to do, coming back to yourselves, your intentions, and what it is that you really want for your children.

We also recommend where possible that schools create or enhance the position of Wellbeing Director/Coordinator. Depending on your context, this may be easier said than done. But when budget and resources are allocated to this, we begin to see substantial opportunities for real change in schools:

Case Study: Mindfulness at Middlesex, MA

There are many ways to integrate mindfulness into a school or organizational community, and what has worked at Middlesex may not be effective in your community culture. Each community has its own philosophy and character and will need to go about this process in its own unique way – utilizing the interests and experience of its mindfulness educators, while at the same time being attentive to the community's particular needs and values.

That said, we believe there are two key elements to the success of the Middlesex program. One is our guiding belief that, while it is important for all Middlesex students to be familiar with mindfulness, participation in any given meditation is always a choice. Our program introduces students to mindfulness through a required course for new students, and occasional presentations at faculty meetings to keep faculty informed, but as always, it is an invitation to practice at Middlesex. We are never trying to mandate practice for anyone not interested in exploring mindfulness in a personal way. Students, faculty, and other community members take from the mindfulness program only what they find useful. In fact, they are always encouraged to have a 'healthy skepticism' and to believe only what they find true in their experience.

The second key element to the development of our program was having a faculty member dedicated to the initiative and committed to practice. Our experience has shown that hiring or empowering a 'Mindfulness Director', an experienced practitioner who is a good fit for your community, will increase the probability of a successful program.

Doug Worthen, Director of Mindfulness, Middlesex School, Concord, MA
Starting in 2009, it took Doug four years to embed mindfulness at Middlesex School, and they have continued to build on these foundations over subsequent years. (You can find further details of the evolution of the program in Worthen, 2018: 'The Mindfulness Program at the Middlesex School: Evolution and Structure', www.mxschool.edu/about-mx/mindfulness/access-to-program-overview).

WholeSchool Mindfulness

The work at Middlesex School has also spawned a new mindfulness organization in the USA called 'WholeSchool Mindfulness', which 'exists to make mindfulness teachers and practices accessible to *all schools*'. To achieve this, WholeSchool Mindfulness helps integrate full-time mindfulness instructors into school communities, working with students, staff, and families to create more sustainable and impactful programs.

WholeSchoolMindfulness.org

Part 2: Other Common Questions

Q8: What if my school community equates mindfulness with religious education?

Mindfulness is about cultivating awareness. It is an innate human capacity that can be developed to support positive mental, emotional, physical and spiritual health. Contemplative practices that promote this awareness through reflection, growth and balance are a part of most religious traditions. Modern applications of mindfulness draw on such practices and in particular on Buddhist psychology in a purely secular context, verified through scientific research.

An important component of introducing ABW to school communities is to clarify what mindfulness **is** – and what it **isn't**. Again, this is very context-dependent. If some people in your school are inclined to equate mindfulness with religion or 'New Age-iness', it is important to approach this carefully and sensitively but in a practical, grounded way. This is why we usually discourage the use of religious bells, essential oils, candles, etc. that might add to misconceptions about mindfulness in education. This is not to say that, depending on your situation, you can't sometimes share these with students as items of interest or aides to calming, but just to take care to not confuse these with mindfulness practice itself. Keeping the focus on the science, such as how calming the mind and body can be achieved through activating the parasympathetic nervous system, or on the benefits of enhancing emotional intelligence for managing mental health, are helpful ways of showing people how mindfulness can have very practical applications in daily life.

Q9: Is there a danger of developing an 'In' group and an 'Out' group?

Yes, this is a real danger. People who get involved in this area, especially in mindfulness, can tend to be passionate about the difference it has made to them and their teaching, and if this enthusiasm becomes overzealous it can push people away.

Author Voice: Lessons Learned

I am definitely guilty of pushing too far too fast! Having seen the benefits of contemplative practices and mindfulness in my own life and having experienced different practices and activities while studying a Master's in Contemplative Education, I was keen to share this with my colleagues at the high school where I taught. In a cringe-worthy memory, I invited all of the staff to write a personal intention for the year – not necessarily a weird thing – but then also asked them to tie their intention to a tree - a very weird thing to do in a suburban high school! I could see my colleagues' eyes roll and I felt the resistance keenly. I learned very quickly how NOT to introduce new ideas to school teachers.

Amy

Resistance is a natural response to anything new and different – and it's important to recognize it, and value it where appropriate. There will always be cynical teachers and leaders, and in fact, in our awareness training, like Doug Worthen (above), we often encourage adults and children to be 'healthily skeptical' – to maintain an openness to new ideas, but not blindly embrace them. There will be resistant teachers just as there will be resistant students. And of course, there will be plenty of opportunities for us to notice our own resistance to personal practice! It's natural. You can't 'make' anybody mindful; all you can do is offer opportunities for exploration, and if someone, a teacher or student, does not feel ready to engage with it at this moment, that is also fine and natural.

As this move towards greater wellbeing gathers momentum, it is important that those involved in helping steer the process do not emphasize any sense of there being an 'In' group as far as mindfulness is concerned. Under the broader concept of 'Wellbeing' however, we have an overarching objective to which all can subscribe. It is hard for anyone to really argue that we *don't* want to be well. *How* we get there, and *which* paths appear best for *which* individuals at *which* times, do however require a flexibility of approach that ensures all feel included.

Expert Advice: No Gurus Allowed!

Continuously talking about mindfulness, forcing mindfulness research on people, and pretending to be more mindful than others is both annoying and the perfect recipe for killing the momentum of a mindfulness program. It helps to remember that sometimes the people who don't practice mindfulness are living balanced lives and simply don't need to practice!

Doug Worthen - Director of Mindfulness, Middlesex School, MA

Q10: How can we change if the system won't change?

In general, our systems of education are unbalanced and expectations on teachers reflect this imbalance. Teachers are overworked and resources for supporting them are often scarce. It can feel hopeless to even begin to contemplate how to change this situation. To be frank, we cannot wait for our education 'systems' to change – they are notoriously difficult beasts to tame! This is why we encourage school communities and even individual teachers and parents to revisit What Really Matters to them. It may seem incongruous for a principal to encourage her staff to 'take care of themselves' while the workload and expectations are so high, but this is not hypocrisy – it is a real tension.

When wellbeing is recognized as an integral part of the school experience, we begin to question how we do things, which begins to shift priorities. We can affect some change at a personal and local level, in our classrooms and in our school communities. We can teach the curriculum and still create an atmosphere of contentment in our classrooms. Research in social neuroscience supports the understanding that we help our young people learn through establishing healthy relationships with them (Cozolino, 2013). This can only happen though if we have a healthy relationship with ourselves. This may sound cheesy, but the truth is, when we take care of our stress and prioritize our health, this can have a significant impact on our classrooms. Shifting our individual perspective is indeed beginning to change the system. (For more on systemic change see the following chapter).

Q11: What if I am feeling too stressed to help kids with their own wellbeing?

Because we are human there are inevitably days or longer periods of time in our lives when we feel overwhelmed and not fully equipped to help the young people around us. This is normal. We can't magically make stress disappear from our lives. What we *can* do is try to bring greater awareness to our situation and state of mind, recognizing and acknowledging whatever our current experience may be. Our stress may be due to personal circumstances or it might be caused by systemic factors or external conditions. Here is an example of how we can support each other in this process of recognition:

Case Study: Teacher Stress in Hong Kong

The 2019 protests in Hong Kong left the country with increased stress and anxiety. Unpredictable outbreaks of violence, blocked roads, school closures and reopenings, the cancellation of many events and the rampant use of tear gas left many, including teachers, feeling an extra layer of distress and worry about the future and their safety and that of the children they teach.

I had been invited to deliver a two-day mindfulness training to a group of kindergarten teachers as part of a three-week professional development visit looking at teaching and learning in the schools. School had been cancelled for students, but teachers were still required to attend. Inviting teachers to discuss how they were

(Continued)

feeling, to accept their emotions, thoughts and feelings related to the protests, was one of the most powerful practices I have participated in. Teachers were able to share with others, some who they worked with and others who they did not know, what their experiences had been and the challenges they were facing. One of the most powerful activities was teachers sharing the analogy of what mental or emotional 'weather' their own state of mind was reflective of. Many teachers said they found comfort in sharing these feelings with their colleagues.

We proceeded with deep breathing exercises and discussion and practice around how these exercises might help the teachers accept, notice and just be with their feelings. One teacher came to me on the second day and said how much the deep breathing had helped her and how she had used some of the practices before bed the evening before and finally had a good night's sleep after three weeks of tossing and turning.

On the second day we continued learning about how our own way of being would influence the children we teach and our own experiences in the classroom. Teachers expressed concern about the trauma their young children might face seeing scary scenes such as groups of police wearing full gas mask gear, the effects of tear gas and the sights of all the vandalism. Teachers agreed that taking care of their own wellbeing would help their students. In groups teachers discussed how they might cultivate more mindful work environments at their own schools and they came up with some innovative ways, such as creating a space in the school for practice, rest and restoration. Others decided to create a five-minute morning practice together before class started or during lunch. One group thought they would go for a mindful walk in their lunch hour together. Throughout, the teachers were highly collaborative and excited about using mindfulness to help their own wellbeing, especially during this turbulent time for schools in Hong Kong.

Dr Helen Maffini – Mindfulness in the Early Years Consultant
and Trainer, https://mindbe-education.com/

It may be somewhat easier in the situation described above to create a sense of shared space and supportive communication because the teachers were all experiencing similar stresses due to the common external conditions. During the COVID-19 pandemic the shared sense of uncertainty and anxiety around the world for teachers, students and families was highly tangible, despite different contexts. But in our experience, whenever we create the conditions for teachers to share their experiences of stress, even when the stress described is more personal, it automatically leads to a shared sense of empathy. Through sharing and supporting each other on this authentic level we build the conditions to help support our students through their own struggles.

Q12: Is mindfulness just a trendy way to make us more passive and accepting of serious systemic issues in our education?

Although we have occasionally heard this concern voiced, and we understand why some people might think this way, in reality nothing could be further from the truth. The practice of mindfulness helps us to 'wake up' – and a heightened awareness is crucial for meaningful social change.

What people may fear is that school leaders or policy makers might support mindfulness training because it can help teachers manage their stress and so perform better, whilst the deeper systemic factors that are causing us and our students to feel overwhelmed by unnecessary stress continue to be ignored. This is a reasonable fear, but it ignores the reality of what normally happens when individuals and groups start to focus on inner growth and outer connections. Once we become more aware of our own stresses and their impact on the body, heart and mind, we naturally also start to question the source of those stressors. Some we have no control over, others we do, and the most obvious place to start is with those immediate factors we can, to some degree, control for our self-care and sanity. Though this first step is essential, we can't just stop there. The impact comes as we apply this heightened awareness to our relationships and our professional situation, with the intention of improving wellbeing for all.

A phrase that is often used in mindfulness is 'With awareness comes choice'. When we are more aware of how our environment impacts us, we are more able to see and sense where changes are necessary. We have found that mindful awareness training inevitably engages individuals more closely in fostering change for the better. In relation to education, it helps people see more clearly where stress in schools is coming from, whether it is self-induced or arising from procedures and processes that are no longer helpful. This naturally leads us to question how we organize schooling; why most exam systems and competitive approaches create such high-stakes stresses for students; and what can be done to help shift the system. Some may feel there is nothing we can do, because 'that's the way things are and always have been', but whilst it is true that educational systems are notoriously resistant to change, the key place to start is with raising awareness. That is why we often begin this work with community dialogue on What Really Matters? and How Well Are We?

As more and more teachers, parents, students, school leaders and policy makers begin to wake up and understand the urgent need for change, we edge closer to potential tipping points where the hard work of so many pioneers in mainstream and alternative education, past and present, will bear fruit. It may well be that the students we are today helping to become more aware, grounded and 'wise as well as clever' will play a central role in future collaborative efforts to create education systems that truly align with the wellbeing of individuals, society and our planet.

Chapter Summary

In this chapter we have articulated and underlined some key themes and common issues that arise when schools focus on supporting wellbeing in their school communities:

- A combination of bottom-up (teacher led) and top-down (leadership supported) approaches helps embed sustainable change.

- Uneven development is the norm at first, but at a certain point, schools that pause and collectively reflect on the way forward produce more coherent approaches.

- The processes used for this work need to model and reflect the outcomes and values of awareness, kindness, listening and compassionate collective action.

- Awareness-based Wellbeing entails an honest understanding of systems and our individual and collective roles in those systems.

Further Reading and Resources

Training

Mindful Schools – Schoolwide Implementation Program, www.mindfulschools.org/
For more Leadership Training resources see the list in Q2.

Books

Brown, V. and Olson, K. (2015) *The Mindful School Leader: Practices to Transform your Leadership and School*. Thousand Oaks, CA: Corwin.

Heilers, T., Iverson, T., and Larrivee, B., eds. (2020) *Educating Mindfully: Stories of School Transformation through Mindfulness*. St. Charles, IL: Coalition of Schools Educating Mindfully.

Maturano, J. (2014) *Finding the Space to Lead: A Practical Guide to Mindful Leadership*. New York: Bloomsbury.

Schonert-Reichl, K. and Roeser, R. (2016) *Handbook of Mindfulness in Education: Integrating Theory and Research into Practice*. New York: Springer.

Weare, K. and Bethune, A. (2021) 'Implementing Mindfulness in Schools: An Evidence-Based Guide', The Mindfulness Initiative. www.themindfulnessinitiative.org/implementing-mindfulness-in-schools-an-evidence-based-guide

Conclusion: Aligning Awareness-based Wellbeing with Societal and Environmental Change

We wrote this book during the COVID-19 pandemic. Over this past year there has been so much suffering around the world, including many who have been unable to be with their loved ones while sick or dying as well as health care workers who have made so many sacrifices, including sometimes even their own lives. All of this continues to happen as we write these concluding words and yet, unbelievably, there exists an even greater challenge to life as we know it. The possibility of further global pandemics has now joined the climate crisis and biodiversity extinction to create a toxic cocktail of threats to our planet that require swift, wise action.

As all this unfolds and unravels around us we seem to be sleepwalking into a highly unstable future where denial or creating 'alternative facts' feels much more comfortable to most than dealing with reality. As democracy falters, political tensions are rising and extreme opinions are becoming commonplace. Our children are growing up amidst unprecedented manipulation, misinformation and deliberate attempts to falsify facts. Truth and understanding are hard to come by as the status quo is defended with desperation by those who seek to preserve their privileges based on exploitation of the environment, systemic racism and ingrained inequalities. As these extreme challenges and our evasive responses combine to create a global crisis for humanity in this century, there is one central message clamouring for our attention:

WE NEED TO WAKE UP!

We need to wake up and to stay woke if we are to stand any chance of creating balanced and sustainable ways of co-existing on this planet. **Awareness** is the single most important capacity we can cultivate in ourselves and in our children. Awareness that helps us know how to open our eyes, our minds and our hearts to what is really going on. Awareness that is clear-sighted and infused with the essential qualities of love and kindness. Awareness that is consciously aimed at finding ways to live together harmoniously on our amazing planet.

If we fail to include self-awareness and self-understanding in our efforts to create a better world, we will forever keep getting tripped up by those 'human factors' that undermine our well-intentioned collaborative efforts. But it's not just *self*-awareness that we need. We need to harness our growing awareness to *understand each other* better and to be able to collaborate with each other more effectively. And, importantly, we need a broader awareness of how *human processes and systems* function so that we don't keep repeating mistakes of the past.

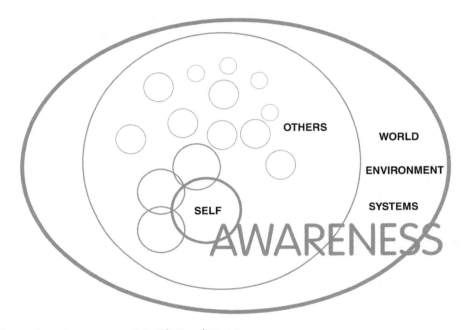

Figure 9.1   Awareness of Self/Other/World

Source: © MindWell

By revisiting and revitalizing our deeper intentions for our educational systems (What Really Matters) we are doing the foundational work of contributing to redesigning our global societies. It is not so difficult to find common agreement on what we want for our children on a deeper, heart level. It's not even so difficult to extrapolate from this that what we want for our children contains the seeds of what we want for the future of communal life on the planet. To promote health, balance and wellbeing in society we need education systems and educators that understand how to help develop these qualities in their students and in themselves. And we can all play a part in this through cultivating awareness-based wellbeing. This book is one small piece amongst a growing wave of ideas and initiatives that show us some simple steps that educators can take to help equip themselves and our children with those essential skills for human development that have so far largely been neglected by our school systems: skills and understandings that promote *wisdom as well as cleverness* and that can help guide our children through the labyrinth of misinformation and distraction; that can help them develop their own inner compass; that can help keep them true to a 'path with heart' that, when combined with their intellectual talents and scientific and technological prowess, can bring creativity, clarity and purpose to efforts to reshape the world for the benefit of future generations.

Within this context we now focus on two key areas:

- **Systems Awareness:** Harnessing our understanding and clear-sightedness to focus on the *actual*, as well as the *intended*, effects of educational systems and processes on learners. The word 'systems' itself sounds mechanistic and perhaps seems to imply an industrial type of factory school system, but we are actually here looking to understand our school systems from a more holistic, humanistic, 'eco'-system perspective.

- **Leadership:** As we see it this includes not only those offices and positions that specify organizational and educational management, but also any efforts taken by any educators to promote and foster positive change in their school cultures and curricula.

'Culture Eats Strategy for Breakfast'

These two areas overlap considerably because a key insight of systems awareness is that we cannot, especially in social systems like schools, separate the individual from the system. When seeking deep change in society and in organizations like schools, we ignore the human factor at our peril. Our own experiences of leading change in schools has underlined this key aspect and we have found it highly beneficial to make time and space for teachers, leaders and parents to engage in collaborative reflection, focusing attention on our own assumptions about learning when re-envisaging our school processes (Hawkins, 2017).

When school leaders and policy makers come up with new strategies, they often fail to fully take account of these human factors, and many initiatives get diverted and diluted by prevailing school cultures and fixed educator mindsets. Brave new ideas can end up in old, familiar boxes that stifle the potential for deeper change. Given the stubborn impermeability of educational systems to change, how can we even begin to hope to impact our own school cultures and ecosystems? We can take heart, inspiration and courage from two key areas:

- The experience and understanding, through research and science, of leading individuals and organizations in the fields of **societal and organizational change**.

- **Aligning our efforts with broader global trends** whilst connecting with others to form networks and build support and trust in the value and purpose of this work.

When it comes to understanding and facilitating deep social and organizational change there are many wonderful examples we can draw from. Some of the smartest and wisest thinkers and activists in this area have been associated with the highly renowned Massachusetts Institute of Technology in the USA. When we look at the examples of Peter Senge, Jay Forrester, Otto Scharmer and Joseph Jaworski, amongst others, we can draw inspiration and practical ideas from their approaches and from the impact of their work around the world. One of the most helpful and successful approaches that is directly relevant to education is 'Theory U'. Otto Scharmer built on the work of those mentioned above to develop this model for activating deep organizational change.

Awareness–based Systems Change

Traditionally, when we want to bring about change in organizations, we first analyse the problems and then seek solutions. This could be seen as moving in a 'V' shape. You go down into the problem then come up with a strategy to solve it. But what Scharmer, Senge and Jaworski learned from their extensive research with leading entrepreneurs is that it is far more effective if those engaged in the change process spend more time at 'the bottom of the curve'. In this way, the curve looks more like a 'U' than a 'V'.

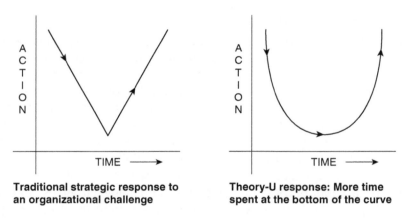

Traditional strategic response to an organizational challenge

Theory-U response: More time spent at the bottom of the curve

Figure 9.2   Theory U – 'the bottom of the curve'

Source: Developed from Otto Scharmer's Theory U (Scharmer, 2016)

The time spent at the bottom is described as 'Presencing' in Theory U, and it's here that we become more familiar with depth and detail and get a more visceral feel for the problem. And it's also here that we can learn to 'sense into the emerging future', exploring *What is it that needs to emerge?* In doing this work leaders adopt a more reflective approach and develop inner skills of 'noticing, tuning in to the system and staying present with what is emerging' (Rowland, 2017). Then, when it is time to act, solutions are coming from a deeper, more creative place, based more on future possibilities than past patterns.

'The Success of an Intervention Depends on the *Interior Condition* of the Intervener'

This key insight from one of the entrepreneurs, Bill O'Brien, helped the MIT researchers develop the Theory U model. O'Brien's experience was that deep and lasting organizational change depends very much on the inner qualities of those leading that change.

This idea is fundamental in Scharmer's (2016: 28) version of Theory U:

'Seeing the system' involves turning the beam of observation back on ourselves.

Figure 9.3   Seeing the System

Source: This work is licensed by the Presencing Institute – Otto Scharmer, under a CC-SA 3.0 license, https://creativecommons.org/licenses/by-sa/3.0/

Author Voice: We are the 'System'

In working as a school principal with my team of teachers, I applied the work of Peter Senge and his books *The Fifth Discipline* (1990) and *Schools That Learn* (Senge et al., 2000). We discovered that what most got in the way of the deeper change we sought was ourselves. The system isn't just out there in the strategies and schedules of the school, it's in ourselves, as educators and leaders, in the mental models we hold and seldom examine in detail. That's why you can't make real change with strategies alone. We have to go deeper, into the messier human realm, if we want implementation of new ideas to be really successful.

Kevin

(For more information see Hawkins, 2017: 145-9)

In the preface to the second edition of *Theory U: Leading from the Future as It Emerges* (2016), Scharmer reflects on some major changes in the world between the two editions, from the late 1990s to 2016. Noting 'the early beginnings of a global awakening – a movement of people, connections, and consciousness' (2016: xxvi) he points to a number of factors contributing to these changes, and the first one he highlights is the emergence of mindfulness and how it has now begun to impact cognitive sciences, health, education and leadership. Mindfulness practice helps us to sustain our attention to be able to be with the discomfort of change rather than running from it into another unsustainable 'solution'. When we can *be with* challenges rather than *run from* them, we allow space for insight to arise and that moves us towards wiser actions.

Cultivating Mindful Leadership in Education

We begin to see how educators involved in promoting systemic change can benefit by cultivating these inner qualities, and one way of working with these inner states is through cultivating Mindful Leadership. Of course some people have natural presence or awareness, but for many of us it helps to be able to train these capacities. As leaders, self-awareness is key. As Deborah Rowland, author of *Still Moving* (2017) and a leading change consultant for major global corporations puts it, 'Change leaders need to first tune into and regulate their inner experience before they can begin to work on the source of their system's routines'. Mindful awareness is a key life skill that we can model in ourselves and nurture in our students, teachers and school communities. Not only as a moment, an activity or a health class, but as something that is woven into our school cultures, helping them function as healthier learning ecosytems.

Mindful Leadership is already a well-established area of professional development in the commercial and business worlds. Otto Scharmer (2016: 12) says, 'Mindfulness practices in leadership development work are being applied not only in tech communities, but also in most forward-leaning global companies.... The lack of pushback is almost shocking. If you do it right (which means promoting mindfulness not as an ideology but as a tool), the positive response is strong, particularly among the next generation of leaders'.

Mindful Leadership is slowly beginning to gain momentum in some educational leadership circles (see Mindful Leadership resources, Chapter 8, p. 178) and whilst the initial emphasis is on building self-awareness and inner qualities on an individual level, practical programmes such as Theory U are showing how collective application of mindful awareness can be employed as a key tool in organizational change.

If we want qualitative change in our schools then we need to use qualitatively different approaches to fostering that change. In Chapter 7 we showed how some schools are using various reflective and contemplative techniques to create conditions for students and teachers to be able to speak and listen to each other on a deeper, more mindful level. Approaches like Council Practice can also be highly effective tools in real-world situations. Creating conditions for meaningful group explorations of a topic is one of the most powerful ways of seeding change when exploring issues such as balance, wellbeing and shifting the focus of our educational systems.

Case Study: Awareness–based Systems Change in Education

'Being Human Together' – The Amsterdam Teacher Shortage Crisis

In 2019, the teacher shortage in schools in Amsterdam reached crisis point with some schools having to close because they could not be staffed (Fransen and Middlebeek, 2020).

Against a background of low salaries and high workload a group of schools in the Nieuw-West area of the city decided to take a different approach to exploring their common challenges. Sixteen primary schools in the area joined up to hold 'A Quality of Education Week' in which over 500 teachers plus education managers and parents shared their ideas and perspectives and produced a new plan for education in their area. The schools met together and separately, each school with their own facilitator who used various structured dialogue techniques to encourage mindful speaking and listening. The community of facilitators was led by Simoon Fransen. Simoon is an experienced facilitator who uses 'Naturalistic approaches to explore pathways to cultural transformation and sustainable solutions, with Theory U as her underlying framework'. She was invited to bring Theory U to the Quality of Education Week by Jo Middlebeek, a well-respected Head of School who had herself worked with Peter Senge on Systems Thinking in education.

The 5,400 children had the week off from school, but thousands attended special classes and activities organized by the parent bodies. Activities included technology, drama and chess classes, and a Student Press Agency was created to report on the week from the students' perspective. Parents enjoyed this chance to get more involved in their children's schools and the possibility was raised of having more days where parents could organize activities so that teachers could meet for professional development. This all raised the awareness amongst parents of the challenges their teachers face – housing and transport issues as well as the stresses of teaching – which in turn helped the teachers to feel more supported and valued by the parent community.

This large-scale collaborative effort proved to be highly effective in clarifying challenges and solutions but also, importantly, in unlocking positive energy within the community. Despite the intense week, teachers reported feeling energized and supported, while increased parental engagement highlighted the value of stepping back and re-establishing the communal context of education. As a result of the week, some schools were able to make important changes to address the key issue of lack of adequate teacher training and support.

(Continued)

Simoon spoke to us openly about the challenges and successes of this approach:

We are not claiming that somehow in five days we solved the future of education issues. There is no quick fix. We produced a manual from all the outcomes and it was presented to the Minister but the issues were still there at the end of the week. For example, you still need new teachers immediately and this is where the real work begins. It takes years to create a pattern, and it takes years to change it, but some qualitative change has occurred, even if it's subtle.

It still gives me goosebumps when I remember the final session on the Friday afternoon. All the school Directors came together and they had thought that they were originally going to each pitch their outcomes as a three-minute presentation. In the end they decided to sit in a circle and talk. The focus was on, 'What's been the most important thing that you have noticed this week?' It was mind blowing to hear them. So many spoke about:

'Finally having time to be together again'.

'To be able to talk about life, to be human together'.

'We became aware that we are a team'.

'How can we make time to be together like this more often?'

In the face of the relentless pace of 'normal' everyday life, it is hard to create this kind of space. But we have established a collective memory for that community – a reminder of what we did that week. We can go back to being human.

Facilitating communal moments of stillness have become an integral part of this approach. As part of the 'presencing' process in Theory U, Simoon usually asks people:

- Where do you have your best ideas?

- What are you doing when you have them?

Responses often include:

- On the toilet.

- In the shower.

- In the forest.

It's never, 'At work behind my computer'! We don't often have our clever moments when we are busy being 'experts'. So we encourage them to go back to music or walking or silence and appreciate the importance of these moments. I think people's capacity for silence these days is increasing. The traditional resistance to it that people have is slowly dissolving – more people are ready for it. The stillness piece is an important element in fostering group awareness.

This crisis in Amsterdam and the way these schools responded to it opened up a deeper conversation about the future of education. The dialogue process enabled each school to look at key issues and solutions from their own perspective, thus creating varying responses impacted by different community contexts, but also feeding into a wider collaborative effort to re-envision schooling in the Netherlands. In the subsequent nationwide teacher strike the following month, other schools chose to use the strike days for similar meetings, exploring fundamental issues in educational Systems Thinking.

I believe the processes of Theory U are very helpful here, for example, developing the three instruments – Open mind, Open heart, Open will.

From the mind we can bring curiosity. 'How come I am/you are doing this?'

From the heart we can bring compassion. 'Ah, now I understand why I was/you were doing this'.

With the will we can find the courage to let go of the old – and that's what creates a space for stuff to happen, for the new to emerge.

Simoon Fransen – Core Team Member, Presencing Institute, www.presencing.org/ (Fransen, 2020)

The work done in Amsterdam highlights a recurring theme in this book – when we want to contribute to shifting the focus in education and changing our education systems, it is vital that the processes we employ are themselves qualitatively different. Such processes need to reflect our intention to create places of learning where adults and children speak and listen to each other with more sensitivity and care, building a greater sense of connection and community, opening minds and hearts to future possibilities.

Although this discussion may start with educators, it is much more meaningful and powerful if we include parents and students when we feel ready to do so. By putting our focus more on the process than the outcome, we are beginning to sow seeds of change in how we relate and interact as a community, and as the ripples from this pool of deep dialogue widen and spread to include more participants, we are already beginning to impact our school cultures. Then, by making collaborative decisions from this space where we are honouring the importance of the 'inner states of the interveners', we are much more likely to design more creative, sustainable solutions.

Bringing greater awareness to the systems we work in is not limited to the adults in the building. There are now many examples of schools that have begun to teach Systems Thinking to even quite young students. Here is one example from the Green School in Bali:

Teacher Voice: Young Systems Thinkers

During a unit on 'Thinking in Systems' we decided to try an experiment with our Grade 4 class. We had been learning about systems and how they can rely on each other, or function independently. We decided to set up a simulation in which we told the kids that each essential system of the school was failing. We wanted to see how they reacted and how they overcame these systematic failings. We started with some of the least important systems (e.g. the rubbish wasn't going to be removed that day) and progressed through to some of the most important systems (e.g. the sewage system in the school was failing). We did this in a strategic way so that there would be less chance they would spot our ruse.

It was fascinating to see different kids react in different ways to different perceived systems failings. We saw examples of collaboration and problem solving; self-interest and self-preservation over community wellbeing; sharing, fear, kindness... And once we revealed our little game, we had a very deep and powerful discussion about what had occurred.

For the rest of the year, this event was referred to and revisited by the students, particularly when world events conspired to affect our world systems. It was a powerful part of our year of teaching, and by 'living' the experiment the students were very much impacted by the learnings and wonderings that they experienced.

Andy Ashton – Grade 4 teacher, Green School, Bali

Following on from the book he co-wrote with Daniel Goleman, *Triple Focus: A New Approach to Education* (2014), Peter Senge joined with Mette Böll and others to work with some schools from around the world to embed a combination of **Mindfulness**, **SEL** and **Systems Thinking** into school curricula. (For further information see 'An introduction to the Compassionate Systems Framework in schools' (Böll and Senge, 2019).)

Aligning Our Work

The other key area that we can draw on to support and sustain our work is through connecting with others and through aligning our efforts with parallel trends in the wider world. In Chapter 8 we looked at the issue of building support within our schools and from our school leaders. But we can also sustain ourselves through connecting with like minds in other schools and even outside of education. As well as the whole tradition of progressive education and school systems such as Steiner Schools, Reggio Emilia, Montessori, Quaker Schools, etc. there are many organizations and groups these days pursuing deep change in education. There is also an increasing commonality amongst various approaches such as Mindfulness, SEL, Positive Education and Systems Thinking as well as amongst many schools of thought interested in 'Re-thinking or Transforming Education'. In complex systems, there can come a point when a combination of diverse factors come together to bring about swift, radical change in what appeared to be intransigent systems resistant to change. Collapse then comes suddenly, new ideas converge and very different conditions can emerge. In many ways it feels like education initiatives around the world may be reaching just such a convergence point.

The Impossible *is* Possible

The concept of 'disruption' in educational change theory is not a new term, but with the advent of the COVID-19 global pandemic we have seen a major, sudden disruption impact education around the planet. What are we learning from this time of disruption?

- Firstly, many schools and school leaders have raised the profile on health and wellbeing and in general there has been a renewed interest in promoting SEL and mental health.

- Secondly, as one school Director put it, 'We have become more aware of what's really *important* and of what's really *possible*'. We are, for example, often frustrated by slow pace of change in education and the dominance of the fixed school schedule, but during the pandemic, overnight, the schedule was changed as committed educators sought to support their communities as seamlessly as possible.

- Thirdly, there has been a significant increase in educational dialogue around seeing this disruption as an opportunity to reflect on making meaningful change. See for example the WISE conference series and e-book 'Education Disrupted, Education Re-Imagined': www.salzburgglobal.org/news/publications/article/education-disrupted-education-reimagined-special-edition-e-book

In many ways, education mirrors the wider world and other large institutions. Our health, education, social service and justice institutions were all created towards the end of the industrial era and all are showing signs of creaking at the seams in the 21st century, when population numbers and social pressures are very different from the societies they were designed to serve. Even our systems of governance and democracy these days are showing the strain of trying to adapt to a post-industrial digital age. At the same time as entropy is pulling at the edges of these systems, there is a growing questioning and deeper awareness pushing us towards rethinking the deeper purposes and redesigning the core of these institutions.

Expert Voice: Finding Hope

Having spent 25 years as a teacher in the UK, and 18 of those at senior leadership level, I witnessed changes that gave rise both to a deep sense of despair and profound hope.

(Continued)

My despair stemmed from the increased focus on assessment, attainment, and accountability. This process, usually based on factual knowledge 'delivered' to students and then assessed through an entirely examination-based process, renders the experience of the student and teacher almost irrelevant in the process, as it does the very 'instrument' of learning: the mind.

My sense of hope arose out of the burgeoning shift of emphasis on mental health and wellbeing as being as much at the heart of teaching and learning as any element of the traditional curriculum. Having now had the great privilege of working with the Mindfulness in Schools Project for eight years, I have witnessed exciting additions to this dialogue, including a broadening of focus from teaching mindfulness in schools to teaching *mindfully*. This represents a radical challenge to both the intention and process of education. It also acknowledges that education needs to evolve in order to meet the needs of an uncertain but rapidly changing world.

The need to reassess not just what we are teaching but also how and with what intention has never been more urgent. Educators and policy makers have an opportunity to step back and recognise the significant choices to be made. We need to find ways to support future generations who will need to be capable of dealing with complexity, cultural difference, and dynamic ethical realities arising out of new technologies and restricted access to resources.

An education that serves both the young person being educated and the society in which they live is one that prepares us for an uncertain future, but one with immense possibilities for change. Mindfulness has a key role to play in how we shape our sense of identity, efficacy, wellbeing, attitudes, ethics, ways of being and acting in the world, and our ability to respond intelligently to life situations. It is certainly an exciting time to be in education!

Claire Kelly – Director of Curricula and Training for the
Mindfulness in Schools Project, UK

There are also many other hopeful signs around us. The most significant may be the increasing questioning of the deeper purposes of government itself. The concept of using Gross National Happiness as a measure of the health and wellbeing of a country rather than Gross Domestic Product arose from the founding fathers of the European Union in the 1970s and more recently has been a stated aim of the government of Bhutan. In 2011 the United Nations adopted a resolution urging other countries to follow this example. More recently, both New Zealand and Iceland made wellbeing the organizing principle for their economic budgets and they joined with Scotland to create a group of Wellbeing Economy Governments. Finland, Denmark, Iceland and Norway regularly top global happiness charts, and what all these countries have in common is a shared understanding that whilst a degree of economic stability is essential for all of us, the primary purpose of government is to promote and protect the wellbeing of its citizens. Economic policies can help establish wellbeing but they are not the end goal. In the last

20 years there have been significant advances on the economics of wellbeing – and new approaches to monitoring wellbeing with the understanding that we should **measure what we value, not value what we measure**. This is also a helpful credo for school assessment policies!

Some of these same countries are beginning to include a stronger emphasis on wellbeing in their curricular frameworks. For example:

- Following in the footsteps of New Zealand, both Iceland and Wales have now identified Health and Wellbeing as a key learning area. In the new national curriculum of Wales 2022, all schools will be required to make Health and Wellbeing one of the six core learning areas. Many schools in both Wales and Iceland are already using mindful awareness training as one of the tools to support student wellbeing, and these initiatives are increasingly drawing attention and support from national agencies.

- In 2019 the UK government launched a large-scale mental health initiative that includes trialling mindfulness in 370 state schools, whilst a large seven-year randomized control study looking at the effectiveness of mindfulness teaching and training in 84 schools was launched in 2015 by the Wellcome Trust.

- In Canada, in 2017, the Ministry of Education in British Columbia defined new core competencies in provincial school curricula to include the development of personal and social competencies. Programmes are now required to focus on personal awareness and responsibility; empathy for others; and social awareness and responsibility, including caring for the community and environment (Mind & Life, 2020). A few teacher training institutions in Canada now offer mindful awareness and resilience courses for new teachers. This crucial next step, which a few other countries are beginning to take, is essential if we really want to embed wellbeing into our education systems.

- In the USA, SEL has become firmly established in many parts of the country, increasingly accompanied by various approaches to MAT. In *Healing America: How a Simple Practice Can Help Us Recapture the American Spirit* (2017), US Congressman Tim Ryan called this movement a quiet revolution and asked: 'Why not teach all of our children this simple, tremendously powerful technique to help increase their capacity to learn and regulate their own emotions? ... It seems so simple and inexpensive, and its effectiveness is backed by scientific research' (pp. 68 and 69).

One example from amongst numerous international efforts in this area is the inspiring framework produced by the Organisation for Economic Co-operation and Development (OECD). 'The future of education and skills 2030' (OECD, 2018) advocates for nations to work with them to transform their education systems and create schools that are '**...committed to helping every learner develop as a whole person, fulfil his or her potential and help shape a shared future built on the well-being of individuals, communities and the planet**'.

Expert Voices: Collective Vision and Equity

How impactful would it be if schools educating mindfully joined forces to support and learn from each other, moving forward together in our collective vision?! Doing so would create even greater momentum for the emergence of mindfulness in education.

This was the shared musing of Barnaby Spring, Director of Mindfulness in Education at New York City Department of Education, that ignited my desire to found the Coalition of Schools Educating Mindfully in 2018. Mindfulness practices provide healthy coping strategies for children AND adults. They help us regulate our nervous system and get our brains in a ready-to-learn state. Mindfulness not only provides the tools to manage the stresses of modern living but also, as Barnaby states, it can be much more, including an ally to democracy.

Tracy Heilers – Founder and Executive Director,
Coalition of Schools Educating Mindfully (COSEM)

Meditation and self-awareness breed compassion and empathy to support the capacity-building of doing equity work. We all have biases that we carry, and as educators, we work with too many people to not be in touch with our biases. Whether implicit or explicit, our biases are a result of our conditioning. Imagine conditioning like an onion and how you can peel back thin layers of an onion only to find more until you get to the centre. That is what it is like to peel back layers of conditioning. Self-awareness from meditation allows us to tap into that conditioning which can be quite unpleasant. If we are going to talk about equity, we have to get really comfortable with the discomfort of being with difficult emotions. We must have the courage to be there and stay engaged. Our mindfulness work, coupled with compassion, can lead us to be more effective leaders of equity so that we can lean in and have real conversations, emotional conversations, authentic race-based, gender-based conversations. This is how we shift the outcomes to be more equitable.

Tovi Scruggs-Hussein – Educational Leader and National Board President, COSEM

Social Justice

Through this work in social-emotional skills and mindful awareness training we are contributing to awareness-based systems change that can help our young people grow up with a more heart-based appreciation of democracy, governance and economics – an ethical awareness that a community or country does not truly thrive and flourish simply through consuming more and more, and that meaningful 'growth' in society actually means personal and social growth rather than pure financial gain. In other words, that we dedicate ourselves to learning how to care for and share this planet more equitably.

When teachers and trainers in schools and organizations working with young people embody these qualities they can provide a powerful vehicle for exploring issues of social justice and inequality. iBme (Inward Bound Mindfulness Education) is one such organization, working alongside young people to help foster this crucial awareness:

Expert Voice: Young People and Social Justice

We recognize that many in our community are actively disadvantaged and encounter systems of oppression every day. These have an especially significant impact on our young people because of the additional disempowerment of children and teens in our society. By supporting young people to deepen awareness, compassion, and ethics and empowering their voices, we are investing in our collective future, one with greater liberation, justice and wellbeing for us all.

iBme's programs aim to guide teens and young adults in their development of self-awareness, compassion, and ethical decision making, empowering them to apply these essential skills to their lives and communities. We have been asked why it is appropriate to consider engaging in social justice as an aspect of teaching mindfulness. As our friend, author and mindful social activist, Rhonda Magee (2019: 20) writes, 'The short and simple answer is that [social] justice, like compassion, is just one form of an ethically grounded, mindful response to suffering in our lives'.

Ultimately, our contemplative practice shows us that life is precious, every moment. And we can experience in the quiet moments of our own minds and in the transformation we see in our teens on retreat, that under conditions that are safe, kind, and unconditionally accepting of the present, the nourished human heart shows up with wisdom and an unbounded ability to love.

With permission from **Jessica Morey** – founding Board Member and Lead Teacher, Inward Bound Mindfulness Education, www.ibme.com

Coping with stress, anxiety, depression and trauma have become key 21st-century life skills. But coping is not enough. We need to equip the next generation with the full range of human capacities that will enable them to work collaboratively and creatively to overcome highly complex global challenges. Understanding and learning how to take care of the mind, body and heart equips a growing child with a toolkit for life. Nurturing key qualities of kindness and curiosity enables our young people to begin to embody the relationship-building qualities and wisdom that our society is so much in need of. In finding ways to share the planet sustainably and equitably, young people will need to be able to understand the deep systemic causes of climate change, inequality and injustice. They will need to be able to understand, with the heart as well as the mind, the impact these factors have on everyone. And they will need to be able to take action together to create a more just, more equal and more caring world.

Expert Voice: Changing the Educational Paradigm

Education is still perceived very one-sidedly as the development of academic skills. But we know that socio-emotional skills and academic development are closely linked and only by encouraging the holistic development of students and teachers can schools fulfil their true potential – the development of compassionate, proactive, creative, and in every sense healthy individuals and societies.

As is the case in many countries, care for teachers, their wellbeing and mental health is still insufficiently recognized and often marginalized in Croatia. During pre-service training, teachers are not sufficiently supported in developing their own socio-emotional and self-care skills and any training they receive once they are certified is almost exclusively focused on students' academic achievement. Consequently, the need to invest in the personal development and wellbeing of teachers has not been recognized.

Over the last few years, researchers in Croatia have conducted interventions focused on teachers' personal development and their mental health based on mindfulness practice and socio-emotional learning. These initiatives were received very positively by teachers and resulted in improvements in their mental health and wellbeing. In order for such programmes to be sustained, it is necessary for educational policy makers to understand the importance of such programmes, but above all, we need the educational paradigm to change.

There can be no learning and prosperity if the wellbeing of the individual is neglected. For that reason, it is time to reconsider the purpose of education in today's society and make sure that we see students and teachers as complex beings – cognitive but also social, emotional, and spiritual beings – capable of great things when nourished holistically.

Mihić, Josipa – Educator and Researcher

In closing this chapter and this book we return to underlining the importance of the work that teachers do and the need to take good care of ourselves. Most countries value education highly, but they often value their teachers somewhat less so. Sometimes as teachers we don't value ourselves highly enough. But the work we do is powerful and meaningful. We literally help shape the brains of the next generation! We can have a profound impact on our students, through our enthusiasm for learning and through who we are as people, in the way we connect and relate. But we need to use that oxygen mask for ourselves first, and make emotional and mental health the foundation of our personal wellbeing.

'Happy Teachers Change the World!'

When we first saw this quote from Thich Nhat Hanh we thought it was perhaps a bit too simplistic. Teaching is hard and stressful and we can't necessarily be happy all the time. But now we understand and appreciate what he is saying. The work of the teacher is so significant for society that if we can truly be well, taking care of ourselves as best we can, we will have a meaningful impact on our students and this will help them contribute to positive change in the world. This is not about being the perfect 'mindful teacher' who never makes mistakes. It's not about perfection, it's about connection.

We need to dedicate time and space to maintaining our emotional and mental health in this highly demanding profession. We can commit to this self-care in the knowledge that the more present and engaged we are, the deeper the connection with our students, and the deeper the learning. In this way we model care for our students and we can help develop more balanced young people, who are wise as well as clever, who know how to take care of themselves and of each other, and who are equipped and motivated to take care of our amazing but threatened planet.

And if ever there was a time when we needed a generation of young people ready and able to take care of our planet, this, surely, must be it.

Further Reading and Resources

Training

Theory U – Free courses from the MIT Presencing Institute, www.presencing.org/
Transforming Educational Leadership – www.teleadership.org/

Books

Bristow, J., Bell, R., and Nixon, D. (2020) 'Mindfulness: Developing agency in urgent times'. The Mindfulness Initiative. www.themindfulnessinitiative.org/agency-in-urgent-times/

Goleman, D. and Senge, P. (2014) *Triple Focus: A New Approach to Education*. Kindle edn. Florence, MA: More than Sound.

Magee, R. (2019). *The Inner Work of Racial Justice: Healing Ourselves and Transforming Our Communities Through Mindfulness*. New York: TarcherPerigee.

Rowland, D. (2017) *Still Moving: How to Lead Mindful Change*. London: Wiley. Also available from: www.deborahrowland.com/still-moving

Scharmer, C. O. (2016) *Theory U: Leading from the Future as It Emerges*. 2nd edn. Oakland, CA: Berrett-Koehler Publishers.

Senge, P., Cambron-McCabe, N. Lucas, T., Smith, B., Dutton, J., and Kleiner, A. (2000) *Schools That Learn: A Fifth Discipline Fieldbook for Educators, Parents, and Everyone Who Cares About Education*. London: Nicholas Brealey.

References

Bethune, A. (2019) *Wellbeing in the Primary Classroom: A Practical Guide to Teaching Happiness*. London: Bloomsbury Publishing.

Biegel, G. (2015) *Stressed Teens Instructor Guide*. Manual of the MBSR-T course. Available at: www.stressedteens.com/training-for-professionals (accessed on 6/5/21).

Biegel, G. and Corbin, T. (2018) *Mindfulness for Student Athletes: A Workbook to Help Teens Reduce Stress and Enhance Performance*. Oakland, CA: New Harbinger Publications.

Böll, M. and Senge, P. (2019) 'An introduction to the Compassionate Systems Framework in schools'. Abdul Latif Jameel World Education Lab, MIT – The Center for Systems Awareness. Available at: https://jwel.mit.edu/sites/mit-jwel/files/assets/files/intro-com passionatesystemsframework-march-2019_0.pdf (accessed on 20/12/20).

Brewer, J. (2021) *Unwinding Anxiety: New Science Shows How to Break the Cycles of Worry and Fear to Heal Your Mind*. New York: Avery/Penguin.

Bristow, J., Bell, R., and Nixon, D. (2020) 'Mindfulness: Developing agency in urgent times'. The Mindfulness Initiative. Available at: www.themindfulnessinitiative.org/agency-in-urgent-times/ (accessed on 18/1/20).

Broderick, T. (2021) *Learning to Breathe: A Mindfulness Curriculum for Adolescents to Cultivate Emotion Regulation, Attention and Performance*. 2nd edn. Oakland, CA: New Harbinger Publications.

Brown, V. and Olson, K. (2015) *The Mindful School Leader: Practices to Transform your Leadership and School*. Thousand Oaks, CA: Corwin.

Burke, A. (2019) 'Contemplative career planning: Helping students draw on their inner guidance counsellor'. *Canadian Teacher Magazine*, Winter Issue. Available at: https://canadianteachermagazine.com/2019/01/18/contemplative-career-planning/ (accessed on 11/9/20).

Burnett, B. and Evans, D. (2016) *Designing Your Life: How to Build a Well-Lived, Joyful Life*. London: Chatto & Windus/Penguin.

Common Sense Media (2018) *Social Media, Social Life: Teens Reveal Their Experiences – Infographic*. September 10. Available at: www.commonsensemedia.org/social-media-social-life-infographic (accessed on 20/9/20).

Cozolino, L. (2013) *The Social Neuroscience of Education: Optimizing Attachment and Learning in the Classroom*. New York: W.W. Norton & Company.

DiOrio, R., illustrated by Eliza Wheeler (2010) *What Does It Mean to Be Present?* San Francisco, CA: Little Pickle Press.

Durlak, J. A., Weissberg, R. P., Dymnicki, A. B., Taylor, R. D., and Schellinger, K. B. (2011) 'The impact of enhancing students' social and emotional learning: A meta-analysis of school-based universal interventions'. *Child Development*, 82(1): 405-32.

Dweck, C. (2006) *Mindset: The New Psychology of Success*. New York: Random House.

Education 4 Peace (2013) *Football – A Path to Self-Awareness: Becoming Master of Your Emotions (Sport-Attitude)*. Available at: www.education4peace.org/ (accessed on 16/7/20).

Edwards, N., illustrated by Katie Hickey (2019) *Happy: A Children's Book of Mindfulness*. London: Little Tiger Press.

Emmons, R. (2010) 'Why gratitude is good'. *Greater Good Magazine*. November 16. Available at: https://greatergood.berkeley.edu/article/item/why_gratitude_is_good (accessed on 10/11/20).

Frank, J., Jennings, P., and Greenberg, M. (2013) 'Mindfulness-based interventions in school settings: An introduction to the special issue'. *Research in Human Development*, 10(3): 205-10.

Fransen, S. (2020) Personal interview, 26 March.

Fransen, S. and Middlebeek, J. (2020) 'The quality of work (WOK) week in Amsterdam'. Presencing Institute Blog. Available at: https://medium.com/presencing-institute-blog/the-quality-of-education-wok-week-in-amsterdam-255c9c3eca3 (accessed on 15/7/20).

Fuster D. and Scholar, M. (2009) 'The relation between executive functioning and emotion regulation in young children'. Pennsylvania State University. Available at: https://pdfs.semanticscholar.org/c17b/b1a731bcc4236bd6836ae17cf80eaf2389bd.pdf (accessed on 13/2/20).

GAIA – Global Activation of Intention and Action (2020) 'Sense making in a time of crisis'. 10 April. Presencing Institute. Available at: https://vimeo.com/showcase/7204406/video/408784159 (accessed on 10/4/20).

Gallwey, T. (1997) *The Inner Game of Tennis: The Classic Guide to the Mental Side of Peak Performance*. New York: Random House.

Ginott, H. (1994 [1972]) *Teacher and Child: A Book for Parents and Teachers*. New York: Simon & Schuster.

Goerling, R. (2014) 'The mindfulness difference: Training ahead can help police recover later'. *Royal Canadian Mounted Police Gazette*, 76(4). Available at: www.rcmp-grc.gc.ca/en/gazette/mindfulness-difference (accessed on 21/10/20).

Goleman, D. and Davidson, J. (2017) *Altered Traits: Science Reveals How Meditation Changes Your Mind, Brain and Body*. New York: Penguin Random House.

Goleman, D. and Senge, P. (2014) *Triple Focus: A New Approach to Education*. Kindle edn. Florence, MA: More than Sound.

Greater Good in Education (2019) 'Mindfulness for students: Why is it important?' *Greater Good in Education: Science Based Practices for Kinder, Happier Schools*. Available at: https://ggie.berkeley.edu/student-well-being/mindfulness-for-students/#tab__2 (accessed on 9/8/20).

Gutierrez, A., Krachman, S., West, M., Scherer, E., and Gabrieli, J. (2019) 'Mindfulness in the classroom: Learning from a school-based mindfulness intervention through the Boston Charter Research Collaborative'. Transforming Education & Centre for Education Policy Research Harvard University. Available at: www.transformingeducation.org/wp-content/uploads/2019/01/2019-BCRC-Mindfulness-Brief.pdf (accessed on 4/11/20).

Hawkins, K. (2016) Personal notes.

Hawkins, K. (2017) *Mindful Teacher, Mindful School: Improving Wellbeing in Teaching and Learning*. London: SAGE.

Heilers, T., Iverson, T., and Larrivee, B., eds. (2020) *Educating Mindfully: Stories of School Transformation through Mindfulness*. St. Charles, IL: Coalition of Schools Educating Mindfully.

Jackson, P. (2006) *Sacred Hoops: Spiritual Lessons of a Hardwood Warrior*. New York: Hyperion.

Jennings, P. (2020) *Teacher Burnout Turnaround: Strategies for Empowered Educators*. New York: W.W. Norton & Company.

Jones, D., Greenberg, M., and Crowly, M. (2015) 'Early social-emotional functioning and public health: The relationship between kindergarten social competence and future wellness'. *American Journal of Public Health*, 105(11): 2283-90.

Kaiser-Greenland, S. (2010) *The Mindful Child: How to Help Your Kids Manage Stress, Become Happier, Kinder and More Compassionate*. New York: Free Press.

Kessler, R. (2000) *The Soul of Education: Helping Students Find Connection, Compassion and Character at School*. Alexandria, VA: ASCD.

Lantieri, L. and Zakrzewski, V. (2015) 'How SEL and mindfulness can work together'. *Greater Good Magazine*. 7 April. Available at: www.greatergood.berkeley.edu/article/item/how_social_emotional_learning_and_mindfulness_can_work_together (accessed on 9/2/20).

Ma, X., Yue, Z., Gong, Z., Zhang, H., Duan, N., Shi, Y., Wei, G., and Li, Y. (2017) 'The effect of diaphragmatic breathing in healthy adults'. *Frontiers in Psychology*. 6 June. Available at: www.frontiersin.org/articles/10.3389/fpsyg.2017.00874/full (accessed on 24/4/20).

MacLean, K. (2009) *Moody Cow Meditates*. Boston, MA: Wisdom Publications.

Magaldi, D. and Park-Taylor, J. (2016) 'Our students' minds matter: Integrating mindfulness practices into special education classrooms'. *The Journal of Special Education Apprenticeship*, 5(2): Article 4. Available at: https://scholarworks.lib.csusb.edu/josea/vol5/iss2/4 (accessed on 29/6/20).

Magee, R. (2019) *The Inner Work of Racial Justice: Healing Ourselves and Transforming Our Communities Through Mindfulness*. New York: TarcherPerigee.

Maturano, J. (2014) *Finding the Space to Lead: A Practical Guide to Mindful Leadership*. New York: Bloomsbury.

Mind & Life (2020) 'Social and emotional learning: A movement comes of age'. *Digital Dialogue: Education of the Heart*. Available at: https://educationoftheheartdialogue.org/social-and-emotional-learning/ (accessed on 4/12/20).

Mumford, G. (2015) *The Mindful Athlete: Secrets to Pure Performance*. Berkeley, CA: Parallax Press.

Muth, J. (2002) *The Three Questions*. New York: Scholastic Press.

New South Wales Government (2020) 'Wellbeing framework for schools'. Available at: www.education.nsw.gov.au/student-wellbeing/whole-school-approach/wellbeing-framework-for-schools (accessed on 21/9/20).

Nhat Hanh, T. (1988) *The Heart of Understanding: Commentaries on the Prajñaparamita Sutra*. Berkeley, CA: Parallax Press.

Nhat Hanh, T. (2011) *Planting Seeds: Practicing Mindfulness with Children*. Berkeley, CA: Parallax Press.

Nhat Hanh, T. and Weare, K. (2017) *Happy Teachers Change the World: A Guide for Cultivating Mindfulness in Education*. Berkeley, CA: Parallax.

OECD – Organisation for Economic Co-operation and Development (2018) 'The future of education and skills 2030' (Position Paper). 5 April. Available at: www.oecd.org/education/2030/E2030%20Position%20Paper%20(05.04.2018).pdf (accessed on 7/1/20).

O'Leary, W. and Willard, C. (2019) *Breathing Makes it Better: A Book for Sad Days, Mad Days, Glad Days and All the Feelings in Between*. Berkeley, CA: Shambhala Publications.

OUSD – Oakland Unified School District (2015) 'PreK-adult social and emotional learning standards'. Available at: www.ousd.org/Page/15358 (accessed on 6/5/21).

Quigley, A., Muijs, D., and Stringer, E. (2018) 'Metacognition and self-regulated learning guidance report'. *Education Endowment Foundation*. Available at: https://educationendowmentfoundation.org.uk/public/files/Publications/Metacognition/EEF_Metacognition_and_self-regulated_learning.pdf (accessed on 20/8/20).

Rechtschaffen, D. (2014) *The Mindful Way of Education: Cultivating Well-Being in Teachers and Students*. New York: W.W. Norton & Company.

Rechtschaffen, D. and Willard, C. (2019) *Alphabreaths: The ABCs of Mindful Breathing*. Boulder, CO: Sounds True.

Ribas, W. B., Brady, D. A., and Hardin, J. (2017) *Social-Emotional Learning in the Classroom: Practical Guide for Integrating All SEL Skills into Instruction and Classroom Management.* Norwood, MA: Ribas Publications.

Rogers, H. and Maytan, M. (2019) *Mindfulness for the Next Generation.* 2nd edn. Oxford: Oxford University Press.

Rowland, D. (2017) *Still Moving: How to Lead Mindful Change.* London: Wiley. Also available from www.deborahrowland.com/still-moving (accessed on 20/6/2020).

Ryan, T. (2017) *Healing America: How a Simple Practice Can Help Us Recapture the American Spirit.* Carlsbad, CA: Hay House.

Saltzman, A. (2018) *A Still Quiet Place for Athletes: Mindfulness Skills for Achieving Peak Performance and Finding Flow in Sports and Life.* Oakland, CA: New Harbinger Publications.

Sanger, K. and Dorjee, D. (2016) 'Mindfulness training with adolescents enhances metacognition and the inhibition of irrelevant stimuli'. *Trends in Neuroscience and Education,* 5(1): 1–11.

Sanger, K., Dorjee, D., and Thierry, G. (2018) 'Effects of school-based mindfulness training on emotion processing and well-being in adolescents: Evidence from event-related potentials'. *Developmental Science,* 21(5): e12646. Available at: www.ncbi.nlm.nih.gov/pmc/articles/PMC6175003/ (accessed on 27/7/20).

Scharmer, C. O. (2016) *Theory U: Leading from the Future as It Emerges.* 2nd edn. Oakland, CA: Berrett-Koehler Publishers.

Scharmer, C. O. (2019) 'Vertical Literacy: Reimagining the 21st Century University'. *Presencing Institute Blog.* April 16. Available at: www.medium.com/presencing-institute-blog/vertical-literacy-12-principles-for-reinventing-the-21st-century-university-39c2948192ee (accessed on 1/7/20).

Schonert-Reichl, K. and Roeser, R. (2016) *Handbook of Mindfulness in Education: Integrating Theory and Research into Practice.* New York: Springer.

Senge, P. (1990) *The Fifth Discipline: The Art and Practice of the Learning Organization.* London: Random House.

Senge, P., Cambron-McCabe, N. Lucas, T., Smith, B., Dutton, J., and Kleiner, A. (2000) *Schools That Learn: A Fifth Discipline Fieldbook for Educators, Parents, and Everyone Who Cares About Education.* London: Nicholas Brealey.

Siegel, D. (2013) *Brainstorm: The Power and Purpose of the Teenage Brain.* New York: Penguin.

Srinivasan, M. (2014) *Teach, Breathe, Learn: Mindfulness In and Out of the Classroom.* Berkeley, CA: Parallax Press.

Srinivasan, M. (2019) *SEL Every Day: Integrating Social and Emotional Learning with Instruction in Secondary Classrooms.* New York: W.W. Norton & Company.

Taylor, R., Oberle, E., Durlak, J., and Weissberg, R. (2017) 'Promoting positive youth development through school-based social and emotional learning interventions: A meta-analysis of follow-up effects'. *Child Development,* 88(4): 1156–71.

Thomas, J. (2016) 'Full speed ahead: Teaching and practicing mindfulness in a special-ed classroom'. *Mindful Schools.* Available at: www.mindfulschools.org/inspiration/teacher-to-teacher-t2t-mindfulness/ (accessed on 3/5/20).

Treleaven, D. (2018) *Trauma-Sensitive Mindfulness: Practices for Safe and Transformative Healing.* New York: W.W. Norton & Company.

van de Weijer-Bergsma, E., Formsma, A., de Bruin, E., and Bögels, S. (2012) 'The effectiveness of mindfulness training on behavioral problems and attentional functioning in adolescents with ADHD'. *Journal of Child and Family Studies,* 21(5): 775–87.

Verde, S., illustrated by Peter Reynolds (2017) *I Am Peace: A Book of Mindfulness*. New York: Abrams Books for Young Readers.

Vo, Dzung X. (2015) *The Mindful Teen: Powerful Skills to Help You Handle Stress One Moment at a Time*. Oakland, CA: Instant Help Books.

Weare, K. and Bethune, A. (2021) 'Implementing Mindfulness in Schools: An Evidence-Based Guide', The Mindfulness Initiative. Available at: www.themindfulnessinitiative.org/imple menting-mindfulness-in-schools-an-evidence-based-guide (accessed on 3/5/20).

White, M., Alcock, A., Grellier, J., Wheeler, B., Hartig, T., Warber, S., Bone, A., Depledge, M., and Fleming, L. (2019) 'Spending at least 120 minutes a week in nature is associated with good health and wellbeing'. *Scientific Reports*, 9: Article 7730. Available at: www.nature.com/articles/s41598-019-44097-3 (accessed on 6/10/2020).

Wilde, S., Sonley, A., Crane, C., Ford, T., Raja, A., Robson, J., Taylor, L., and Kuyken, W. (2018) 'Mindfulness training in UK secondary schools: A multiple case study approach to identification of cornerstones of implementation'. *Mindfulness* 10: 376-89.

Willard, C. (2014) *Mindfulness for Teen Anxiety: A Workbook for Overcoming Anxiety at Home, at School and Everywhere Else*. Oakland, CA: Instant Help Books.

Willard, C. and Weisser, O. (2020) *The Breathing Book*. Boulder, CO: Sounds True.

Williams, J. M. G. (2010) 'Mindfulness and psychological process'. *Emotion*, 10(1): 1-7.

Williams, M. and Penman, D. (2011) *Mindfulness: A Practical Guide to Finding Peace in a Frantic World*. London: Piatkus.

Wooden, J. (1997) *Wooden: A Lifetime of Observations and Reflections On and Off the Court*. New York: McGraw Hill.

Worthen, D. (2018) 'The Mindfulness Program at the Middlesex School: Evolution and Structure'. Available at: www.mxschool.edu/about-mx/mindfulness/access-to-program-overview (accessed on 20/9/2020).

Yeoman, B. (2017) 'Mindful policing: The future of force'. *Mindful Magazine Online*. Available at: www.mindful.org/mindful-policing-the-future-of-force/ (accessed on 23/7/2020).

Index